EXTERIOR and INTERIOR TRIM

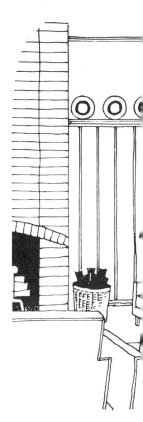

EXTERIOR and INTERIOR TRIM

JOHN E. BALL

11

LIBRARY OF CONGRESS CATALOG CARD NUMBER: 75-6060
ISBN: 0-8273-1120-6

Printed in the United States of America
Published simultaneously in Canada
by Nelson Canada,
A Division of International Thomson Limited

CONTENTS

SECTION I   EXTERIOR TRIM

Unit   Page

1   Roofing Materials   1

2   Wood Shingles and Shakes   11

3   Asphalt Shingles   17

4   Closed Cornices   25

5   Open Cornices   34

6   Doors   41

7   Windows   51

8   Door and Window Trim   63

9   Exterior Sidewall Covering   69

SECTION II   INTERIOR TRIM

10   Gypsum Wallboard Construction   82

11   Paneling   92

12   Acoustical Ceilings   98

13   Base, Ceiling, and Wall Molding   105

14   Wood Flooring   112

15   Joints in Cabinet Construction   120

16   Kitchen Cabinets   130

17   Cabinet Drawers and Doors   140

18   Stairs Built on Open Stringers   148

19   Stairs Built on Semihoused Stringers   155

20   Stairs Built on Housed Stringers   162

21   Built-In Furniture   169

22   Finish Hardware   177

Appendix   185

Acknowledgments   188

Index   189

The author and editorial staff at Delmar Publishers are interested in continually improving the quality of this instruction material. The reader is invited to submit constructive criticism and questions. Responses will be reviewed jointly by the author and source editor. Send comments to:

Delmar Publishers Inc.
2 Computer Drive-West
Box 15-015
Albany, New York 12212

NOTICE TO THE READER

Section I *EXTERIOR TRIM*

Unit 1 Roofing Materials

The roof is one of the most important features of a building. Without the proper installation of the roof, the interior would be damaged by rain, wind, snow, dust, and heat. The roof is expected to shed water and protect the interior from the elements, and add to the visual appeal of the house.

At one time, wood shingles were almost totally used for roofing framed structures. During recent years, however, wood shingles have been replaced for the most part by composition materials in the form of strip and individual shingles. In addition to the shingles, accessories such as sheathing, underlayment, flashing, and fasteners are used to produce a finished roof that is structurally sound and free of defects.

SHEATHING

Solid sheathing usually consists of 1" x 6" (nominal thickness) boards with *tongue-and-groove* construction, figure 1-1, or *shiplap* boards, figure 1-2, tightly notched and nailed with 8d common nails. The boards may be square edged, but because of the possibility of air and dust infiltrating through the cracks, this type is not usually used in roof sheathing. The edges of the tongue-and-groove and shiplap boards fit together to make a tight joint. The vertical joints should be placed directly over the rafters, and when nominal one-inch stock is used, the rafters should be spaced no more than 24 inches on center.

Spaced sheathing, figure 1-3, is sometimes used for wood shakes and wood shingles. Usually consisting of nominal 1" x 3", 1" x 4" or 1" x 6" boards, spaced sheathing should be used only in areas that are not subjected to excessive amounts of snow or wind. The spacing of roof sheathing varies according to the weather conditions of the area and the amount of exposure; however, the distance on center never exceeds 10 inches. The vertical joints should be staggered and placed directly over the rafters. They are then attached with 8d common nails.

There is a difference of opinion as to whether solid roof sheathing of boards or spaced sheathing is more durable and efficient. The solid sheathing generally gives the roof more stability and provides better insulation and resistance to fire than spaced sheathing. However, some authorities claim that shingles over spaced sheathing are better ventilated and, therefore, less subject to decay than shingles over solid roof boards.

Plywood roof sheathing, figure 1-4, has recently gained great popularity and is now used on more construction jobs than other types of sheathing. The primary reason for its popularity is an economic one. The large panels can be laid quickly, waste is minimal, and, in some cases, costs may be cut by using fewer rafters.

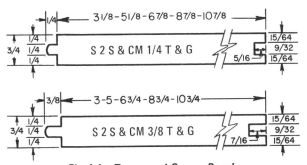

Fig. 1-1 Tongue-and-Groove Boards

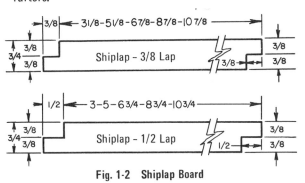

Fig. 1-2 Shiplap Board

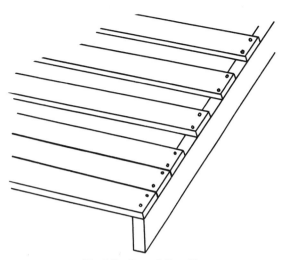

Fig. 1-3   Spaced Sheathing

Plywood is available in two basic types, interior and exterior, and should conform to the U.S. Product Standard PSI for Softwood Plywood. Exterior plywood has a 100% waterproof glueline, while interior plywood has a glueline which resists most moisture. Plywood used for sheathing is classified into three types: Structural I, Structural II, and C-C Exterior. The sheathing is marked with an identification index number, figure 1-5. The index number is a two-element number separated by a slash, such as 32/16. The number on the left is the maximum recommended spacing of the rafters; the number on the right is the maximum recommended spacing of floor joists. If the

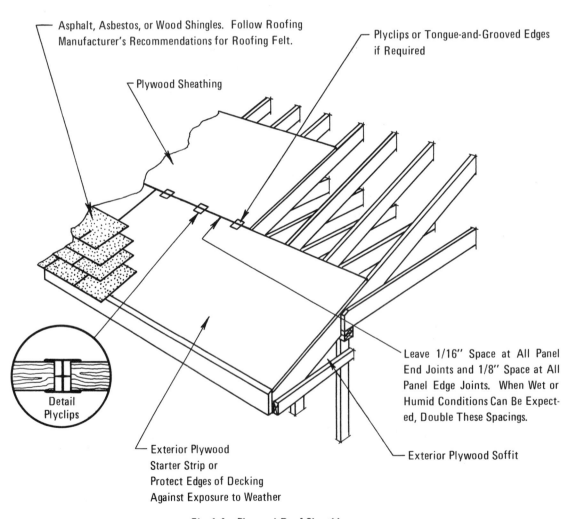

Asphalt, Asbestos, or Wood Shingles. Follow Roofing Manufacturer's Recommendations for Roofing Felt.

Plyclips or Tongue-and-Grooved Edges if Required

Plywood Sheathing

Detail Plyclips

Leave 1/16'' Space at All Panel End Joints and 1/8'' Space at All Panel Edge Joints. When Wet or Humid Conditions Can Be Expected, Double These Spacings.

Exterior Plywood Starter Strip or Protect Edges of Decking Against Exposure to Weather

Exterior Plywood Soffit

Fig. 1-4   Plywood Roof Sheathing

number on the right is stated as 0, the plywood may be used for roof sheathing, but is not recommended for subflooring. Figure 1-6 is a guide to the index numbers on plywood sheathing.

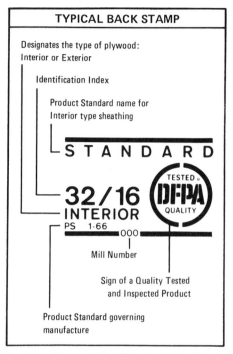

Fig. 1-5   Plywood Identification Index Number

DECKING

Decking may be defined as material used to protect a flat surface from the weather. Plywood decking is nailed with 6d common smooth, ring-shank, or spiral-thread nails if it is 1/2 inch or less in thickness. If the plywood decking is thicker than 1/2 inch, 8d common smooth, ring-shank, or spiral-thread nails should be used. The nails are spaced 6 inches apart at panel edges and 12 inches apart at intermediate rafters.

UNDERLAYMENT

Underlayment is an asphalt-saturated felt that has three basic purposes.

- It keeps the roof sheathing dry until the shingles can be applied.

- Once the shingles have been laid, it acts as a secondary barrier against wind-driven rain and snow.

- The underlayment does not allow the shingles to come in direct contact with resinous areas produced by the roof sheathing. The resin, because of chemical incompatibility with shingles, could be damaging.

GUIDE TO IDENTIFICATION INDEX ON ENGINEERED GRADES ([1])

Thick-ness (inch)	Standard (C-D) INT-DFPA (2) C-C EXT-DFPA			Structural I (3) C-D INT-DFPA Str. I C-C EXT	Structural II (3) C-D INT-DFPA Str. II C-C EXT	
	Group 1	Group 2 or 3 (4)	Group 4 (5)	Group 1 only	Group 1	Group 2 or 3 (4)
5/16	20/0	16/0	12/0	20/0	20/0	16/0
3/8	24/0	20/0	16/0	24/0	24/0	20/0
1/2	32/16	24/0	24/0	32/16	32/16	24/0
5/8	42/20	32/16	30/12	42/20	42/20	32/16
3/4	48/24	42/20	36/16	48/24	48/24	42/20
7/8		48/24	42/20			48/24

Notes:

(1) Identification Index numbers shown in the table appear in DFPA grade-trademarks on Standard, C-C, Structural I and Structural II grades. They refer to maximum recommended spacing of supports in inches when panels are used for roof decking and subflooring with face grain across supports. The left hand number shows spacing for roof supports. The right hand number shows spacing for floor supports. Numbers are based on panel thickness and species makeup detailed in Product Standard PS 1-66. Under each grade, the table identifies the species classification of the veneer used for outer plys. Where face and back veneers are not from the same species group, the number is based on the weaker group.

(2) Also available with exterior or intermediate glue.

(3) Manufactured with exterior glue only.

(4) Panels made with Group 2 outer plys may carry the Identification Index numbers shown for Group 1 panels when they conform to special thickness and construction requirements detailed in PS 1-66.

(5) Panels made with Group 4 outer plys may carry the Identification Index numbers shown for Group 3 panels when they conform to special thickness and construction requirements detailed in PS 1-66.

Fig. 1-6   Guide to The Index Numbers on Plywood Sheathing

Tar-saturated materials, coated felts, waterproof papers, or any other material that would act as a vapor barrier should be avoided when choosing underlayment. A material of this type traps moisture between the underlayment and roof sheathing, causing decay and structural damage.

One layer of 15-pound, asphalt-saturated felt is normally used as underlayment. The underlayment should have a top horizontal lap of 2 inches, a 4-inch sidelap of all joints, and a 6-inch extension over all hips and ridges, figure 1-7.

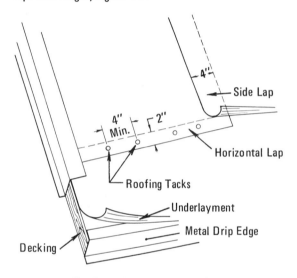

Fig. 1-7   Underlayment Application

FLASHING

If some provision is not made to control the effects of weather, several features of the roof may be prone to leakage, such as the projection of soil stacks and chimneys through sheathing, the intersection of a vertical wall with the roof, and the intersection of two sloping sides of the roof. *Flashing,* made of a metal or composition material, is used in these places to prevent leakage. The durability of the roof depends to a great extent on the application of the flashing.

Flashing Valleys

A *valley,* the intersection of two sloping roofs, may be flashed by the open valley technique or the closed valley technique. Open valleys are construc-

ted by placing metal flashing or 90-pound, mineral-surfaced, asphalt roll roofing in a color to match or contrast with the roof shingles over number 15-pound, asphalt-saturated felt in the valley, figure 1-8. Before the shingles are applied, chalk lines are snapped the entire length of the valley. At the *ridge,* the top of the roof, the chalk lines are 6 inches apart, each being 3 inches from the center of the valley, and slope toward the bottom of the valley at a rate of 1/8 inch per foot. The chalk lines serve as a guide for cutting the shingle units. The upper corner of each shingle unit is cut so that it may divert water into the valley and prevent water from penetrating the roof between courses.

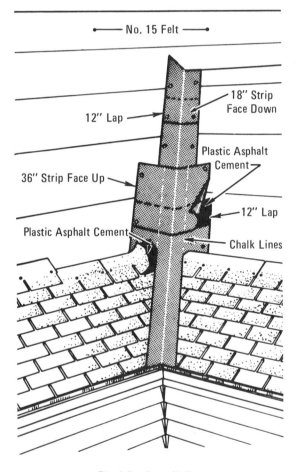

Fig. 1-8   Open Valley

The *closed* or *woven valley,* figure 1-9, is preferred by some contractors, but may be constructed only with the application of strip-type shingles. These shingles are usually 36 inches long, 12 inches wide,

and are divided into three equal parts. In this technique, the valley is lined with 55-pound, asphalt-saturated underlayment; then 55-pound felt is applied over 15-pound underlayment. The valley is then given extra coverage of shingles by laying the shingles on adjacent roof surfaces at the same time, making alternate overlaps with the strip shingles, or by working the shingles in an upward direction to a point within 3 feet of the valley. After the entire roof is shingled, the valley shingles are woven in place.

One of the most efficient methods of flashing the intersection of a vertical wall and a sloping roof is a technique known as *step flashing*, figure 1-10. The type of flashing used is made from metal strips about 6 inches long and 8 inches wide. The strips are bent so that approximately 4 inches of the metal extends up the vertical wall and 2 inches is covered by a shingle. Each flashing strip is placed just above the exposed edge of a shingle and is secured to the vertical wall sheathing with one nail in the top corner. The finish siding is then nailed over the flashing.

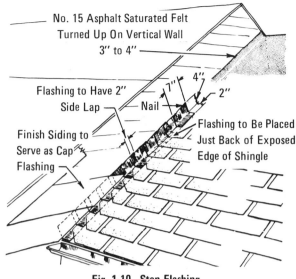

Fig. 1-10   Step Flashing

Flashing Chimneys

Because of differential settling of chimneys, flashing should consist of *base flashing* secured to the roof, figure 1-11 and *deck and counter*, or *cap flashing* secured to the chimney, figure 1-12. Before any flashing is installed, a *cricket*, or *saddle*, should be

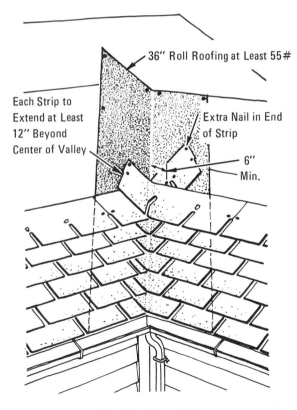

Fig. 1-9   Closed Valley

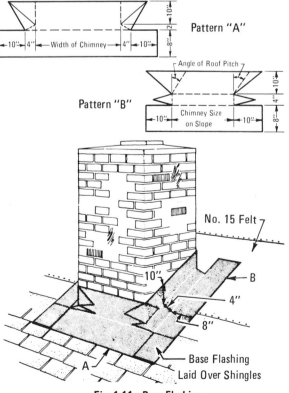

Fig. 1-11   Base Flashing

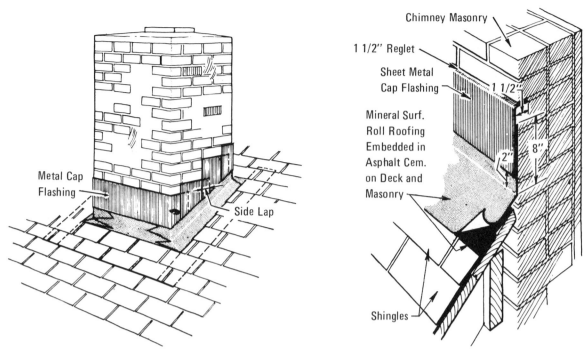

Fig. 1-12   Counter Flashing

built, figure 1-13, and the shingles laid over the under-layment to the front of the chimney.

The cricket, installed where two larger surfaces meet at an angle, is located behind the chimney. It diverts water around the chimney and prevents build-up of snow and ice. To construct a cricket, the base flashing is cut and the lower section is placed over the shingles in a bed of asphalt-plastic cement. The upper

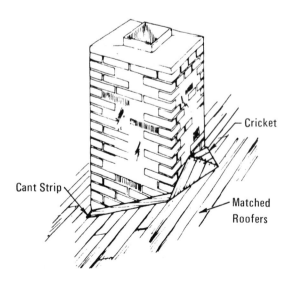

Fig. 1-13   Cricket

section is secured to the chimney with asphalt-plastic cement and nails are driven into the mortar joints. The triangular tips are then bent around the corners of the chimney and cemented in place. The side section is cut and bent to shape, and then placed in a bed of asphalt-plastic cement. The triangular tips are folded around the chimney corners and cemented in place over the front base flashing.

One of the better materials for cap flashing is sheet copper which is at least 16 ounces in weight. To install cap flashing, the mortar joint is cleaned to a depth of 1 1/2 inches and the flashing is inserted. The joint is then refilled with portland cement mortar. The cap, or counter, flashing is then bent down to cover the base flashing.

Flashing Pipes

Pipes that protrude through roof sheathing require special flashing techniques, figure 1-14. When using metal flashing, the shingles are fitted around the pipe. The metal flashing is then fitted over the stack, adjusted to the roof, and the flashing sleeve is turned down into the stack. When asphalt products are used, a rectangular piece of 55-pound roll roofing is cut and fitted over the stack, figure 1-15. The rectangular

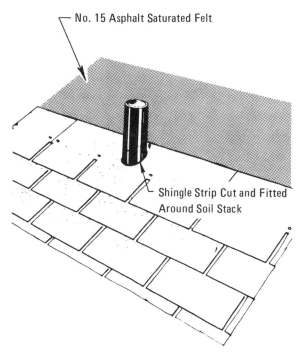

Fig. 1-14   Soil Stack Flashing

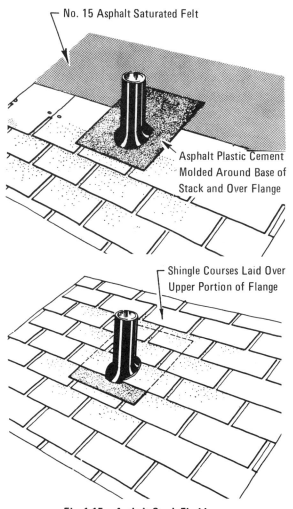

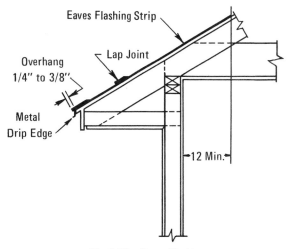

Fig. 1-15   Asphalt Stack Flashing

piece, or flange, should be large enough to extend 4 inches below, 8 inches above and 6 inches on each side of the stack.   The flange is placed over the pipe and flat on the roof with a collar of plastic cement extending 2 inches up the pipe and 2 inches over the flange.

Flashing Eaves

In areas where the temperature drops below freezing for an extended period of time, there is a possibility of ice forming along the eaves line.   To prevent a problem of this nature, eaves flashing is used.   *Eaves flashing* includes placing 55-pound, or heavier, roll roofing from a point 1/4 to 3/8 inches below the metal drip edge to a point 12 inches inside the interior wall line, figure 1-16.   If the area of the flashing exceeds 36 inches, the joint created should be cemented and located at a point beyond the building line.   *Snow slides,* 26-gage aluminum sheets, may also be used to protect against damage caused by snow and ice backing up under the eaves.   Snow slides are recommended for houses in areas that frequently receive heavy snowfalls.

Fig. 1-16   Eaves Flashing

FASTENERS

The nails used on asphalt shingles should be of corrosion-resistant steel or aluminum. They should be large-headed, 3/8 to 7/16 inch in diameter, and have barbed or deformed shanks made of 11- or 12-gage wire. Aluminum nails should be threaded with a 12 1/2-degree thread angle. If steel nails are threaded, they should have annular threads.

The nails used on wood shakes and wood shingles should also be made of corrosion-resistant materials, such as hot galvanized steel or aluminum. If the shakes are applied over plywood sheathing, threaded nails should be used. However, if the shingles are applied over solid lumber sheathing or spaced sheathing, smooth shank nails can be used. If the nails used are threaded, the steel nails should have annular threads and the aluminum nails should have a thread angle of 12 1/2 degrees. If a wood shake or shingle has a butt thickness of 3/4 to 1 1/4 inches, 6d nails are adequate; if the butt thickness ranges from 3/8 to 3/4 inch, 5d nails are used.

REVIEW

A. Choose the best answer or answers to complete each statement.

1. Eaves flashing should extend _____ inch below the metal drip edge.

    a. 1
    b. 3/4
    c. 3/8
    d. 1/2

2. If a shake has a butt thickness of 3/4 inch, a ___ nail should be used.

    a. 5d
    b. 8d
    c. 6d
    d. 4d

3. Exterior plywood has a _____ -percent waterproof glue line.

    a. 99
    b. 100
    c. 50
    d. 75

4. If a piece of plywood is stamped with an index number of 24/16, the recommended spacing of the rafters is _____ inches on center.

    a. 24
    b. 16
    c. 48
    d. 32

5. If 1/2-inch plywood decking is used, it should be nailed with ____ nails.

    a. 5d
    b. 7d
    c. 8d
    d. 6d

6. The diameter of a nailhead used for asphalt shingles should be ___ inch.

    a. 7/16
    b. 5/8
    c. 3/4
    d. 1

7. When using nominal 1-inch, tongue-and-groove boards, the rafters should be spaced no more than _____ inches on center.

    a. 16
    b. 12
    c. 24
    d. 36

8. Spaced sheathing should be spaced on center no more than ___ inches apart.

   a. 6   c. 10
   b. 8   d. 12

9. Plywood decking should be nailed along the edge with 6d nails ___ inches on center.

   a. 2   c. 6
   b. 4   d. 8

10. One layer of ___ -pound asphalt-saturated felt is usually used as underlayment.

    a. 50   c. 30
    b. 45   d. 15

B. Place the correct answer in the space provided for each of the following questions.

1. The nominal size of shiplap most often used for decking is _____ .

2. A type of sheathing that is sometimes used for wood shakes is called _____ _____ .

3. The two basic types of plywood are _____ and _____ .

4. If 1/2-inch plywood decking is used, it should be nailed with _____ nails.

5. Aluminum nails should be threaded with a _____ thread angle.

6. Underlayment should have a top horizontal lap of _____ .

7. A _____ is the intersection of two sloping roofs.

8. The flashing of the intersection of a vertical wall with a sloping roof is called _____ flashing.

9. A _____ is used to divert water from a chimney.

C. In space provided sketch

1. an end view of shiplap and tongue-and-groove boards.

2.   a closed or woven valley.

3.   step flashing.

4.   base flashing for a chimney.

Unit 2 Wood Shingles and Shakes

At one time, framed structures were always roofed with wood shingles or shakes. In recent times, however, asphalt shingles have virtually replaced wood shingles and shakes. In the past, many building codes had prohibited the use of wood shingles and shakes because of their low fire resistance. However, they can now be treated to offer better resistance and are used at times to add to the visual appeal of the structure.

SHAKES

Shakes are split wood shingles which have rough faces and are made primarily of western red cedar. The backs may also be split to produce a rough surface, or may appear smooth. Both sides of the shingle are sawed.

Shakes are manufactured in three basic types: taper split, straight split and hand split and resawed, figure 2-1. Cedar shakes are available only in Number 1 grade. They are 100 percent clear wood and are graded from the split face. Taper split and straight split shakes are 100 percent edge grain, in which the grain forms a 45-degree angle with the surface, while the hand split and resawed shakes may have up to 10-percent flat grain, with the growth rings in the wood forming an angle of less than 45 degrees with the surface. Shakes are available in lengths of 18, 24, and 32 inches with thicknesses varying from 3/8 to 1 1/4 inches.

Starter-finish shakes are used as the first course at the eaves and as last course at the ridge. They are available in 15-inch lengths. Hip and ridge units are factory cut, mitered, and assembled in lengths of 18 and 24 inches. They come prefabricated to fit a 6 in 12 slope but can be adjusted to fit slopes between 4 in 12 and 8 in 12. A roof that has a 4 in 12 slope rises 4 inches for every 12 inches on the level.

SHINGLES

The best wood shingles are sawed from cypress, western red cedar, or redwood. In some sections of the country, eastern white cedar, white pine, and soft southern pines are used. The basic grades of shingles are: Number 1, Blue Label; Number 2, Red Label; and Number 3, Black Label, figure 2-2.

Number 1 grade shingles are considered the premium grade. The shingles are 100-percent heartwood, clear, and edge grain. The shingles come in lengths of 16, 18 and 24 inches and in random widths of 3 or more inches. The *butts,* or thickened ends, come in thicknesses of .40, .45, and .50 inch.

Number 2 grade shingles should be used for structures in areas with light weather exposure. They are available in lengths of 16, 18, and 24 inches and have the same butt thickness as do Blue Label Shingles.

Number 3 grade shingles are primarily used for economical applications and should be used only in areas where weather exposure is minimal: The lengths and butt thickness are the same as those specified for Number 1 and Number 2 grade shingles.

The approximate square foot coverage of one square of hand split shakes, based on weather exposure, is given in figure 2-3; the approximate coverage of one square (4 bundles) of shingles based on weather exposure is given in figure 2-4.

HOW TO LAY WOOD SHINGLES OR WOOD SHAKES

Note: Assume that a straight roof with gable ends is to be shingled with Number 1, 18-inch wood shingles.

1. Snap a chalk line 16 1/2 inches from the first sheathing board. The 16 1/2 inches will allow the shingle to project 1 1/2 inches beyond the board.

2. Nail a shingle at one end of the roof, allowing one inch to project over the *rake,* the end of a gable roof that slopes upward.

   Note: The nails should be long enough to penetrate 1/2 inch of the sheathing. Usually 6d nails are used; however, the thickness of the shingles may vary and longer nails may be necessary.

CERTI-SPLIT RED CEDAR HANDSPLIT SHAKES

Grade	Length and Thickness	20" Pack		18" Pack		Shipping Weight	Description
		# Courses Per Bdl.	# Bdls. Per Sq.	# Courses Per Bdl.	# Bdls. Per Sq.		
No. 1 HANDSPLIT & RESAWN	15" Starter-Finish	8/8 10/10	5 4	9/9	5	225 lbs. 220 lbs.	 These shakes have split faces and sawn backs. Cedar logs are first cut into desired lengths. Blanks or boards of proper thickness are split and then run diagonally through a bandsaw to produce two tapered shakes from each blank.
	18" x ½" to ¾"	10/10	4	9/9	5	250 lbs.	
	18" x ¾" to 1¼"	8/8	5	9/9	5	225 lbs.	
	24" x ⅜"	10/10	4	9/9	5	280 lbs.	
	24" x ½" to ¾"	10/10	4	9/9	5	350 lbs.	
	24" x ¾" to 1¼"	8/8	5	9/9	5	450 lbs.	
	32" x ¾" to 1¼"	6/7	6				
No. 1 TAPERSPLIT	24" x ½" to ⅝"	10/10	4	9/9	5	260 lbs.	 Produced largely by hand, using a sharp-bladed steel froe and a wooden mallet. The natural shingle-like taper is achieved by reversing the block, end-for-end, with each split.
No. 1 STRAIGHT-SPLIT	18" x ⅜" True-Edge*	14 Straight	4			120 lbs.	 Produced in the same manner as tapersplit shakes except that by splitting from the same end of the block, the shakes acquire the same thickness throughout.
	18" x ⅜"	19 Straight	5			200 lbs.	
	24" x ⅜"	16 Straight	5			260 lbs.	

Fig. 2-1   Grades of Handsplit Shakes

Summary of Grades, Sizes and Shipping Weights

CERTIGRADE RED CEDAR SHINGLES

Grade	Length	Thickness (at Butt)	No. of Courses Per Bundle	Bdls/Cartons Per Square	Shipping Weight	Description
No. 1 BLUE LABEL	16" (Fivex) 18" (Perfections) 24" (Royals)	.40" .45" .50"	20/20 18/18 13/14	4 bdls. 4 bdls. 4 bdls.	144 lbs. 158 lbs. 192 lbs.	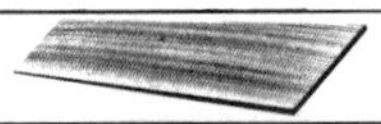 The premium grade of shingles for roofs and sidewalls. These top-grade shingles are 100% heartwood, 100% clear and 100% edge-grain.
No. 2 RED LABEL	16" (Fivex) 18" (Perfections) 24" (Royals)	.40" .45" .50"	20/20 18/18 13/14	4 bdls. 4 bdls. 4 bdls.	144 lbs. 158 lbs. 192 lbs.	 A good grade for most applications. Not less than 10" clear on 16" shingles, 11" clear on 18" shingles and 15" clear on 24" shingles. Flat grain and limited sapwood are permitted in this grade.
No. 3 BLACK LABEL	16" (Fivex) 18" (Perfections) 24" (Royals)	.40" .45" .50"	20/20 18/18 13 14	4 bdls. 4 bdls. 4 bdls.	144 lbs. 158 lbs. 192 lbs.	 A utility grade for economy applications and secondary buildings. Not less than 6" clear on 16" and 18" shingles, 10" clear on 24" shingles.
No. 1 or No. 2 REBUTTED-REJOINTED	16" (Fivex) 18" (Perfections) 24" (Royals)	.40" .45" .50"	33/33 28/28 13/14	1 carton 1 carton 4 bdls.	60 lbs. 60 lbs. 192 lbs.	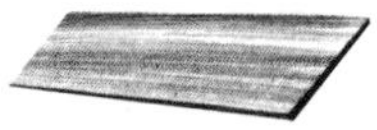 Same specifications as above but machine trimmed for exactly parallel edges with butts sawn at precise right angles. Used for sidewall application where tightly fitting joints between shingles are desired. Also available with smooth sanded face.
No. 4 UNDER-COURSING	16" (Fivex) 18" (Perfections)	.40" .45"	14/14 or 20/20 14/14 or 18/18	2 bdls. 2 bdls. 2 bdls. 2 bdls.	60 lbs. 72 lbs. 60 lbs. 79 lbs.	 A utility grade for undercoursing on double-coursed sidewall applications or for interior accent walls.

Fig. 2-2   Grades of Wood Shingles

	Approximate sq. ft. coverage of one square of handsplit shakes based on these weather exposures												
	5½"	6½"	7"	7½"*	8"	8½"	10"	11½"	13"	14"	15"	16"
18" x ½" to ¾" Handsplit-and-Resawn	55*	65	70	75**	80	85†	. . .	. . .	. . .	140‡	. . .	. . .
18" x ¾" to 1¼" Handsplit-and-Resawn	55*	65	70	75**	80	85†	. . .	. . .	. . .	140 ‡	. . .	. . .
24" x ⅜" Handsplit	. . .	65	70	75***	80	85	100††	115†	. . .	. . .	. . .	. . .
24" x ½" to ¾" Handsplit-and-Resawn	. . .	65	70	75*	80	85	100**	115†	. . .	. . .	. . .	. . .
24" x ¾" to 1¼" Handsplit-and-Resawn	. . .	65	70	75*	80	85	100**	115†	. . .	. . .	. . .	. . .
32" x ¾" to 1¼" Handsplit-and-Resawn	. . .	. . .	. . .	. . .	. . .	. . .	100*	115	130**	140	150†	. . .
24" x ½" to ⅝" Tapersplit	. . .	65	70	75*	80	85	100**	115†	. . .	. . .	. . .	. . .
18" x ⅜" True-Edge Straight-Split	. . .	. . .	. . .	. . .	. . .	. . .	. . .	. . .	. . .	100	106	112‡
18" x ⅜" Straight-Split	65*	75	80	90	95	100†	. . .	. . .	. . .	. . .	. . .	. . .
24" x ⅜" Straight-Split	. . .	65	70	75*	80	85	100	115†	. . .	. . .	. . .	. . .
15" Starter-Finish Course	Use supplementary with shakes applied not over 10" weather exposure.											

NOTES: * Recommended maximum weather exposure for 3-ply roof construction.
** Recommended maximum weather exposure for 2-ply roof construction
*** Recommended maximum weather exposure for roof pitches of 4/12 to 8/12.
† Recommended maximum weather exposure for single-coursed wall construction.
†† Recommended maximum weather exposure for roof pitches of 8/12 or steeper.
‡ Recommended maximum weather exposure for double-coursed wall construction.

Fig. 2-3   Square Foot Coverage of Shakes

LENGTH AND THICKNESS	Approximate coverage of one square (4 bundles) of shingles based on following weather exposures																									
	3½"	4"	4½"	5"	5½"	6"	6½"	7"	7½"	8"	8½"	9"	9½"	10"	10½"	11"	11½"	12"	12½"	13"	13½"	14"	14½"	15"	15½"	16"
16" x 5/2"	70	80	90	100*	110	120	130	140	150Σ	160	170	180	190	200	210	220	230	240†	. . .	. . .	. . .	. . .	. . .	. . .	. . .	. . .
18" x 5/2¼"	. . .	72½	81½	90½	100*	109	118	127	136	145½	154½Σ	163½	172½	181½	191	200	209	218	227	236	245½	254½†	. . .	. . .	. . .	. . .
24" x 4/2"	. . .	. . .	. . .	. . .	. . .	80	86½	93	100*	106½	113	120	126½	133	140	146½	153Σ	160	166½	173	180	186½	193	200	206½	213†

NOTES: * Maximum exposure recommended for roofs.   Σ Maximum exposure recommended for single-coursing on sidewalls.   † Maximum exposure recommended for double-coursing on sidewalls.

Fig. 2-4   Coverage of One Square of Shingles

3. Continue to lay the shingles side by side 1/4 inch apart and over the entire length of the roof. These shingles need to be nailed only at the butts. The nails should be kept 1 inch from the edge and 1 1/4 inches from the butt.

   Note: Use only straight grain shingles and split all shingles which are over 9 inches wide, nailing the split sections as individual shingles. All shingles should be nailed with two nails unless they are less than 4 inches wide. Keep the heads of the nails flush with the surface.

4. Lay another course of shingles on top of the first course, figure 2-5. Be sure to keep the nails far enough above the butts so that they will be covered by at least 1 inch of the succeeding course.

5. Snap a chalk line 5 1/2 inches from the butt of the double course.

   Note: The surface exposed for a 16-inch shingle should be 5 inches, 5 1/2 inches for an 18-inch shingle, and 7 1/2 inches for a 24-inch shingle.

6. Nail the second course of shingles in the same manner as the starting course, with the butts along the chalk line.

   Note: Break all side joints of the second course of shingles 1 1/2 inches away from the side joints of the starting course. No joint should be directly over another joint on any three consecutive courses.

7. Continue laying the courses of shingles up the roof in the same manner as described for the second course.

   Note: If the roof has a slope greater than 6 in 12, secure a footrest every 6 feet up the roof. Wood shingles or shakes should not be used on roofs that have a slope of less than 4 in 12.

HOW TO BUILD A FOOTREST FOR WOOD SHINGLES OR WOOD SHAKES

1. Select a 2 x 4 that is free of knots or fractures and about 12 feet long. Lay it parallel to the shingle line on the roof with one end even with the edge of the roof.

2. Place three 4-inch or 5-inch shingles on the face of the 2 x 4, with one about 4 inches from each end and one in the center. Place the butts of the shingles on the 2 x 4. Be certain that the butts extend at least 1 1/2 inches across the 2 x 4 and that they are centered on the joints of the shingle course above. Nail each shingle to the 2 x 4 in this position with about five shingle nails, figure 2-6.

3. Nail a shingle in a similar fashion to additional 2 x 4s every 6 feet. Use enough pieces to cover the entire length of the roof.

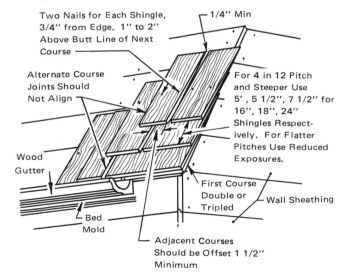

Fig. 2-5   Laying of Wood Shingles

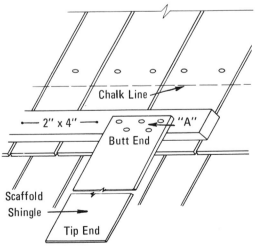

Fig. 2-6   Footrest

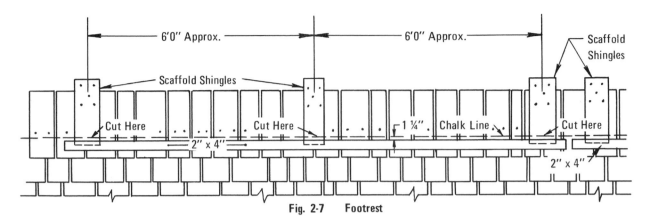

Fig. 2-7   Footrest

4. Turn the 2 x 4 over so that the shingles take a position of being nailed to the course marked by the chalk line. Adjust the 2 x 4 so that the top edge reaches about 1/4 inch below the chalk line.

5. Nail the scaffold shingles to the roof. Keep the nails in a similar position to those of the other shingles but drive at least five nails into each of these shingles, figure 2-7.

Note: When the scaffold is of no further use, the scaffold shingles should be cut off on a line with the shingle course and the 2 x 4 should be removed from the roof.

HOW TO SHINGLE HIPS AND RIDGES

Note: Hips and ridges can be constructed from prefabricated units. If preassembled units are not used, the shingles should be laid in a "Boston" fashion, figure 2-8.

1. Measure 5 inches on either side of the ridge or hip and snap a chalk line, or tack two wooden straightedges to the roof at this point.

2. Starting at the bottom, nail the first shingle on the hip, using the line or straightedge as a guide.

3. Cut the edge of the shingle that is projecting over the hip back on a bevel.

4. Secure the shingle on the opposite side.

5. Cut the projecting edge to fit.

6. Going up the roof, continue to lay the first layer of shingles.

7. Alternate a second layer of shingles in reverse order.

Note: These shingles are applied over the top of the regular shingle courses and may be mitered instead of being alternately lapped. *Mitering* is the joining of two surfaces at an evenly divided angle. Most miter joints have a 45-degree angle.

HOW TO SHINGLE A VALLEY

Note: The grain of valley shingles should match the grain in the body of the roof.

1. Measure 3 inches from the center of the valley and establish a point on both sides at the ridge. At the eaves line measure 3 inches from the center of the valley adding 1/8 inch for every running foot from the ridge to the eaves line.

2. Mark a line between these two points by snapping or by using a straightedge tacked to the roof.

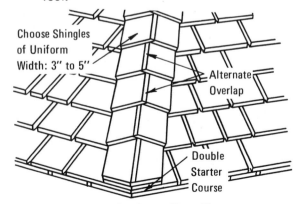

Fig. 2-8   Boston-Type Hip

3. Place a cut valley shingle on each side of the valley with the cut edge along the shingle guideline.

4. Place a regular shingle against the valley shingle, allowing a distance of 1/4 inch between the two.

5. Secure another valley shingle on top of the first valley shingle.

6. Continue the double course of shingles, placing regular shingles against valley shingles.

REVIEW

A.   Choose the best answer or answers to complete each statement.

1. A hip shingle should extend _____ inches on either side of the hip.

   a. 5   c. 9
   b. 7   d. 12

2. The starter course for a hip should be a _____ course.

   a. double   c. triple
   b. single   d. quadruple

3. The difference between a valley shingle and a regular shingle should be ___ inch.

   a. 3/8   c. 1/4
   b. 1/2   d. 1/8

4. To establish the width of the valley at the eaves line, add _____ inch for every running foot up to a total of 3 inches.

   a. 3/4   c. 1/4
   b. 1/2   d. 1/8

5. The correct exposure for an 18-inch shingle is _____ inches.

   a. 5   c. 6
   b. 5 1/2   d. 7 1/2

6. All side joints of the second course should be _____ inch(es) from the side joint of the starting course.

   a. 1   c. 2
   b. 1 1/2   d. 2 1/2

7. Shingles that are 4 inches wide or larger should be nailed with ____ nails.

   a. 2   c. 1
   b. 3   d. 4

8. The butts of shingles come in thicknesses of .40 inch, .45 inch and ___ inch.

   a. .50   c. .80
   b. .60   d. .75

9. A square of 24-inch x 3/8-inch hand split shakes with an 8-inch weather exposure will cover _____ square feet.

a. 90   c. 75
b. 85   d. 80

10. Hip and ridge units are preassembled to fit a _____ slope.

a. 4 in 12   c. 6 in 12
b. 5 in 12   d. 8 in 12

B. Place the correct answer in the space provided for each of the following questions.

1. The primary difference in wood shakes and wood shingles is_____ .

2. Starter-finish shakes are produced in _____ -inch lengths.

3. The _____ wood shingle is used primarily for economy applications.

4. A shingle should project _____ beyond the first sheathing board.

5. Shingle nails should be placed ___ from the edge and ___ from the butt.

6. The exposure for a 16-inch shingle is _____ .

7. A footrest should be about _____ feet long.

8. Hips and ridges should be laid in a _____ fashion.

9. The shingle at the top of the ridge should be _____ from the center of the valley.

C. In the space provided sketch

1. the steps necessary for shingling a valley.

2. a ridge with shingles laid in a Boston-type fashion.

Unit 3 Asphalt Shingles

Asphalt roofing shingles are made from felt that is saturated and coated with asphalt. The felt is made from products containing cellulose fibers (rags, paper, and wood). Asphalt is a by-product of the petroleum industry and goes by the trade name of Asphalt Flux. The saturation of the asphalt increases the preserving and waterproofing properties of the asphalt shingle.

In addition to the asphalt, flux mineral stabilizers are sometimes used to coat asphalt shingles. It has been found that the products will better resist effects of the weather and generally be more stable if they contain a small percentage of minerals such as silica, slate dust, talc, dolomite, and trap rock. The mineral granules also reflect the rays of the sun, increase the fire resistance of the shingle, and enhance the architectural style of the home, primarily because of the variety of colors and color blends.

Asphalt shingles are manufactured in weights from 145 pounds to 330 pounds per square, figure 3-1. A *square* is an area which measures 10 feet by 10 feet, or 100 square feet; three or four bundles of 36-inch shingles will cover a square. The most common weights of the asphalt composition shingle used in light construction are 235 and 240 pounds. As shingles increase in weight, the life expectancy of the shingle also increases.

If a roof is covered with asphalt shingles and has a slope of less than 4 in 12, a double thickness of underlayment should be placed over the roof sheathing. The roof should also be provided with eaves flashing in areas that are subjected to freezing temperatures for an extended period of time. Only shingles with adhesives on the tabs should be used on a roof with a slope of less than 4 in 12, or a spot of adhesive should be placed under the free tab. Most manufacturers will not guarantee shingles used on a roof with a slope of less than 4 in 12.

STRIP SHINGLES

Strip shingles, figure 3-2, come in many weights and styles and are packed in three to four bundles to cover one square. The rectangular-shaped shingles are available 12 inches wide and 36 inches long and are stamped or slotted to appear as individual shingles when they are laid. To prevent the shingle from buckling from the effects of sun and wind, spots of special adhesive are applied to the tabs of the shingles, figure 3-3. Application of the shingles in small sheets allows for their expansion and contraction which otherwise could also have a buckling effect on the shingles.

INDIVIDUAL ASPHALT SHINGLES

The *individual asphalt shingle* is very similar in composition and weight to the strip shingle. The hexagonal and angular shapes have the same locking features and factory-applied adhesives as the strip type. The individual hex shingle comes in two basic types, those which are secured by a staple, figure 3-4, and those with a locking device, figure 3-5. In most cases, the individual hex shingle is used for reroofing old structures, but it is occasionally used in new construction.

Giant individual shingles are 12 inches wide and 16 inches long and are used primarily for reroofing. The shingles can be applied over most types of old roofing, but applications on roofs with a rise of less than 4 inches per foot should be avoided.

HOW TO APPLY STRIP SHINGLES

1. Place a starter course of inverted shingles along the eaves line, allowing 1/4 to 3/8 inch to extend over the eaves and rake edges, figure 3-6. The first inverted shingle should be the size of a full shingle minus 3 inches.

    Note: It is sometimes helpful to snap a horizontal chalk line 11 3/4 inches from the eaves line. This line will serve as a guide and prevent the shingles from being placed out of alignment.

    Lay the first course of shingles, starting with a full shingle. The first shingle of the succeeding courses will be either a full or cut strip.

1	2	3	4	5	6	7	8	9	10
Product	Approx. Shipping Weight Per Square	Packages Per Square	Length	Width	Shingles Per Square	Side or End Lap	Top Lap	Head Lap	Exposure
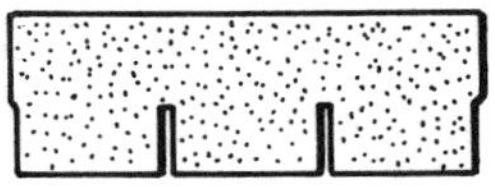 3 Tab Self Sealing Strip Shingle	235 lb. 300 lb.	3 or 4	36" 36"	12" 12"	80 80		7" 7"	2" 2"	5" 5"
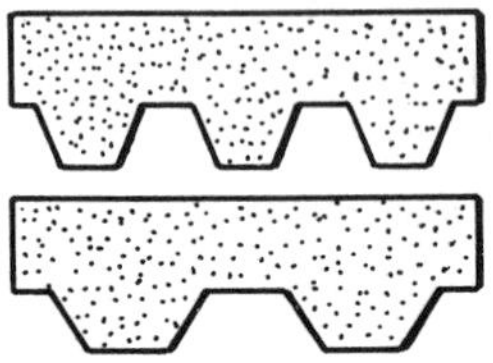 2 and 3 Tab Hex Strip	195 lb.	3	36"	11 1/3"	86		2"	2"	5"
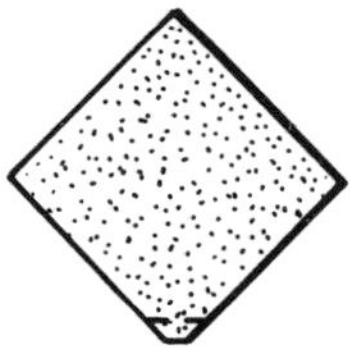 Individual Lock Down	145 lb.	2	16"	16"	80	2½"			
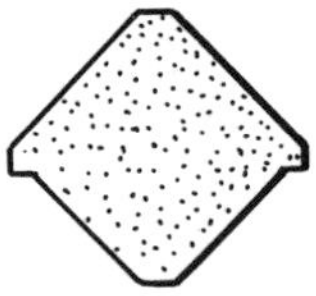 Individual Staple Down	145 lb.	2	16"	16"	80	2½"			
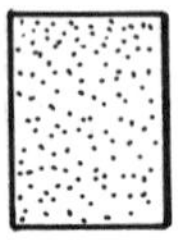 Giant Individual American	330 lb.	4	16"	12"	226		11"	6"	5"
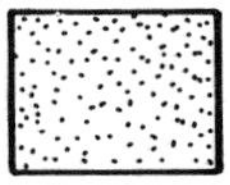 Giant Individual Dutch Lap	165 lb.	2	16"	12"	113	3"	2"		10"

Fig. 3-1   Asphalt Shingles

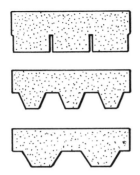

Fig. 3-2   Strip Shingles

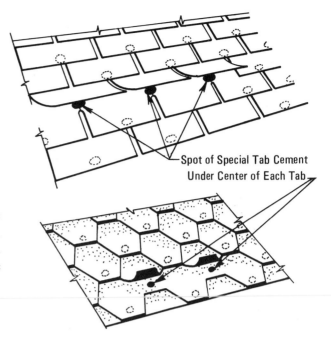

Spot of Special Tab Cement
Under Center of Each Tab

Fig. 3-3   Application of Tab Cement

Note: Roofs that are 30 feet or less in length may have the strip shingle laid from either rake. However, if the length exceeds 30 feet, it is useful to snap a vertical chalk line in the center of the roof and work from the vertical line.

3. Lay the second course, starting with a full-sized shingle minus 4 inches.

   Note: Chalk lines are often used as a means of controlling the alignment of each course. However, some contractors prefer to use the shingler's hatchet equipped with a sliding gage, figure 3-7. The gage is used for quick, accurate checking of shingle exposure.

4. Start the third course with a full-sized shingle minus 8 inches and proceed to lay the course.

5. Start the fourth course with a full-sized shingle and lay the course.

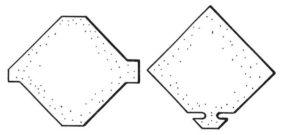

Fig. 3-4   Individual Hex Shingle   **Fig. 3-5   Self-Locking Device for an Individual Shingle**

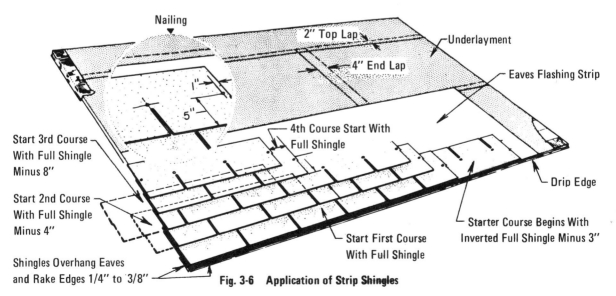

Nailing

2" Top Lap — Underlayment

4" End Lap

Eaves Flashing Strip

1"

5"

4th Course Start With Full Shingle

Start 3rd Course With Full Shingle Minus 8"

Start 2nd Course With Full Shingle Minus 4"

Drip Edge

Shingles Overhang Eaves and Rake Edges 1/4" to 3/8"

Start First Course With Full Shingle

Starter Course Begins With Inverted Full Shingle Minus 3"

Fig. 3-6   Application of Strip Shingles

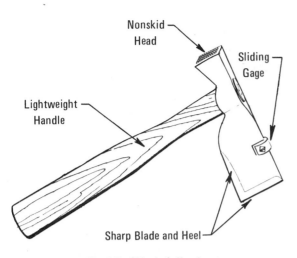

Nonskid Head

Sliding Gage

Lightweight Handle

Sharp Blade and Heel

Fig. 3-7 Shingler's Hatchet

HOW TO APPLY SHINGLES BY THE RIBBON COURSING METHOD

Many contractors apply massive roofing to a home for a special appearance effect. To achieve this special effect, *ribbon coursing*, a technique involving a special starting procedure repeated every fifth course, is used.

1. Cut 4-inch strips from full-sized 12-inch shingles. The strip will act as a starter strip, figure 3-8.

2. Lay the 4-inch starter strip along the eaves line, allowing 1/4 inch to 3/8 inch to project over the eave and rake edge.

3. Cover the starter strip with the remaining 8-inch strip. The cutouts should be laid down to the eave.

4. The first full course of 12" x 36" shingles is then laid over the 4-inch and 8-inch strips.

5. The next three courses are laid in the same manner as are the strip shingles.

6. The ribbon coursing technique is completed by aligning the ribbon course to the top of the cutouts of every fifth course.

HOW TO SHINGLE HIPS AND RIDGES

1. Cut 9" x 12" hip and ridge shingles. Precut hip and ridge shingles may be used.

2. Bend each shingle in the center.

   Note: In cold weather, bending will be easier if the shingles are heated first.

3. Starting at the bottom of the hip or at the end of the ridge, apply the shingles, leaving 5 inches exposed.

4. Nail the shingle 5 1/2 inches from the exposed end and one inch up from the edge.

   Note: All hips and ridges using asphalt shingles should be applied in a similar manner.

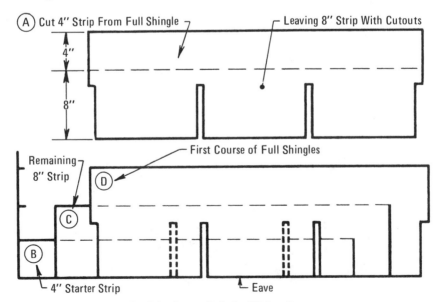

(A) Cut 4" Strip From Full Shingle

Leaving 8" Strip With Cutouts

4"

8"

Remaining 8" Strip

First Course of Full Shingles

(D)

(C)

(B)

4" Starter Strip

Eave

Fig. 3-8 Starter Strip for Ribbon Course

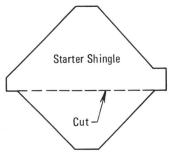

Fig. 3-9   Starter Shingle

HOW TO APPLY INDIVIDUALLY-STAPLED HEX SHINGLES

1. Cut hex shingles below the shoulder to make starter shingles, figure 3-9.

   Note: Use vertical and horizontal chalk lines to keep the hex shingles in correct alignment.

2. Starting from either the center of the building or the edge of the rake, place the cut edge flush with the overhang. Each shoulder tab should be

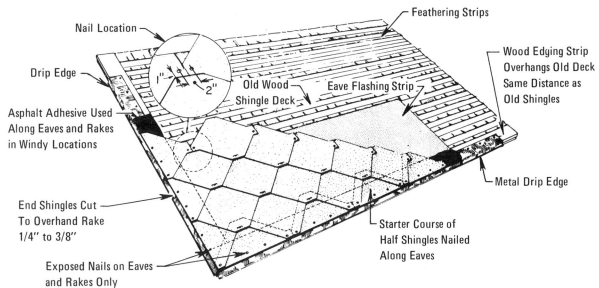

Fig. 3-10   Application of Individual Stapled Shingles

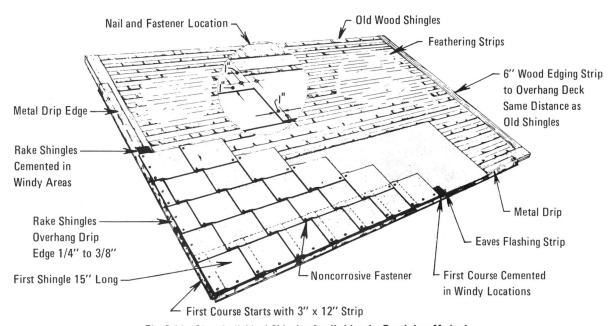

Fig. 3-11   Giant Individual Shingles Applied by the Dutch Lap Method

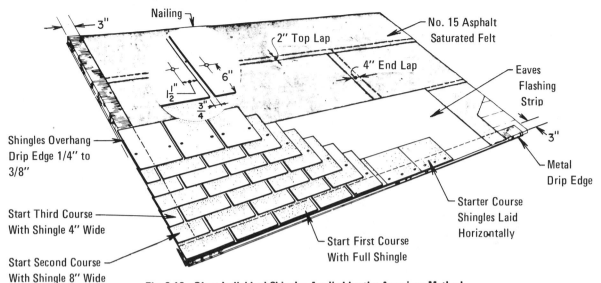

Fig. 3-12 Giant Individual Shingles Applied by the American Method

fastened with a nail, and the edges of the shingle along the eaves line should have two exposed nails, figure 3-10.

Note: In areas that are subjected to high winds, place asphalt cement under the eave and rake shingles.

3. Apply the first course of shingles. The bottom of each shingle should be flush with the edge of the eave and centered over the shoulder tabs of the starter course.

4. Apply the succeeding courses in the same manner, fastening the bottom of each shingle with wire fasteners.

HOW TO APPLY GIANT SHINGLES BY THE DUTCH LAP METHOD

1. Snap a chalk line 12 inches above the eaves line.

2. Place a 3" x 12" piece of shingle flush with the rake and the chalk line, figure 3-11.

3. Place a full-sized unit over the 3" x 12" piece, aligning it with the chalk line and allowing 1/4 to 3/8 inch to overhang the drig edge.

Note: The shingles should be secured with non-corrosive fasteners, and the lower left-hand corner of each shingle should have an exposed nail.

4. Continue the first course, overlapping each unit 3 inches.

5. Run the remaining courses. Start with a full shingle aligned with the vertical exposed edge of the shingle in the preceding course.

Note: In windy areas, the rake and eave shingles should be cemented down.

HOW TO APPLY GIANT INDIVIDUAL SHINGLES BY THE AMERICAN METHOD

1. Snap a chalk line along the short dimension of the shingle, measuring from the eaves line up the roof.

2. Lay the starter course, keeping the first unit flush with the rake and chalk line. Lay the starter course with the long side of the shingle in a horizontal position and the units butted to each other, figure 3-12.

3. Apply the first course of shingles, aligning the first shingle with the eave. Allow the shingle to project 1/4 to 3/8 inch over the rake edge. Place the remainder of the shingles flush with the eaves line and spaced 1/2 inch apart.

4. Apply the succeeding courses, breaking joints every third shingle. The second course starts with an 8-inch shingle; the third with a 4-inch shingle; and the fourth with a full-sized shingle.

REVIEW

A.   Choose the best answer or answers to complete each statement.

1.   Asphalt is a by-product of _____ .

   a. petroleum   c. gypsum
   b. gas   d. coal

2.   Asphalt shingles are manufactured in weights of _____ .

   a. 100 pounds to 300 pounds   c. 145 pounds to 330 pounds
   b. 150 pounds to 350 pounds   d. 75 pounds to 165 pounds

3.   Giant individual shingles are _____ inches wide.

   a. 12   c. 16
   b. 18   d. 10

4.   Strip shingles should extend _____ inch over the rake edge.

   a. 1/8   c. 1/2
   b. 3/4   d. 3/8

5.   When giant individual shingles are applied by the American method, the second course starts with a(an) _____ -inch unit.

   a. 8   c. 6
   b. 4   d. 12

6.   Individually stapled hex shingles are secured at the bottom with _____ _____ .

   a. nails   c. wire fasteners
   b. tacks   d. brads

7.   In applying giant individual shingles by the Dutch lap method, each shingle should have a _____ -inch side lap.

   a. 2   c. 5
   b. 3   d. 6

8.   If a chalk line is not used to aligh shingles, a _____ is sometimes used.

   a. hammer   c. nail
   b. tape measure   d. shingler's hatchet

9.   Shingles used on a hip or ridge should measure _____ .

   a. 9" x 12"   c. 12" x 12"
   b. 10" x 10"   d. 15" x 12"

10.   In applying a ribbon course, the starter strip is _____ -inches wide.

   a. 8   c. 9
   b. 6   d. 4

B. Place the correct answer in the space provided for each of the following questions.

1. Asphalt roofing shingles are made from _____ , _____ , and _____ .

2. The two most common weights of asphalt composition shingle used in residential construction are _____ and _____ .

3. Factory-applied adhesives are found on the _____ of the strip shingle.

4. The individual hex shingle is available in two basic types, _____ , and _____ .

5. If a massive appearance for a roof is desired, the _____ technique is used.

6. The second course of strip shingles should be started with a full-sized shingle minus _____ inches.

7. A hip or ridge shingle should have an exposure of _____ inches.

8. Hex shingles are kept in correct alignment by using _____ .

9. Giant individual shingles should be secured with _____ .

10. The tearing of a shingle is sometimes prevented by _____ .

Unit 4 Closed Cornices

The *cornice* is that section of the exterior trim which is formed by the projection of the rafters. In some areas, the cornice is known as the *eave* of the structure. The cornice, or eave, is vital to the architectural design of the home.

One classification of cornice construction is the *closed* or *boxed cornice*. In this particular type of construction, the rafter tails are enclosed by a fascia, soffit, and trim.

A closed cornice may continue completely around the building, or extend along two sides and return a short distance around the ends of the building. This structure is known as a *return cornice*, figure 4-1. A *rake cornice*, figure 4-2, is extended up the slope of the roof at the intersection of the wall and the roofline.

A closed cornice provides a means of decorating the section where the roof and walls of a building meet and is often used to extend the rooflines so that the lines are in agreement with the general style of the building. A projecting cornice protects the wall of the building by shedding water and provides a surface for the installation of gutters, which carry drainage to downspouts.

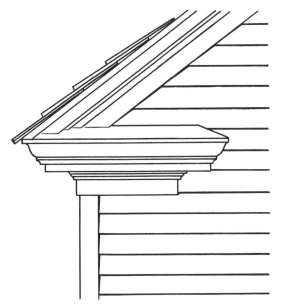

Fig. 4-1 Return Cornice

CORNICE MEMBERS

A closed cornice with a level soffit has eight basic structural members: rough fascia, finish fascia, soffit, lookouts, molding, drip edge, frieze and lookout ledger, figure 4-3. Each item contributes to the total design and function of the structure.

The *rough fascia*, usually a 1 x 4 or 2 x 4, provides an even nailing surface for the finish fascia. The top of the rough fascia should be beveled to match the slope of the roof. A fascia is used to enclose and enhance the beauty of the cornice, and provide a nailing surface for a gutter. The *finish fascia*, usually a 1 x 6, is nailed directly to the rough fascia. In some cases, the fascia may be provided with slots to receive the soffit, figure 4-4.

The *soffit*, or *plancier*, is the underside of the cornice. It is usually made of 1/4- or 3/8-inch plywood; however, hardboard, metal, or plaster may be used. For ventilation purposes, the soffit may have numerous openings or ventilation holes covered by an aluminum grill.

Lookouts are usually 2 x 2 or 2 x 4 horizontal structural members and are used to support the soffit. The lookouts are spaced 16 to 48 inches on center and extend from the lookout ledger to the end of the rafter.

Molding consists of narrow strips of wood designed to present a depressed or extended surface. They are used for decorating flat surfaces and for covering joints created by the intersection of structural members. Crown molding, figure 4-5, is generally used on cornices at the fascia and roofline. Bed and cove molding, figure 4-6, is sometimes used instead of or in combination with, crown molding.

The *drip edge*, figure 4-7, is placed over the roof sheathing and along the fascia to protect the sheathing and fascia by allowing water to drip free of the cornice construction.

The *frieze* provides a closing space for the brick and fills the void between the top of the window and the soffit. In brick veneer construction the frieze is

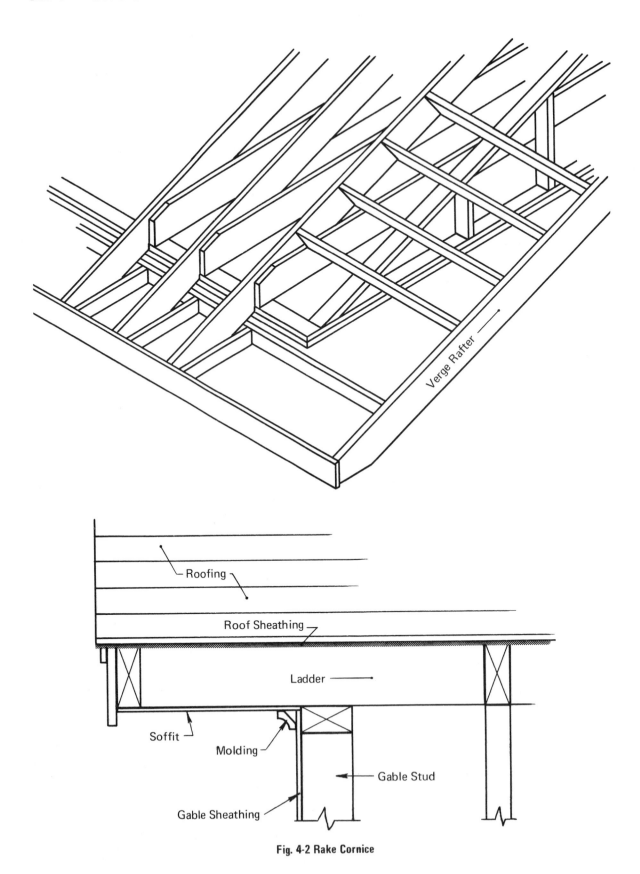

Fig. 4-2 Rake Cornice

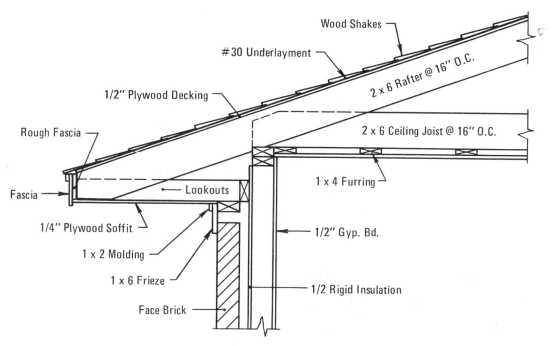

Fig. 4-3 Closed Cornice With a Level Soffit

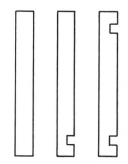

Fig. 4-4 Plain and Grooved Fascia

usually a 1 x 6, a 1 x 8, or a piece of molding. The *lookout ledger* is a horizontal 1 x 4 nailed to the stud wall. The ledger provides a nailing base for the lookout and is usually placed 1/2 inch below the bottom of the rafter tails.

SLOPING SOFFIT

Contractors sometimes prefer to use a sloping soffit rather than a cornice with a level soffit. A closed or box cornice with a sloping soffit, figure 4-8, is constructed by eliminating the lookouts and lookout ledger. The soffit is nailed directly to the

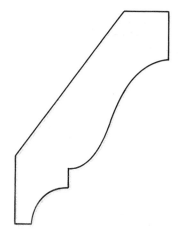

Fig. 4-5 Crown Molding

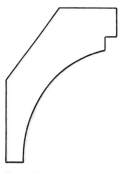

Fig. 4-6 Cove Molding

Fig. 4-7   Drip Edges

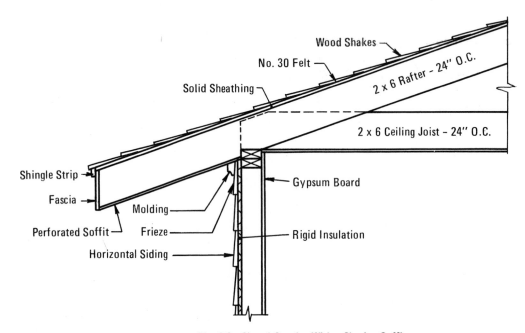

Wood Shakes

No. 30 Felt

Solid Sheathing

2 x 6 Rafter – 24'' O.C.

2 x 6 Ceiling Joist – 24'' O.C.

Shingle Strip

Gypsum Board

Fascia

Molding

Perforated Soffit

Frieze

Rigid Insulation

Horizontal Siding

Fig. 4-8   Closed Cornice With a Sloping Soffit

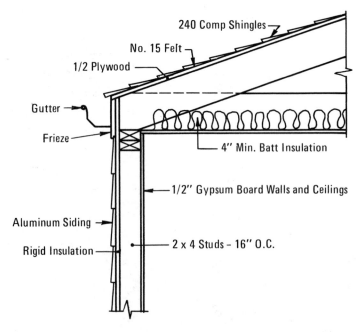

240 Comp Shingles

No. 15 Felt

1/2 Plywood

Gutter

Frieze

4'' Min. Batt Insulation

1/2'' Gypsum Board Walls and Ceilings

Aluminum Siding

2 x 4 Studs – 16'' O.C.

Rigid Insulation

Fig. 4-9   Snub Cornice

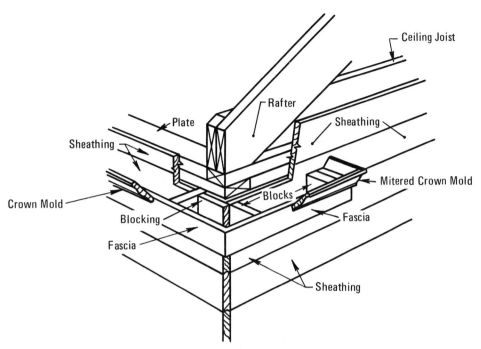

Fig. 4-10   Box Cornice Return

underside of the rafter tails. The closed cornice with
a level soffit is sometimes preferred, even though it
may be more costly, because of the difficulty in fitting
the sloping soffit and the general appearance of the
sloping cornice.

SNUB CORNICE

The *snub cornice*, figure 4-9, is another type of
closed cornice, but is not used extensively. In the
construction of a snub cornice, the ends of the rafters
are flush with the exterior wall, and a fascia is nailed
directly to the rafter tails. A gutter, made to resemble
large crown molding, is usually attached to the fascia.
The absence of the soffit adds a note of simplicity to
the project and is economical to construct.

CORNICE RETURNS

The *return* of a cornice, figure 4-10, is used
where the cornice is terminated, such as at the ends of
the sidewalls, or where a gable is located at the sidewall
and the cornice does not extend across the gable. The
design of the cornice return should be consistent with
the design of the cornice itself. The soffit, fascia, and

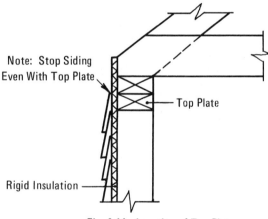

Fig. 4-11   Location of Top Plate

crown molding should project beyond the building
line the same distance on the end of the building as
they do on the side. In colonial cornices, the return is
snubbed as it returns around the corner of the building.

HOW TO CONSTRUCT A CLOSED CORNICE WITH A LEVEL SOFFIT FOR A BRICK VENEERED STRUCTURE

1.   Snap a chalk line 1/2 inch lower than the bottom
     of the rafter tails.

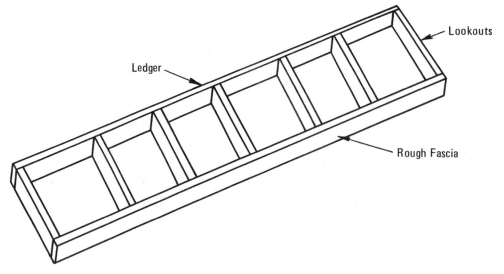

Fig. 4-12 Soffit Ladder

2. Using the chalk line as a guide, nail the 2 x 4 lookout ledger against the stud wall. Allow the lookout ledger to extend the length of the overhang past the end of the house.

3. Nail the rough fascia to the end of the rafter tails, being certain that it is level with the lookout ledger.

4. Nail the lookouts to the rough fascia and the lookout ledger.

5. Straighten the rough fascia, using a stretched string as a guide.

6. Measure perpencidular to the stud wall 5 1/2 inches and snap a chalk line on the lookouts.

7. Using the chalk line as a guide, nail a 2 x 4 stringer to the lookouts. The stringer acts as a nailing surface for the frieze.

8. Nail the soffit to the bottom of the lookouts. Allow the soffit to project 1/16 inch past the rough fascia.

9. Nail the fascia in place with 1/2 inch projecting below the bottom of the soffit.

10. Nail the drip edge in place.

11. Nail the frieze in place.

12. Nail the molding in place.

HOW TO CONSTRUCT A CLOSED CORNICE WITH A SLOPING SOFFIT

1. Nail the fascia to the ends of the rafters. If the fascia is not aligned properly, stretch a nylon string along the full length of the fascia and straighten the fascia by tapping it.

2. Place the soffit against the back of the fascia and nail it to the underside of the rafters.

3. Snap a chalk line along the length of the wall to show the location of the bottom of the frieze. Allow the top of the frieze to extend within 1/2 inch of the soffit.

4. Place and nail the frieze board against the building.

5. Nail the molding in place at the intersection of the soffit and frieze.

6. Nail the drip edge to the fascia.

HOW TO CONSTRUCT A SNUB CORNICE

Note: When placing the ceiling joists and rafters, be certain that the ends do not extend past the stud wall.

1. Secure the siding to the wall frame, aligning the siding with the top plate. The *top plate* is the horizontal member nailed to the top of the stud.

2. Snap a chalk line 1/2 inch below the top of the siding. This line will establish the location of the bottom of the frieze.

3. Nail the frieze board in place against the rafter tails, using the chalk line as a guide.

4. Install the gutter system. A *gutter* is a wooden or metal channel that carries off rainwater and water from melting snow.

HOW TO CONSTRUCT A CLOSED CORNICE WITH A LEVEL SOFFIT FOR A FRAMED STRUCTURE

Note: The technique used in the construction and erection of the soffit ladder can also be used in the construction of a closed cornice for a brick veneer.

1. Cut the lookout ledger and rough fascia to the proper length. The length should equal the length of the house plus twice the length of the overhang.

2. Cut the lookouts to the proper length.

3. Assemble the lookouts, lookout ledger, and rough fascia to form the soffit ladder, figure 4-12.

4. Snap a chalk line on the sheathing 1/2 inch lower than the bottom of the rafter tails.

5. Raise the soffit ladder, placing the bottom of the lookout ledger against the chalk line.

6. Nail the lookout ledger to the studs and the rough fascia to the rafter tails.

7. Cut and place the soffit against the underside of the soffit ladder. Allow 1/16 inch to project past the edge of the rough fascia.

8. Nail the fascia in place with 1/2 inch projecting below the bottom of the soffit.

9. Nail the drip edge in place.

10. Nail the molding in place.

REVIEW

A. Choose the best answer or answers to complete each statement.

1. The cornice is sometimes called the _____ .
   - a. stoop
   - b. eave
   - c. rake
   - d. ridge

2. The soffit is nailed to the _____ .
   - a. ceiling joist
   - b. rafter
   - c. lookout
   - d. plancier

3. The narrower strips of wood that are placed in internal corners are called _____ .
   - a. molding
   - b. eaves
   - c. rakes
   - d. fascia

4. To protect the sheathing and fascia from excessive amounts of water, a _____ is used.
   - a. frieze
   - b. soffit
   - c. drip edge
   - d. lookout

5. The lookout ledger is nailed to the _____ .

   a. rafters
   b. ceiling joist
   c. stud wall
   d. fascia

6. In the construction of a level soffit, a chalk line is snapped _____ inch below the rafter tails.

   a. 1/4
   b. 1/2
   c. 3/4
   d. 1

7. The stringer is placed _____ inches from the stud wall.

   a. 5 1/2
   b. 4
   c. 12
   d. 6 1/2

8. The soffit projects _____ inch past the rough fascia.

   a. 1
   b. 1/2
   c. 1/8
   d. 1/16

9. The drip edge is nailed to the _____ .

   a. soffit
   b. frieze
   c. fascia
   d. plancier

10. The length of a rough fascia is _____ .

    a. 33 feet
    b. the length of the house plus twice the length of the overhang.
    c. the length of the house minus 8 feet.
    d. the length of the house minus twice the length of the overhang.

B. Place the correct answer in the space provided for each of the following questions.

1. The _____ is that part of the exterior trim formed by the projection of the rafters.

2. If a cornice extends up the slope of the roof, it is called a _____ cornice.

3. The soffit is sometimes called a _____ .

4. Lookouts are spaced _____ to _____ inches on center.

5. The _____ provides a closing space for the brick.

6. The rough fascia is nailed to the _____ .

7. The fascia projects _____ inch below the bottom of the soffit.

8. In addition to a hammer, a _____ is used to align the finish fascia.

9. The frieze board is nailed to the _____ in a snub cornice.

10. The lookouts, lookout ledger, and rough fascia framed together form the

    _____ .

C. Identify the parts of the closed cornice in the figure.

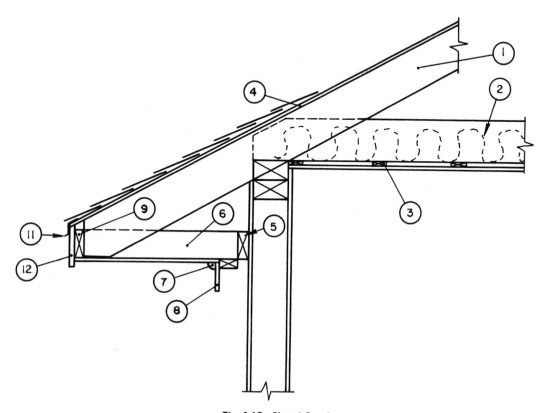

Fig. 4-13 Closed Cornice

Unit 5 Open Cornices

An *open cornice*, figure 5-1, is a cornice in which the rafter tails and roof sheathing are exposed. The rafter tails are usually straight, with a plumb cut at the end for the installation of a fascia or gutter, figure 5-2. Rafter tails are sometimes cut with an ornamental curve at the bottom and a plumb cut at the end, figure 5-3. The ornamental cut serves no structural purpose; it is placed on the rafter only to complement a particular architectural style.

In the construction of an open cornice, a wide frieze board extends from the siding to the bottom of the rafters, while a narrower frieze board extends from the top of the wide frieze to the roof sheathing. The narrower frieze is placed between each rafter and is capped with a piece of molding where it intersects with the roof sheathing.

At a corner of a structure, where the open cornice returns up the rake, the horizontal frieze board will sometimes also extend in that direction, figure 5-4. The return of the horizontal fascia extends beyond the end of the building and in an upward direction along the rake. The *bargeboard*, the decorative board which extends up the rake, is sometimes thicker and wider than the horizontal fascia.

The roof sheathing nailed over an open cornice may be either an exterior grade of plywood or dressed beaded ceiling stock. Plywood sheathing over the open cornice adds a note of simplicity to the cornice while dressed beaded ceiling stock, figure 5-5, is more decorative. If the thickness of the sheathing covering the open cornice is not the same thickness as the sheathing that covers the roof, a wedge should be used to feather out the difference, figure 5-6. The ceiling stock for an open cornice should also be thick enough to prevent protrusion of nails or staples.

It is especially important to consider insulation for roofs built with open cornices since heat may escape through the ceiling above the wall line in buildings which are not properly insulated. In winter months, the heat may melt snow on the roof. The water then drains from the roof surface until it reaches the section of the roof which extends beyond the building line. The outer section of the roof is exposed to cold winds on the underside, thereby causing the draining water to freeze on the roof above the open cornice and in the hanging gutter. The accumulating ice causes the water to back up underneath the shingles to a point above the building line where it

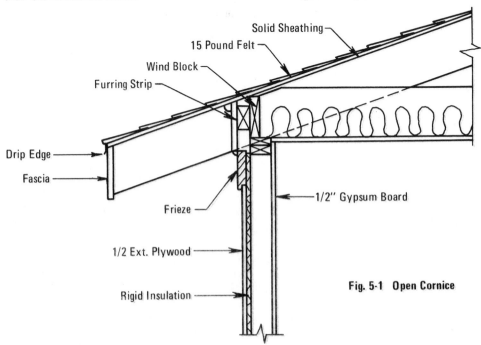

Fig. 5-1 Open Cornice

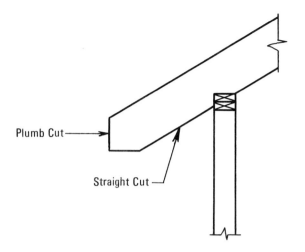

Fig. 5-2 Straight Rafter Tail With Plumb Cut

Plumb Cut

Straight Cut

seeps into the building, causing serious problems. This decided disadvantage of the large overhanging open cornice, together with the extra labor of installation and costly upkeep, has tended to make this type of

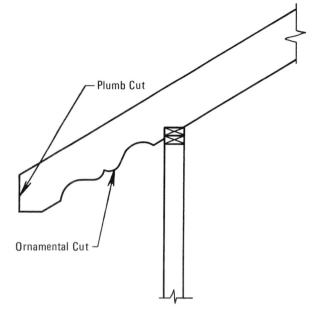

Plumb Cut

Ornamental Cut

Fig. 5-3 Ornamental Rafter Tail With Plumb Cut

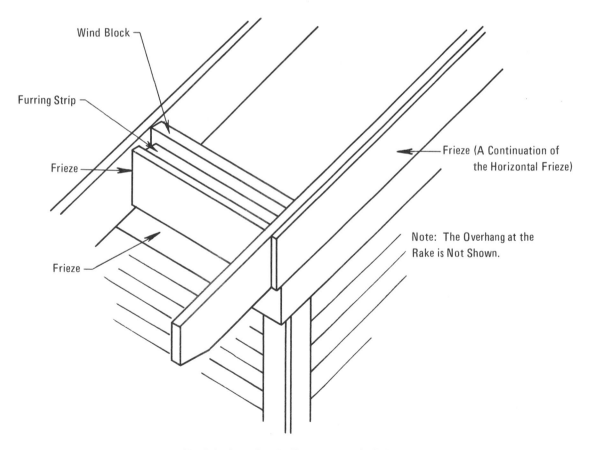

Wind Block

Furring Strip

Frieze

Frieze

Frieze (A Continuation of the Horizontal Frieze)

Note: The Overhang at the Rake is Not Shown.

Fig. 5-4 Open Cornice Returning up the Rake

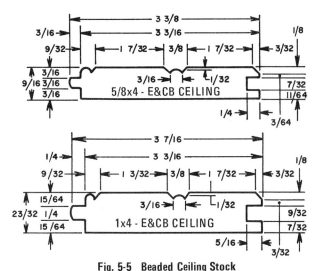

Fig. 5-5 Beaded Ceiling Stock

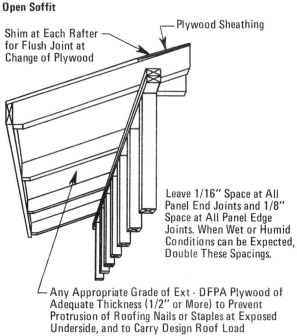

Open Soffit

Shim at Each Rafter for Flush Joint at Change of Plywood

Plywood Sheathing

Leave 1/16" Space at All Panel End Joints and 1/8" Space at All Panel Edge Joints. When Wet or Humid Conditions can be Expected, Double These Spacings.

Any Appropriate Grade of Ext - DFPA Plywood of Adequate Thickness (1/2" or More) to Prevent Protrusion of Roofing Nails or Staples at Exposed Underside, and to Carry Design Roof Load

Fig. 5-6 Shimming Plywood Sheathing

cornice obsolete, especially in the northern part of the United States.

GUTTERS

Gutters, or *eaves troughs,* are used to collect and divert water away from eaves lines and foundation systems. Gutters are usually made of metal or plastic and are available in a wide variety of styles and sizes. At one time, molded wood gutters were frequently used, but for economic reasons the metal gutter has now replaced the wooden gutter in popularity.

Metal gutters come in a variety of shapes and can be quickly assembled on the job site. In addition to the gutter itself, there are numerous accessories, figure 5-7. These parts include joint connectors, outside mitered corners, strap hangers, slip joints, connectors, and expansion joints. The different parts are held together by means of Pop®rivets or sheet metal screws. Joints are kept tight by means of a gutter seal.

HOW TO CONSTRUCT AN OPEN CORNICE

1. Cut and secure wind blocks between each rafter. A *wind block,* usually a 2 x 6, serves as a nailing surface for the frieze.

   Note: Most contractors construct the cornice before sheathing the roof, since it is more

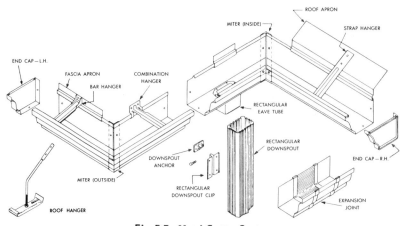

Fig. 5-7 Metal Gutter System

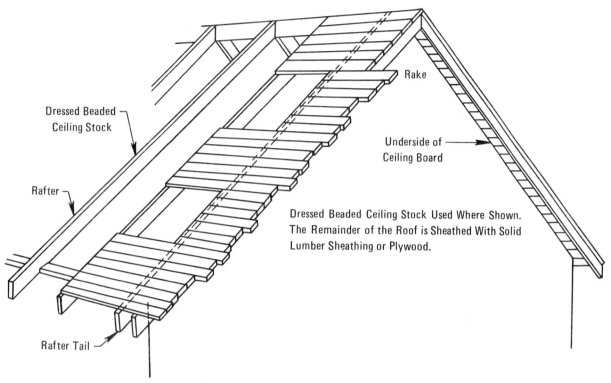

Dressed Beaded
Ceiling Stock

Rafter

Rafter Tail

Rake

Underside of
Ceiling Board

Dressed Beaded Ceiling Stock Used Where Shown.
The Remainder of the Roof is Sheathed With Solid
Lumber Sheathing or Plywood.

Fig. 5-8 Application of Ceiling Board to Rake

convenient to place the wind blocks and trim before the roof sheathing is installed.

2. Snap a chalk line the length of the wall to show the location of the bottom of the frieze board. Allow the top of the frieze to extend 1/2 inch below the bottom edge of the rafter tails.

3. Cut and secure furring strips to the wind blocks. A *furring* strip is a piece of lumber used to build up a surface. The thickness of the furring strips should equal the thickness of the sheathing and wide frieze.

4. Nail the frieze board between the rafters and against the furring strips. The boards should be wide enough to extend from the top edge of the rafter to 1 inch below the bottom of the rafter tail.

5. Nail and fit cove molding against the bottom edge of the frieze. Fit and nail quarter round molding, which shows a profile of a quarter of a circle, or a bed molding flush with the tops of the rafters.

6. Nail the fascia to the end of the rafter tails. Allow the fascia to project 1/2 inch below the rafter tail.

7. Nail shingle molding or a drip edge to the fascia.

HOW TO PLACE BEADED CEILING STOCK ON AND OPEN CORNICE

Note: For illustrative purposes, beaded ceiling stock 3 7/16 inches wide is used.

1. Locate a point 3 3/8 inches from the bottom of the two end rafters.

2. Snap a chalk line between these two points.

3. Place a piece of stock along the chalk line being certain that the beaded side is down.

4. Face nail the stock with 6d nails, toenailing only where the boards do not join tightly. Be certain that there are no loose knots between the rafter tails.

5. Allow the boards to project beyond the end rafter, the length of the rake overhang.

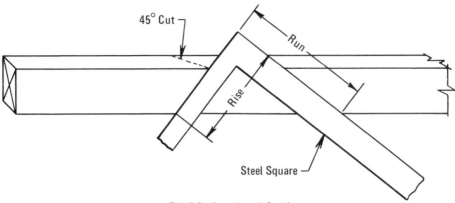

Fig. 5-9 Bargeboard Stock

HOW TO BUILD THE RAKE FOR AN OPEN CORNICE

1. Align the outside common rafter with the rake of the roof by temporarily nailing a stay across the bottom edges of about four common rafters. A *stay* is a temporary brace.

2. Apply the ceiling boards to the rake. Allow six or eight lengths of the boards to extend to the second common rafter to support the overhang, figure 5-8. These sections should be placed about every 2 feet up the rafter. The other ceiling boards should extend from the first common rafter to the edge of the overhang.

3. Determine the distance from the sheathing to the outside face of the bargeboard. Mark this distance at the top of the ceiling boards near the ridge and at the eaves.

4. Snap a chalk line connecting these two points and saw off the ceiling boards along this line.

   Note: The bargeboard is the outermost exposed rafter that extends up the rake of the roof. It is nailed to the underside of the roof ceiling boards and forms a surface upon which the crown or shingle molding is nailed. The bargeboard is actually the horizontal fascia returned up the rake.

5. Form a plumb 45-degree miter joint on the lower end of a length of bargeboard stock, figure 5-9. Use the figures on the steel square that were used to lay out the plumb of the common rafter for the plumb cut of the bargeboard.

   Note: This joint is fitted to the miter joint of the horizontal fascia board.

6. Nail the bargeboard to the underside and outer edge of the ceiling boards.

7. Mark the length of bargeboard that is required to reach to the ridge of the roof. The place where the top cut of the bargeboard meets the bargeboard on the opposite side of the gable is determined by using the square that is used in finding the plumb cut of the common rafter.

8. Nail the bargeboard to all of the roof boards.

9. Fit the crown, or shingle, molding against the face of the bargeboard. The cuts at the lower and upper ends of the molding are made parallel to the respective cuts of the bargeboard. Keep the top edge of the shingle molding flush with the top surface of the roof boards.

10. Nail the molding to the bargeboard, using nails that will not protrude through the bargeboard.

HOW TO INSTALL A METAL GUTTER

1. Locate the high and low points of the gutter and snap a chalk line between them. If there are to be two conductor pipe outlets in the gutter, the high point should be located midway between the outlets.

2. Secure a fascia hanger along the chalk line.

3. Place the gutter lengths in hangers, using joint connectors or expansion joints to assemble different pieces.

4. Attach an inside or outside miter to the straight run in cases where the gutter must turn a corner.

5. Close the end of the gutter with end caps.

6. Seal the joints with gutter seal.

REVIEW

A.   Choose the best answer or answers to complete each statement.

1. Gutters are sometimes called _____ .
   - a. leaders
   - b. eaves troughs
   - c. eaves
   - d. cornices

2. Gutters are usually made of plastic or _____ .
   - a. wood
   - b. metal
   - c. neoprene
   - d. copper

3. The top of the frieze should extend _____ inch(es) below the bottom edge of the rafter tails.
   - a. 3/4
   - b. 1/8
   - c. 2
   - d. 1/2

4. A _____ strip is a piece of lumber used to build up a surface.
   - a. furring
   - b. day
   - c. purlin
   - d. wind

5. The fascia should project _____ inch(es) below the rafter tails.
   - a. 1
   - b. 3
   - c. 1/2
   - d. 2

6. Beaded ceiling stock should be nailed with _____ .
   - a. 16d nails
   - b. 12d nails
   - c. 3d nails
   - d. 6d nails

7. To straighten a common rafter temporarily, a _____ may be used.
   - a. run
   - b. stay
   - c. purlin
   - d. beam

8. The _____ is the outermost exposed rafter that extends up the rake of the roof.
   - a. bargeboard
   - b. hip rafter
   - c. lookout
   - d. cornice

9. The end of a metal gutter is closed with a(an) _____ .
   - a. starter cap
   - b. fascia
   - c. end cap
   - d. expansion joint

B. Place the correct answer in the space provided for each of the following questions.

1. If a gutter is turning an inside corner, a (an) _____ is used.

2. The lower end of a bargeboard has a plumb _____ miter joint.

3. The various parts of the gutter are held together by _____ and _____ .

4. Wind blocks are usually _____ in size.

5. In order for a gutter to drain, it is usually _____ .

6. In a building that is not well insulated, there is a loss of _____ .

7. The roof sheathing over an open cornice may be constructed of either _____ or _____ .

8. In the open cornice, the _____ and _____ are exposed.

9. The best time to finish the cornice is before the roof is _____ .

C. Identify the parts of the open cornice in the figure.

A. _____   F. _____

B. _____   G. _____

C. _____   H. _____

D. _____   I. _____

E. _____   J. _____

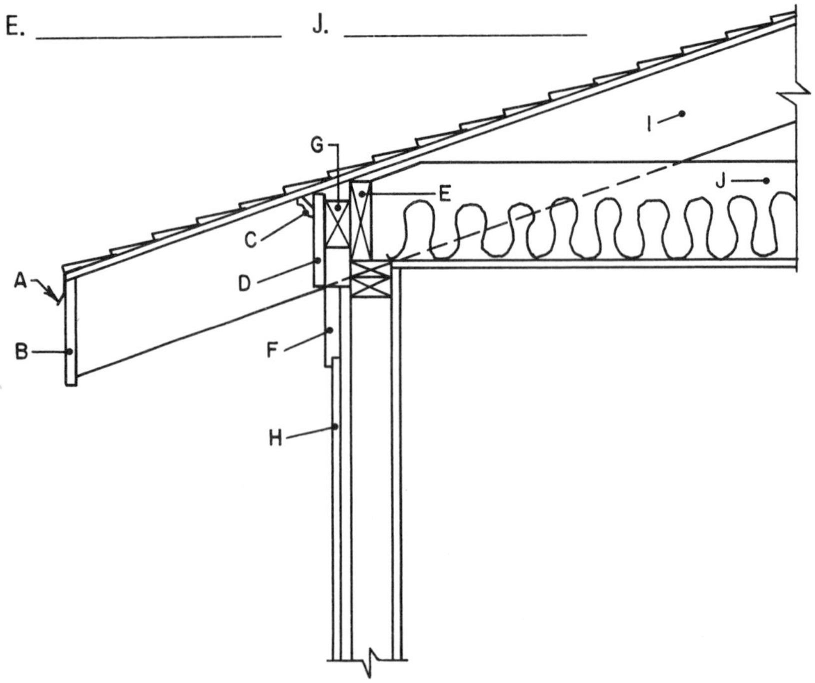

Fig. 5-10 Open Cornice

Unit 6 Doors

Fig. 6-1 Solid Core Door
(Lumber Blocks)

Fig. 6-2 Solid Core Door
(Bonded Wood Particles)

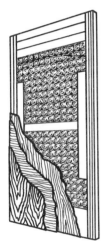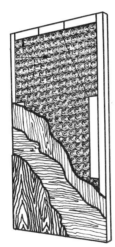

Fig. 6-3 Hollow Core Door
(Wood Spiral)

Exterior and interior doors provide privacy in rooms and a means of access into the home and individual rooms. Exterior doors are a prominent feature of the exterior trim and may be simple or elaborate in design. At one time, doors were primarily constructed from solid stock. Because of advancements in technology, however, both exterior and interior doors are now constructed of wood, glass, plastic, wood chips, or metal.

There are two general types of doors in light construction, *flush* and *panel*. Flush and panel doors operate by swinging, sliding, or folding.

FLUSH DOORS

The *flush door* consists of two face panels of either a hardwood or softwood veneer, with a core built in between the two. There are two types of cores, solid and hollow. A solid core door may be constructed of hardwood lumber blocks bonded together, figure 6-1, which provide great strength and durability, or bonded particles of wood, figure 6-2. Softwood *rails,* the horizontal members in the door, and *stiles,* the vertical members in the door, usually band the core. A two- or three-ply veneer is bonded to each side of the core.

Hollow core doors are constructed in a number of lightweight styles. The doors may have a wood spiral core, figure 6-3; a ladder-type core which is

Fig. 6-4 Hollow Core Door
(Ladder Core)

Fig. 6-5 Hollow Core Door
(Angled Struts)

Fig. 6-6 Hollow Core Door
(Corrugated Honeycomb Core)

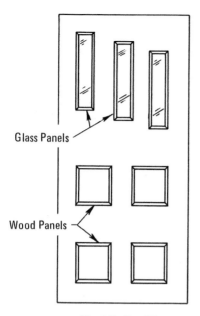

Fig. 6-7 Panel Door

notched into the sides of the stiles, figure 6-4; struts, which are placed at an angle against the rails, figure 6-5; or corrugated honeycomb cores, figure 6-6. A *strut* is a piece of lumber that is used to keep two structural members apart.

PANEL DOORS

Panel doors consist of rails and stiles with wood or glass panels, figure 6-7. These doors are constructed in a variety of styles, utilizing many different types of wood and materials. Most of the doors, however, are constructed in ponderosa pine or Douglas fir. The rails and stiles of panel doors are fastened together by means of *dowel joints,* figure 6-8, or *mortise and tenon joints*, figure 6-9. The panels are either inserted into grooves in the rails and stiles or placed in *rabbet joints* on the rails and stiles and covered with molding, figure 6-10. The rabbet joint consists of a groove cut across the edge or end of two boards which are joined together. A dowel joint is a joint used to reinforce boards that are glued edge to edge. The mortise and tenon joint is used in frame construction.

Sliding Doors

Sliding, or *bypassing,* doors operate on overhead tracks and nylon rollers attached to the door, figure 6-11. To keep the doors from swinging in or out, floor guides are sometimes provided. Sliding doors

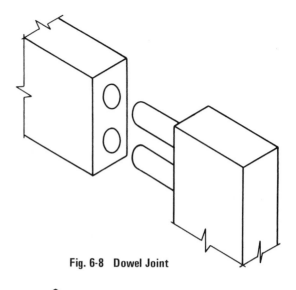

Fig. 6-8 Dowel Joint

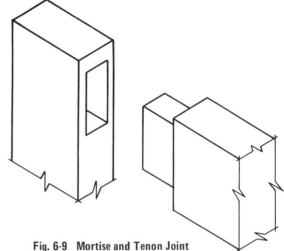

Fig. 6-9 Mortise and Tenon Joint

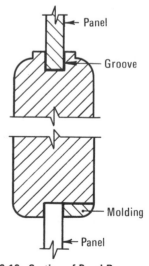

Fig. 6-10 Section of Panel Door

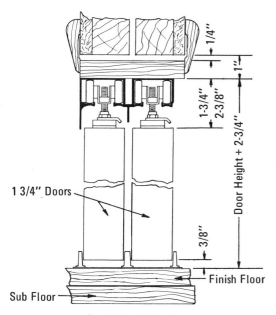

Fig. 6-11   Sliding Door

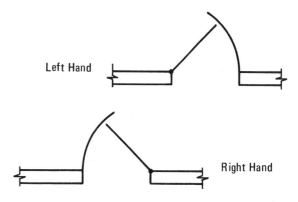

Fig. 6-12   Left-Hand and Right-Hand Door

are used extensively in closets and other areas where privacy, sound isolation, and weather resistance are not a major concern. These doors are manufactured in different sizes, heights, and widths and are available with one, two, three, or four doors.

Swinging Doors

Swinging doors usually operate on two or three hinges fastened to one of the door jambs. A swinging door is typically classified as a left-hand or right-hand door, depending on the location of the hinges. If the hinges are on the left side as a person faces the door, the door is classified as a left-hand door; if the hinges are on the right side of the door, it is classified as a right-hand door, figure 6-12. Swinging doors afford maximum security. Entrance and passage doors are typical examples.

Folding Doors

Folding doors, like sliding doors, operate on an overhead track and nylon rollers. They are available in different widths and heights., figure 6-13. There are three types of folding doors: flush, louvered, and panel. They usually act as room dividers and closet doors. The folding door offers little sound isolation or resistance to weather.

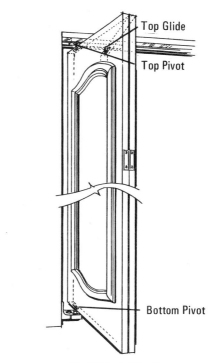

Fig. 6-13   Folding Door

HOW TO INSTALL A DOOR FRAME

Note: In many cases the door frame, complete with hung door, arrives at the job site ready for installation.

1. Place the frame in the rough opening.

2. Level the sill; use wedges if necessary.

3. Nail the side jambs at the bottom.

4. Plumb the side jambs with a level and nail each side to a 2 x 4 cripple.

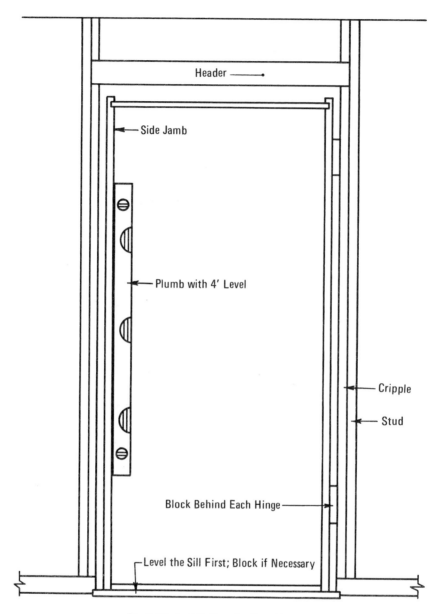

Fig. 6-14   Installation of a Door Frame

5. At each hinge location place blocks between the door frame and cripple, figure 6-14.

6. Finish nailing the side and head casings, spacing the nails about 14 inches apart.

7. Set all nails. *Setting* is a process in which the nailhead is driven below the surface of the wood.

HOW TO FIT A SWINGING DOOR

1. Plane the top of the door smooth and square it with the stiles or the side of the door.

Note: To properly fit a door, an equal amount of the door's wood should be trimmed from both the top and bottom. Never trim more than 3/4 inch from one end.

2. Measure the height of the door frame and cut the door to the proper length, leaving approximately 1/8-inch clearance at the top and 3/4-inch clearance at the bottom for carpeting.

3. Measure the distance between the two side jambs and plane the door to the proper width,

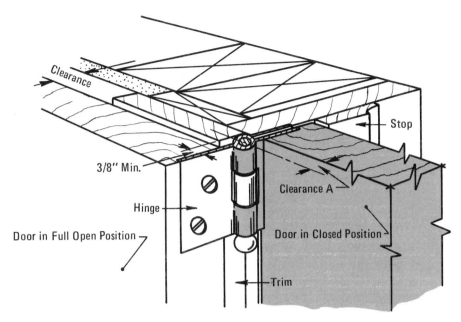

Fig. 6-15 Clearance of butts. Shaded portion shows cross-sectional view of door in closed position.

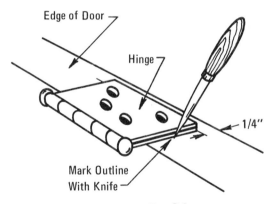

Fig. 6-16 Laying Out Gain

leaving approximately 3/32-inch clearance on each side.

Note: On exterior doors, all surfaces that are cut or machined should be sealed with an exterior sealer.

HOW TO FIT MORTISE HINGES FOR FLUSH DOORS

1. Select hinges large enough to clear the casings of the door trim.

    Note: In installing full butt hinges on any type of door that is flush with the edge of the jamb, there should be a clearance from the edge of the

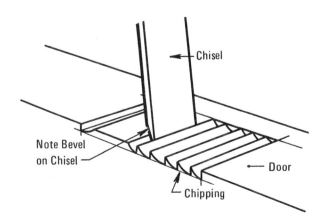

Fig. 6-17 Cutting Out Gain

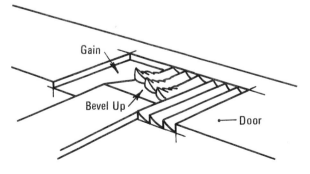

Fig. 6-18 Paring Butt Gain

SPECIFICATIONS				STANDARD EQUIPMENT	ACCESSORY EQUIPMENT					
					Templet Guides		Hinge Butt Routing Bits	Features	Net Wt., lbs.	Ship. Wt., lbs.
*No.	Door Length	Door Thickness	Size Hinge	Extra Templet Nails	91 015 R88	91 264 91 267 90 150				
83 002	6'6'' 6'8'' 7'	1 3/8'', 1 3/4'' 2'', 2 1/4''	2 1/2'' to 5 1/2''	83 008	USE	USE	USE	Wood Doors and Jambs	5 1/4	6 1/4
83 000	8'	1 3/8'' to 2''	3'' to 5''	83 008				Wood Doors and Jambs	4 3/4	6 3/4
83 001	7'	1 3/8'' to 2''	3'' to 5''	83 008	82 854	82 864	85 159	Folding	3	3 3/4
†T3	8'	1 3/8'' to 2 1/2''	3'' to 5'' with bushings	83 006			**85 249	For Steel and Wood Jambs	5	7

DOOR AND JAMB BUTT TEMPLATES

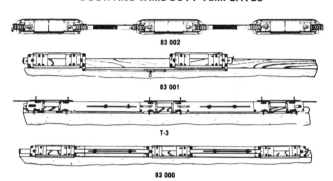

83 002

83 001

T-3

83 000

Fig. 6-19   Router, Door and Jamb Butt Templates

jamb to the center of the hinge pin. The clearance varies with the thickness of the door, the thickness of the trim, and the size of the hinge.

2. Locate the position of the hinges on the jamb.

Note: Inside doors up to and including those 60 inches in height require two hinges. Those which are 60 inches to 90 inches in height require three hinges, and those from 90 inches to 120 inches, four hinges. If three butts are used, the middle butt should be halfway between the top and bottom hinges. The top hinge should not be less than 6 inches from the top of 1 3/8- or 1 3/4-inch door, and the bottom hinge should not be less than 9 inches from the floor. On 1 1/8 inch thick doors, the hinges may be from 2 inches to 4 inches from the top and bottom, depending on the height of the door.

3. Make a gage line on the edge of the door and on the face of the jamb at the hinge locations so that the center of the hinge pin will project the correct distance beyond the face of the door, figure 6-15.

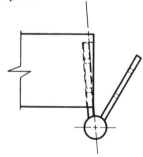

Fig. 6-20   Shifting Butt Angle

4. Place the hinge on the door along the gaged line and mark the length of the hinge, figure 6-16.

5. Gage the thickness of the hinge along the edge of the jamb and the face of the door.

6. Use a 1 1/2-inch butt chisel to chip out the outlined gain, figure 6-17.

7. Pare the chips from the gain, holding the back of the chisel toward the bottom of the gain and paring along the gage line which shows the depth of the gain, figure 6-18.

Note: A router and template can be used for steps 3 through 7, figure 6-19.

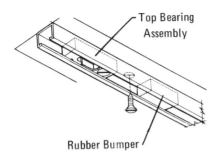

Fig. 6-21 Top Bearing Assembly

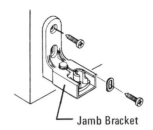

Fig. 6-22   Jamb Bracket

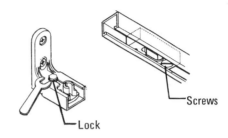

Fig. 6-23   Adjustment Devices

8. Place the hinge in the gain to be certain that the top surface of the hinge is flush with the edge of the door.

9. When the butt fits the gain properly, fasten the butt with screws.

    Note: If the hinge surface is below the door surface, figure 6-20, shim it with cardboard until it is flush. If the hinge is above the surface, pare the gain until the butt is flush.

10. Fit the opposite half of the butt to the door jamb in exactly the same manner as the other half was fitted to the door.

    Note: Be sure to use the proper half of the butt on the door and on the jamb so that the loose pin will be inserted from the top of the hinge.

11. Fit the other door butts in the same manner.

12. Hang the door on the hinges of the jamb by first placing the loose pin in the top butt. Then tap the bottom half butts together and insert the lower pin.

13. Test the door to see if it swings into the opening properly. If it does not fit well, do not force it into the opening; locate the problem.

    Note: There are several common reasons and remedies for a poor-fitting door.

    • If the door strikes on the jamb at the side, examine the door butts to see that the flat-head screws are perfectly flat with the surface of the butt. If they are not, they may be preventing the hinge from closing properly. Check the depth of the butt gains to see that the surface of the butts are not above the

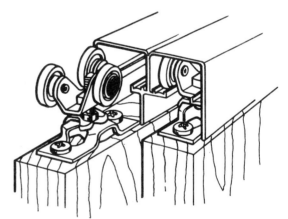

Fig. 6-24   Track System

surface of the door or jamb. If they are make them flush or slightly below the surface.

• If the door binds, the door butts are probably too far below the surface of the door or jamb and should be shimmed.

    These conditions may also be corrected by beveling the bottom of the gain in the door so that the butt pin center is shifted toward or away from the lock jamb. This procedure pulls the edge of the door toward or away from this jamb.

• If the top or bottom of the door strikes the sill or head, the top or bottom must be planed. Do not try to drive the hinge butts up or down to correct this condition.

HOW TO INSTALL A FOLDING DOOR

1. Locate the center of the top jamb and mark a line the length of the jamb.

2. Place the track over the line and mark the locations of the screw holes.

3. Drill pilot holes for the track screws. A *pilot hole* is a drilled hole smaller than the diameter of the screw.

4. Secure the track to the head jamb with screws placed in the pilot holes.

5. Secure the top bearing assembly and the rubber bumper in the track, figure 6-21.

6. Secure the door jamb bracket at the bottom of the door jamb and flush with the floor, figure 6-22.

7. Place the door in the top bearing assembly and door jamb bracket.

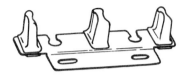

Fig. 6-25 Door Guide

8. Adjust the door with the lock screws in the top track and bottom jamb pivot, figure 6-23.

HOW TO INSTALL A SLIDING DOOR

1. Locate and mark the center of the head jamb.

2. Place the track system over the centerline.

3. Mark the location of the screw openings.

4. Drill pilot holes for the track system.

5. Secure the track system to the head jamb, figure 6-24.

6. Secure the door guide, figure 6-25, to the finish floor. Be sure that the door guide is in alignment with the track system.

7. Install the doors in the track system and in the door guides.

REVIEW

A. Choose the best answer or answers to complete each statement.

1. The rails and stiles of panel doors are fastened together by dowel joints and

   _____ .

   a. rabbet joints   c. mortise and tenon joints
   b. dado joints   d. dovetail joints

2. Sliding doors are sometimes referred to as _____ .

   a. bypassing doors   c. louvered doors
   b. swinging doors   d. folding doors

3. The door sill is sometimes leveled by using _____ .

   a. nails   c. wedges
   b. screws   d. purlins

4. The side jamb of a door is nailed to a _____ .

   a. cripple   c. stud
   b. header   d. ledger

5. The top of a door should be square with the _____ .

    a. rails   c. ledger

    b. stiles   d. purlin

6. A door 60 inches high requires _____ .

    a. two butt hinges   c. four butt hinges

    b. three butt hinges   d. five butt hinges

7. The bottom hinge should not be less than _____ inches above the floor.

    a. 12   c. 3

    b. 6   d. 9

8. The top of a folding door is adjusted with _____ .

    a. a jamb pivot   c. a jamb bracket

    b. lock screws   d. track screws

9. The top hinge should not be less than _____ inches from the top of the door.

    a. 5   c. 12

    b. 3   d. 6

10. In trimming a swinging door, no more than _____ inch(es) should be cut from one end.

    a. 1/2   c. 1

    b. 3/4   d. 1 1/4

B. Place the correct answer in the space provided for each of the following questions.

1. The two types of doors used in light construction are _____ and _____ .

2. A solid core door is constructed of _____ and _____ .

3. Panel doors consist of _____ and _____ which frame wood or glass panels.

4. Two types of doors that operate on overhead tracks and nylon rollers are _____ and _____ .

5. A _____ should be placed behind each door hinge.

6. If the distance between two side jambs is 3 feet, what should the width of the swinging door be? _____

7. If the height of a door frame is 6' 8'', what is the approximate height of the door? _____

8. A _____ or _____ is used to cut the gain for a butt hinge.

9.   The butt is fastened to the door with _____ .

10.   What should be done if the bottom of the door strikes the sill? _____

_____

C.   In the space provided sketch

1.   a panel door.

2.   a sliding door.

3.   a left-hand door.

4.   a folding door.

Unit 7 Windows

Window units provide light and, in some cases, serve as a source of ventilation. The most popular window units available are: double hung, casement, horizontal sliding, awning, hopper, and fixed. These six categories of window units can be further subdivided into three basic units: sliding, swinging, and fixed.

Window units are usually constructed of wood, steel, or aluminum. Moisture collection on wooden units is not as great as that on the aluminum and steel units, since wood does not conduct heat as readily as the other types. However, wood is subject to decay and must be carefully maintained. Aluminum units need no painting; steel window units have the advantage of strength.

WINDOW PARTS

A window unit is composed of many working parts, including the jamb, sash, sill, stool, and mullion, figure 7-1. The *sash* is a frame into which the glass is placed. The *sill* is the lowest horizontal member below the window; the *stool* is the horizontal member placed at the bottom of a window. The *mullion* is the structural piece that creates the division between multiple windows, and the *jamb* is the vertical structural member of the window.

TYPES OF WINDOWS
Double-Hung Windows

Double-hung windows, figure 7-2, have two operating sash. The sash, figure 7-3, moves vertically,

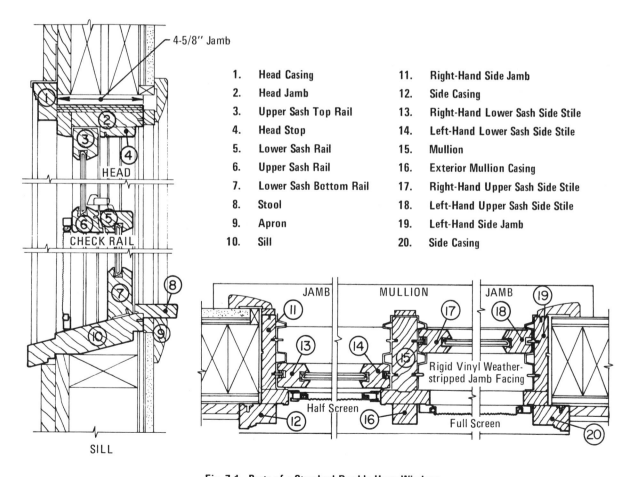

1. Head Casing	11. Right-Hand Side Jamb
2. Head Jamb	12. Side Casing
3. Upper Sash Top Rail	13. Right-Hand Lower Sash Side Stile
4. Head Stop	14. Left-Hand Lower Sash Side Stile
5. Lower Sash Rail	15. Mullion
6. Upper Sash Rail	16. Exterior Mullion Casing
7. Lower Sash Bottom Rail	17. Right-Hand Upper Sash Side Stile
8. Stool	18. Left-Hand Upper Sash Side Stile
9. Apron	19. Left-Hand Side Jamb
10. Sill	20. Side Casing

Fig. 7-1 Parts of a Standard Double-Hung Window

Perma-Shield® Narroline®

Fig. 7-2 Double-Hung Window. Courtesy of the Andersen Corporation, Bayport, Minn.

allowing a maximum of 50 percent ventilation. It is held in position by either friction or a balancing device. Double-hung units come in a number of sizes, figure 7-4. To determine the unit dimensions, rough opening, and sash opening, the window schedule or the manufacturer's catalog should be consulted.

Casement Windows

Casement windows, figure 7-5, are hinged on one side and may swing in or out by means of a crank or lever, figure 7-6. The unit may have two or more operating sash, and when open, may give up to 100 percent ventilation. If the window swings out from the building, it is an *outswinging casement;* if it swings into the building, it is called an *inswinging casement.*

Horizontal Sliding Windows

Horizontal sliding windows, figure 7-7, have a minimum of two sash, with at least one operating sash which slides horizontally. In a three-sash unit, the middle sash is usually fixed and the two side units are operable. Three sash units are easily adapted to

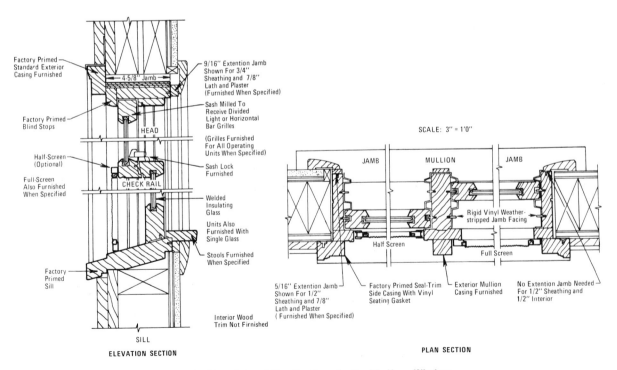

Fig. 7-3 Elevation and Plan Section of a Double-Hung Window

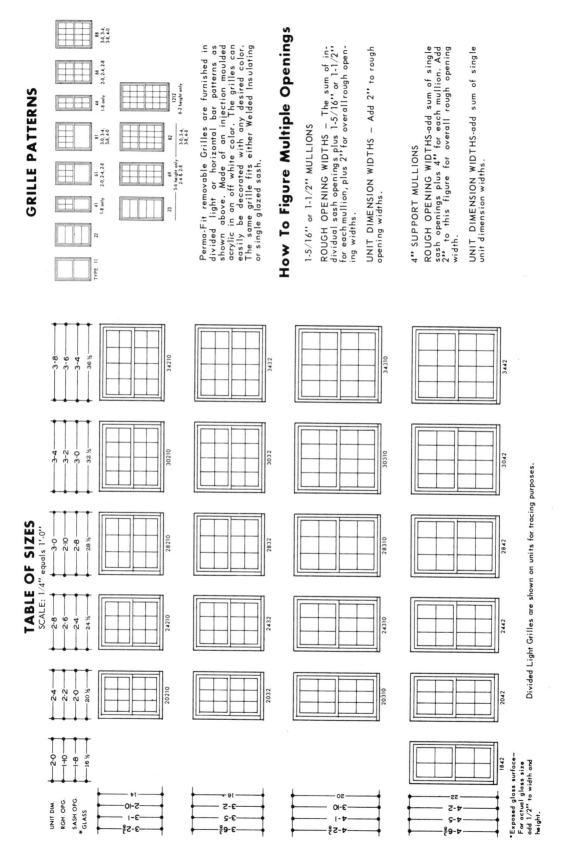

GRILLE PATTERNS

Perma-Fit removable Grilles are furnished in divided light or horizontal bar patterns as shown above. Made of an injection moulded acrylic in an off white color. The grilles can easily be decorated with any desired color. The same grille fits either Welded Insulating or single glazed sash.

How To Figure Multiple Openings

1-5/16" or 1-1/2" MULLIONS

ROUGH OPENING WIDTHS — The sum of individual sash openings plus 1-5/16" or 1-1/2" for each mullion, plus 2" for overall rough opening widths.

UNIT DIMENSION WIDTHS — Add 2" to rough opening widths.

4" SUPPORT MULLIONS

ROUGH OPENING WIDTHS-add sum of single sash openings plus 4" for each mullion. Add 2" to this figure for overall rough opening width.

UNIT DIMENSION WIDTHS-add sum of single unit dimension widths.

TABLE OF SIZES

SCALE: 1/4" equals 1'-0"

Divided Light Grilles are shown on units for tracing purposes.

*Exposed glass surface— For actual glass size add 1/2" to width and height.

Fig. 7-4 Sizes of Double-Hung Windows

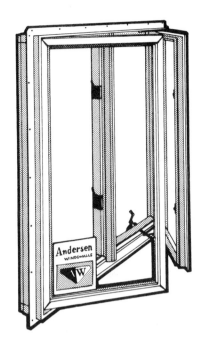

Fig. 7-5 Casement Window. Courtesy of the Andersen Corporation, Bayport, Minn.

**Perma-Shield®
Casement Windows**

Aluminum Flashing Furnished.

1 5/16" x 2" Seal-Trim Casing Furnished

When Other Casing is Used, 1 1/16" Thickness Must be Maintained to Receive the Hinge Member at Head.

Sash 2" Thick and Groove Glazed With Select Quality Grade Welded Insulating Window Glass.

Also Available Glazed With Single Glass and Removable Double Glazing Panels.

Extension Hinge Provides 100% Ventilation and Allows Room to Clean Outside of Glass From the Inside.

Perma-Clean Aluminum Frame Screen

HEAD

Roto-Release Under Screen Operator

SILL

Scale: 3" equals 1' 0"

Handing of Hardware is Determined by the Side Which Sash are Hinged as Viewed From the Outside.

JAMB

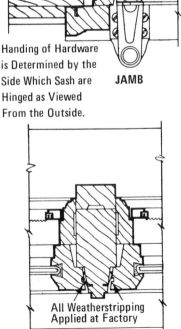

All Weatherstripping Applied at Factory

MULLION

Fig. 7-6 Parts of a Casement Window

Perma-Shield ® Gliding Windows

Fig. 7-7 Horizontal Sliding Window
Courtesy of the Andersen Corporaration, Bayport, Minn.

different construction materials, figure 7-8, and are available in several different sizes, figure 7-9.

Awning Windows

Awning windows, figure 7-10, are hinged at the top and may open into the building or away from it. Single awning units may be combined with other types of window units, or they may operate independently by means of a crank that opens each individual unit or all of the units simultaneously. The units vary in size, figure 7-10, and provide 100-percent ventilation.

Hopper Windows

Hopper windows, figure 7-11, are similar to awning windows with the exception that they are hinged on the bottom rather than the top. In some cases, a hopper window is simply an awning window turned upside down. The units are used extensively in basements and allow 100-percent ventilation.

Fixed Windows

Fixed windows, figure 7-12, usually consist of a stationary sash built into a frame. In some cases, fixed

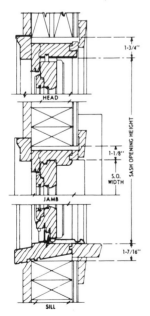

DETAIL NO. G-20. Brick veneer wall construction with blind stop flush with 3/4'' sheathing. Extension jambs and wood trim.

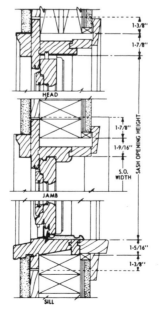

DETAIL NO. G-17. Frame wall with stucco applied over 3/4'' sheathing.

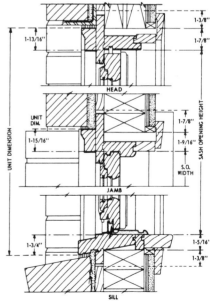

DETAIL NO. G-13. Single-frame wall construction with 3/4'' exterior and 1/2'' interior. Note blind stops cut off flush with back of jambs.

Fig. 7-8 Horizontal Sliding Windows in Brick Veneer, Stucco, and Single-Frame Construction

STOCK SIZES AND LAYOUTS

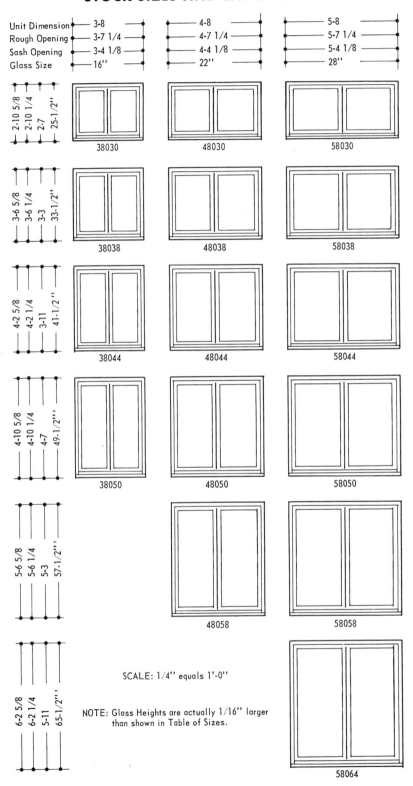

Unit Dimension — 3-8 — / — 4-8 — / — 5-8 —
Rough Opening — 3-7 1/4 — / — 4-7 1/4 — / — 5-7 1/4 —
Sash Opening — 3-4 1/8 — / — 4-4 1/8 — / — 5-4 1/8 —
Glass Size — 16" — / — 22" — / — 28" —

2-10 5/8 / 2-10 1/4 / 2-7 / 25-1/2"   38030   48030   58030

3-6 5/8 / 3-6 1/4 / 3-3 / 33-1/2"   38038   48038   58038

4-2 5/8 / 4-2 1/4 / 3-11 / 41-1/2"   38044   48044   58044

4-10 5/8 / 4-10 1/4 / 4-7 / 49-1/2"   38050   48050   58050

5-6 5/8 / 5-6 1/4 / 5-3 / 57-1/2"   48058   58058

6-2 5/8 / 6-2 1/4 / 5-11 / 65-1/2"   58064

SCALE: 1/4" equals 1'-0"

NOTE: Glass Heights are actually 1/16" larger
than shown in Table of Sizes.

Fig. 7-9   Sizes of Horizontal Sliding Windows

DETAIL

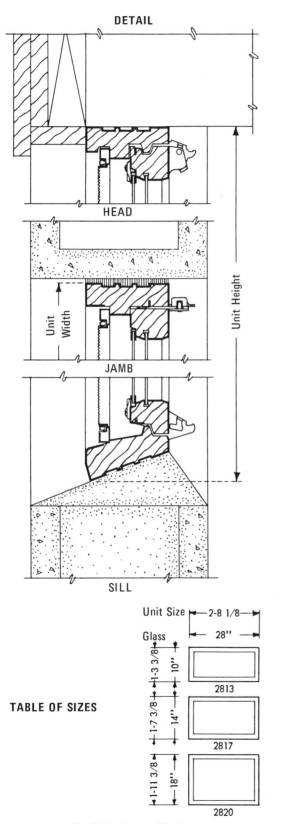

HEAD

Unit Width

JAMB

Unit Height

SILL

TABLE OF SIZES

Unit Size — 2-8 1/8

Glass — 28"

1-3 3/8   10"

2813

1-7 3/8   14"

2817

1-11 3/8   18"

2820

Fig. 7-11   Hopper Window

Perma-Shield® Awnings

Fig. 7-10   Awning Window. Courtesy of the Andersen Corp-oration, Bayport, Minn.

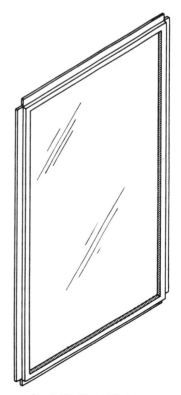

Fig. 7-12   Fixed Window

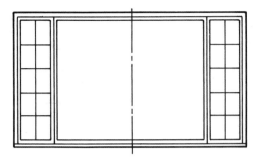

Fig. 7-13   Fixed Unit Flanked by Casement Windows

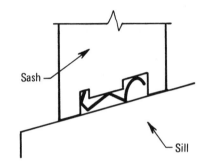

Fig. 7-14   Spring-Tension Weatherstripping

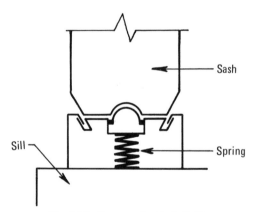

Fig. 7-15   Compression Sash Guide

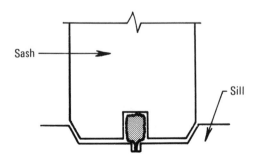

Fig. 7-16   Woven Felt Weatherstripping

units are flanked by double-hung, casement, or awning windows, figure 7-13. They provide no ventilation.

WEATHERSTRIPPING WINDOWS

Properly installed weatherstripping reduces heat loss and guards against the infiltration of outside air, dust, and windblown rain, thereby providing a savings on both heating and air conditioning. Weatherstripping is usually applied in the factory since windows require a very accurate fit.

Spring-tension weatherstripping, constructed of aluminum or rigid vinyl, is the most common material used for weatherstripping a wooden window, figure 7-14. Other techniques involve the use of a compression sash guide, figure 7-15; woven felt, figure 7-16; and a compressible bulb, figure 7-17.

Storm windows are sometimes used to reduce heat loss and resist the elements. They are one of the better means of providing insulation at window openings because they prevent wind and rain from entering between the sash edges and the frame, and provide a double thickness of glass with a dead air space between the storm sash and the regular sash. This dead air space acts as an excellent insulator and helps to avoid condensation of moisture on the glass surfaces in cold weather. Most storm windows come equipped with single glazing or insulating glass, figure 7-18, and are secured to the window sash by face glazing, wood stop glazing, or groove glazing.

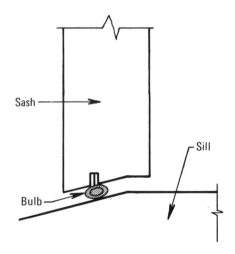

Fig. 7-17   Compressible Bulb Weatherstripping

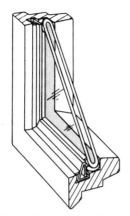

Fig. 7-18   Insulating Glass

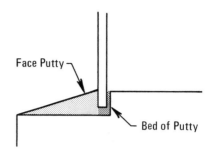

Fig. 7-19   Face Glazing

Face glazing involves placing the glass in a bed of putty, securing the glass with glazing points, and sealing the glass to the rabbet joint with face putty, figure 7-19. *Wood stop glazing* entails placing the glass on a bed of putty in a rabbet joint and securing a wood stop flush to the glass and rabbet joint, figure 7-20. In the *groove glazing* technique, glass is placed in a groove that is filled with glazing compound, figure 7-21.

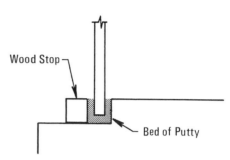

Fig. 7-20   Wood Stop Glazing

HOW TO INSTALL A WINDOW

Note: Before the window frame is set into the opening, the edges of the opening should be flashed so that the joint between the back of the window casing and the sheathing is weathertight. The flashing is usually heavy building paper or plastic about 6 inches wide.

1. Check the window unit and rough opening for proper size.

2. Place the window in the rough opening.

3. Center the bottom of the frame in the opening at the sill. Temporarily nail the bottom of one side.

4. Level the sill by first holding the level across the inside edge of the sill and then upright against the side jamb. Use a straightedge and level if the frame is large, and a large level is not available.

5. Set a nail in the bottom of the opposite side jamb. When the sill is level, nail the casing to the sheathing.

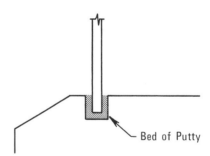

Fig. 7-21   Groove Glazing

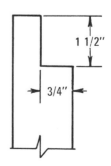

Fig. 7-22   Rabbet Joint

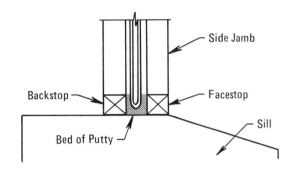

Fig. 7-23 Wood Frame for a Fixed Unit

6. Finish nailing the side and head casing, spacing the nails about 14 inches apart. Set all nails.

    Note: If the side jamb horns of the frame do not rest on the 2 x 4 sill, they should be blocked so that the frame has a solid bearing on the rough opening. Care should be exercised in putting the wedges between the 2 x 4 and the bottom of the jamb so as not to disturb the levelness of the frame sill.

HOW TO BUILD A FRAME FOR A FIXED UNIT

Note: Most window units come preassembled. However, it may be necessary for the carpenter to construct a window frame at the job site. This is often the case for fixed units.

1. Select stock for the sill, sides, and top of the window. The sill should be constructed from a 2 x 8; use a 2 x 6 for the two sides and top.

2. Cut the two side jambs to the proper length. The inside clearance should be 1/2 inch on each side. Insulating glass should usually be used on a fixed unit.

3. Lay out the rabbet joints at the top and bottom of each side jamb. The bottom rabbet joints and the rabbet joint at the top of the side jamb should be 1 1/2 inches wide and 3/4 inch deep.

4. Cut the sill and head jamb to the proper length.

5. Place the sill in the rabbet joints of the two side jambs and nail the side jambs to the sill.

6. Place the head jamb into the rabbet joints of the two side jambs and nail the side jambs to the head jamb.

HOW TO INSTALL A FRAME AND INSULATING GLASS FOR A FIXED UNIT

1. Place the frame into the rough opening.

2. Level the sill by holding a level across the inside edge of the sill.

3. Plumb the side jambs and nail them into place. If a long level is not available, a short level and a straightedge can be used.

4. Nail the backstop into place, using mitered joints on all corners.

5. Place a bed of putty against the backstop.

6. Place setting blocks on the insulating glass. *Setting blocks* are small blocks, usually plastic, which frame insulating glass and prevent glass from sliding on the frame.

7. Place the bottom edge of the insulating glass in position on the sill and press the glass and setting blocks against the backstops.

8. Nail the facestops in position, figure 7-23.

    Note: Do not toenail the facestops in position, since nails driven at an angle may hit and fracture the insulating glass.

REVIEW

A. Choose the best answer or answers to complete each statement.

1. Window units are usually constructed of wood, steel, or _____ .

    a. plastic
    b. aluminum

    c. neoprene
    d. polyethylene

2. Window glass is placed in the _____ .

   a. sash   c. sill
   b. stool   d. mullion

3. Windows that operate vertically and have two operating sash are called _____ windows.

   a. single-hung   c. sliding
   b. casement   d. double-hung

4. Windows that operate by a crank and are hinged on one side are called _____ windows.

   a. casement   c. sliding
   b. single-hung   d. double-hung

5. Spring-tension weatherstripping is made of aluminum or _____ .

   a. rubber   c. felt
   b. vinyl   d. copper

6. Window flashing is usually made of felt or _____ .

   a. plastic   c. sheet metal
   b. copper   d. asphalt

7. The first part of a window that is leveled is the _____ .

   a. sill   c. head
   b. jamb   d. sash

8. The nails placed in the side casing should be spaced about _____ inches apart.

   a. 6   c. 3
   b. 24   d. 14

9. A rabbet joint for a fixed unit should be about _____ inch deep.

   a. 1/4   c. 1
   b. 3/4   d. 7/8

10. Before placing the insulating glass in the frame, _____ are usually spaced around the glass.

    a. setting blocks   c. insulating blocks
    b. starting blocks   d. miter blocks

B. Place the correct answer in the space provided for each of the following questions.

   1. Side jambs should be plumbed with a _____ .

   2. A _____ joint is used to join backstops.

   3. Sill stock for a fixed unit is usually _____ in size.

   4. Most window units are built and assembled at the _____ .

5. The flashing for a window is about _____ in width.

6. The placing of glass in a groove that is filled with glazing compound is called _____ glazing.

7. Weatherstripping, _____ and _____ reduce heat loss.

8. Horizontal sliding windows have a minimum of _____ sash.

9. The most popular window units are: _____ , _____ , _____ , _____ , _____ , and _____ .

10. The _____ is the horizontal member placed at the bottom of a window.

C. Identify the parts of the window in the figure.

1. _____ 11. _____
2. _____ 12. _____
3. _____ 13. _____
4. _____ 14. _____
5. _____ 15. _____
6. _____ 16. _____
7. _____ 17. _____
8. _____ 18. _____
9. _____ 19. _____
10. _____ 20. _____

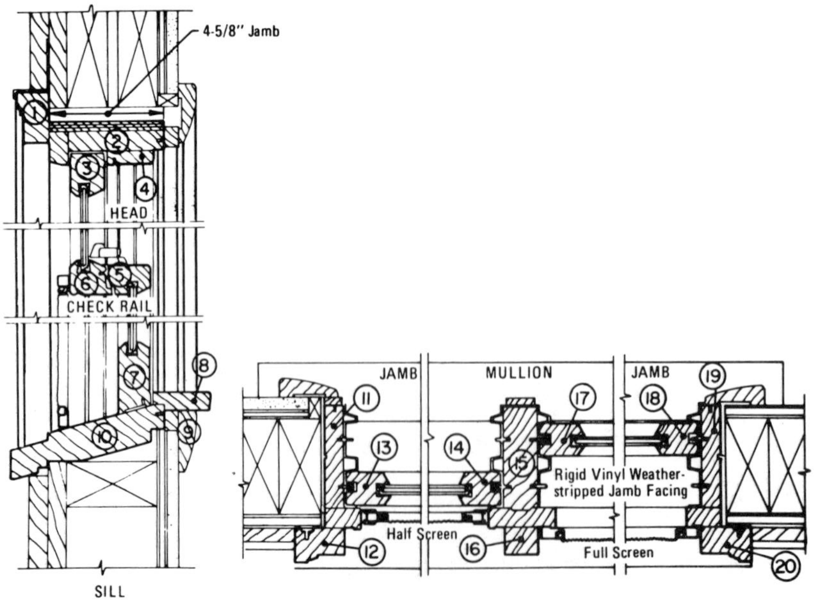

Fig. 7-24 Section of a Double-Hung Window

Unit 8 Door and Window Trim

Because defects in the interior trim are very noticeable, care should be taken in its selection. There should be no dents on the surface of the trim, and all joints should be tight and secure.

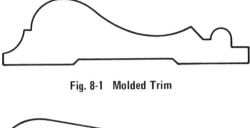

Fig. 8-1 Molded Trim

Fig. 8-2 Plain Trim

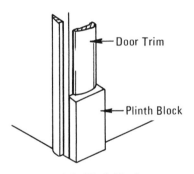

Fig. 8-3 Plinth Block

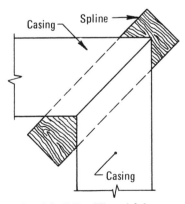

Fig. 8-4 Spline Mitered Joint

DOOR TRIM

Door casing is the wooden trim attached to both the sides and head of the door jamb. Its primary functions are to protect the edges of the interior wall finish and to form an ornamental finish for the door jamb. The trim is available in a variety of patterns so that it can complement particular styles of architecture. Molded patterns, figure 8-1, are best suited for panel doors. Simple patterns complement a contemporary style of architecture, figure 8-2. The trim, whether plain or molded, may extend from the floor or be butted against a *plinth block*, a small block of wood that is a little thicker and wider than the trim around the door, figure 8-3. The corners of door casings are usually mitered, but they may be cut square and butted against each other. If a mitered joint is used, the joint should be fastened with glue and a *spline*, a thin strip of wood that is placed in the groove of a miter to stiffen the joint, figure 8-4.

The strip on the inside face of a door frame which a door closed against is the *doorstop*, figure 8-5. They vary in thickness, width, and style. Their edges may be round or molded, except for the edge next to the door, which is always square. The device which holds a door to an open position is also known as a doorstop.

WINDOW TRIM

Side and head casings of windows are generally of the same design as door casings. Door trim consists of two sides and a head casing; window trim includes a casing, stool, and apron. The trim is used to

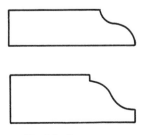

Fig. 8-5 Doorstops

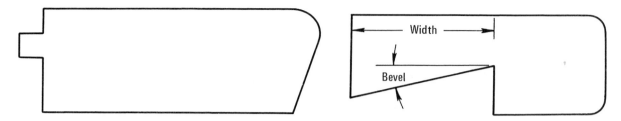

Fig. 8-6   Window Stool

cover joints where intersections occur and protect the edges of gypsum board, plaster, or paneling, while complementing the decor of the room.

The *stool*, figure 8-6, is usually 1 1/16" x 3 1/2" in size and extends beyond the sides of the side casing. It may be plain or rabbeted to fit the bevel of the sill. The stool provides a level top upon which the side casing may be fitted.

The dimensions of window casing, figure 8-7, vary from 11/16" x 2 1/2" to 5/8" x 3 1/4". Casing gives the window a finished look by concealing termination of the sidewall covering and inner window construction. The top casing has two 45-degree miters which butt against a 45-degree miter on the side casing.

The *stop bead*, figure 8-8, forms one edge of the runway for the lower sash. The stop is fastened to the head and side jambs. The joint at the two top corners may be mitered; the lower ends of the stop bead are butted against the stool. Stop beads vary in shape and size.

The *apron*, an added support for the stool, is a means of forming a trim at the bottom of the window opening. The size and shape varies, but the length of the apron is dimensioned to correspond to the side casings of the window trim.

HOW TO FIT PLAIN CASINGS

1. Select straight casing stock and lay off what is needed for the side and head casings. Allow enough material for the joints.

2. Cut the bottom ends of the two side casings square.

3. Place a side casing next to the side jamb. Allow a margin of 3/16 inch between the edge of the casing and the edge of the jamb.

4. Mark a point 3/16 inch above the bottom face of the head jamb on the inside edge of the casing. This point shows the short end of the 45-degree cut to be made at the top of the casing. Mark the two side casings in this manner.

   Note: A convenient way of scribing a true margin along the edge of the jamb is to set the combination square so that the blade projects 3/16 inch beyond the face of the square head. The square may then be used as a gage to mark the margin.

5. Place the head casing in position on the head jamb. Mark a point on the inside lower edge of the casing 3/16 inch beyond the inside edge of the side jamb. Mark both ends of the head

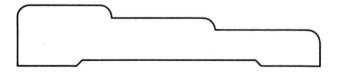

Fig. 8-7   Window Casing

Fig. 8-8   Stop Bead

casing in the same way. These points show the short end of the miter cuts. Mark the miter cuts.

6. Cut the miters on the casings with the use of a miter box and finish the surfaces with a plane if necessary. A *miter box* is a device used for guiding a saw at the proper angle when making a miter joint in wood.

7. Form a kerf for the spline in the miters by running a saw cut in the edge of the miter to a depth of 1 inch. The *kerf* is the groove made by the teeth of the saw.

    Note: The kerf may be conveniently cut with a portable electric saw. The saw blade should be equipped to saw a kerf of about 3/16 inch. A double cut may be made by running the saw with the fence against one face and then with it against the other. A hand ripsaw may also be used for this purpose.

8. Make a spline of about 1/4" x 6" x 2" and fit it into the kerfs of both sections of the mitered joint. Assemble the joint to see if the spline is fitted properly and is stable. If necessary, refit the spline.

9. Beginning at the bottom, nail the side casing to the edge of the side jamb with 8d finishing nails. Space the nails about 14 inches apart and maintain the 3/16-inch margin as the nails are being driven.

    Note: In maintaining the 3/16-inch margin, be certain that the jamb is not pulled out of line. A nail driven in at too great an angle will sometimes pull the jamb out of alignment.

10. Nail the opposite edge of the casing to the cripple and stud, keeping the nails opposite those driven into the jamb. Set the nails. The *cripple* and *stud* are framing members used in wall openings.

    Note: When spacing the nails, do not locate a nail where the lock strike plate will interfere with the jamb.

11. Nail the opposite side casing in the same manner.

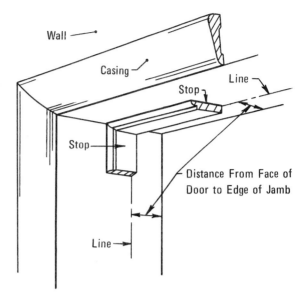

Fig. 8-9 Installation of Doorstops

12. Cover the splines with glue and place them in the miter cuts of the head casing.

13. Slip the casing in place and nail it in the same way as the side casings were nailed. Drive the nails into the stud at an angle so that the miter joint is tight.

14. Using a sharp chisel, trim the edges of the spline off flush with the casing edges. Sand the edges smooth.

HOW TO INSTALL DOORSTOPS

1. Select the doorstop material and cut the head stop to fit between the two side jambs.

2. Cut doorstops long enough to reach from the head jamb to the bottom of the side jamb for both side jambs.

3. Mark the thickness of the door on the face of the head and side jambs, figure 8-9.

4. Nail the head and side stops in place along these lines. When the door is closed, the square edge of the stop should be against the face of the door.

    Note: After the door has been hung and the lock fitted, the stops may be adjusted so that the door closes properly.

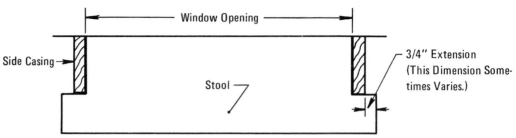

Fig. 8-10 Stool Size

HOW TO INSTALL WINDOW TRIM

1. Measure and cut the stool to the proper length. The length should equal a total of the width of the window opening from side jamb to side jamb, an allowance for the two side casings, and a 3/4-inch extension allowance on each side of the casing, figure 8-10.

2. Place the stool against the window jambs at the sill line. Keep the ends of the stool flush with the 3/4-inch extension point.

3. Place a combination square against the inside face of the window jamb with the blade extending across the window stool. Draw a line on the stool along the blade. Repeat this process on the other side of the window.

4. Measure the distance between the inside face of the sash rail and the back edge of the sill. Transfer this measurement to the ends of the stool and cut the scribed notch from each end of the stool. When cutting the notch, cut on the waste side of the line.

5. Place the stool in the windowsill. Trim the stool if necessary.

6. Nail the stool to the windowsill, using 8d nails spaced about 10 inches apart. There should be a 1/16-inch space between the stool and the bottom sash.

7. Cut the apron stock to the proper length. The length should equal the distance from the outside edge of one side casing to the outside edge of the other side casing.

   Note: If the apron is molded, return the profile on the ends.

8. Fit the apron against the bottom of the stool and nail it in place. Insert nails into the sill at the top of the apron and into the subsill of the rough window opening. Use 6d finishing nails spaced 14 inches apart.

9. Square the bottom of the two side casings.

10. Mark a point 3/16 inch above the bottom face of the head jamb on the inside edge of the casing. This point shows the short end of the 45-degree cut to be made at the top of the casing.

11. Measure the distance from the top of the stool to 3/16 inch above the head jamb and cut the side casing to this length.

12. Place the head casing in position on the head jamb. Allowing a 3/16-inch margin, mark a point on the inside lower edge of the casing 3/16 inch beyond the inside edge of the side jamb. Mark both ends of the head casing in the same manner. These points show the short end of the miter cuts. Mark the miter cuts.

    Note: Some contractors prefer to use splined mitered joints to connect the side casing to the head casing.

13. Starting at the bottom, nail the side casings to the edge of the side jambs and studs with 8d finishing nails. Space the nails approximately 14 inches apart. Maintain the 3/16-inch margin as the nails are being driven.

14. Place the head casing and nail it to the head jamb and header. The *header* is a structural member that is placed above a door or window opening.

REVIEW

A.   Choose the best answer or answers to complete each statement.

1.   The _____ of a window may be plain or rabbeted.

     a. sill   c. casing

     b. stool   d. stop bead

2.   The _____ forms one edge of the runway for the lower sash.

     a. sill   c. casing

     b. stool   d. stop bead

3.   The bottom of the two side casings are cut _____.

     a. square   c. at a 30-degree angle

     b. at a 45-degree angle   d. at a 60-degree angle

4.   A margin of _____ inch exists between the edge of the casing and the edge of the jamb.

     a. 1/2   c. 3/16

     b. 3/4   d. 5/8

5.   The spline for a miter joint is about _____ inch thick.

     a. 3/16   c. 1/16

     b. 1/2   d. 3/8

6.   Splines are constructed of wood or _____ .

     a. plastic   c. neoprene

     b. metal   d. rubber

7.   The side casing is nailed to the side jamb with _____ finishing nails.

     a. 6d   c. 8d

     b. 12d   d. 16d

8.   Splines are usually covered with _____ before they are placed in miter cuts when fitting casings to windows.

     a. a damp cloth   c. nails

     b. water   d. glue

9   The stool of a window is attached to the _____ .

     a. windowsill   c. side casing

     b. head casing   d. stop bead

10.   When installing window trim, the head casing is nailed to the head jamb and

     _____ .

     a. stop bead   b. header   c. sill   d. stool

B.   Place the correct answer in the space provided for each of the following questions.

1.   A _____ pattern of trim is best suited for panel doors.

2.   A _____ is a small block of wood that is a little thicker and wider than the trim around the door.

3.   A _____ is a thin strip of wood that is placed in a groove.

4.   Window trim includes _____ , _____ , and _____ .

5.   The _____ conceals the raw edge of sidewall covering.

6.   Miters are cut on a _____ -degree angle.

7.   In fitting plain casings, a spline which is _____ in thickness, _____ in width, and _____ in length should be inserted into the kerf.

8.   The edges of the spline are trimmed with a _____ .

9.   In the installation of doorstops, the thickness of the door is marked on the _____ and _____ .

10. A _____ is a tool used in laying out the window stool.

C.   Describe the procedure used in

1.   fitting a stool. _____

_____

2.   fitting a miter. _____

_____

3.   fitting an apron. _____

_____

Unit 9 Exterior Sidewall Covering

HARDBOARD SIDING

Hardboard siding is manufactured in panels and siding strips, figure 9-1. Siding strips are available in lengths of 8 to 16 feet with 2-foot increments and in widths of up to 12 inches. Panel siding is available in nominal lengths of 4, 6, 7, 8, 9, 10, 12, and 16 feet with a nominal width of 4 feet. The nominal thickness of lap siding is 3/8 inch or 7/16 inch, while the nominal thickness of panel siding is 1/4 inch, 3/8 inch, or 7/16 inch.

Hardboard siding is comprised of wood chips and fibers pressed together, which forms a hard, dense material. Oils and resins are sometimes impregnated in the wood chips and fibers to produce a harder and more water-resistant product known as *tempered hardboard*.

Hardboard is available with unfinished or primed surfaces with an option of an embossed or machined pattern on one side.

PLYWOOD SIDING

Plywood is made by gluing a number of layers of wood together with 100 percent waterproof phenolic resin, with the grain in each layer at a right angle to each successive layer. Nominal dimensions of plywood panels include a width of 48 inches, and lengths of 8, 9, and 10 feet. A thickness of 3/8 inch in direct-to-stud application and a 5/16 inch thickness in application over sheathing are usually required. The cross-lamination of plies in plywood siding adds strength to structures and provides natural thermal insulation properties.

Plywood siding is available in many grades, including N, the highest grade, A, B, C, and D, the lowest grade. In addition to the grades, plywood siding has many surface textures. Some of these are reverse board and batten, rough sawed, perfect, channel grooved, brushed, fine-line, and striated, figure 9-2.

SIDEWALL SHINGLES

Sidewall shingles are manufactured from select quartered logs, with no two shingles being exactly alike. The shingles have a smooth, resawed, flat back which enables them to lie flat without cupping or curling. These shingles are extremely durable and require no painting or staining to increase their longevity. Sidewall shingles are produced in three lengths: 1 inch, 18 inch, and 24 inch, figure 9-3, and four grades: Number 1, Number 2, Number 3, and undercoursing. The recommended exposure for single-course walls is 8 1/2 inches for 18-inch shingles and 11 1/2 inches for 24-inch shingles. If a double course is used, 18-inch shakes may have a 16-inch exposure, and the 24-inch shake may have an exposure of 22 inches.

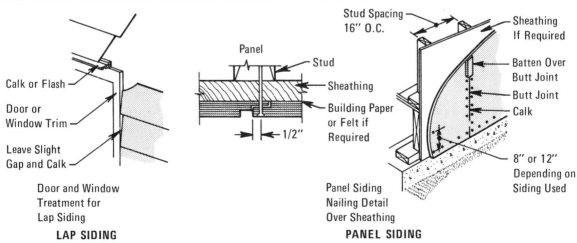

LAP SIDING

Calk or Flash

Door or Window Trim

Leave Slight Gap and Calk

Door and Window Treatment for Lap Siding

Panel

Stud

Sheathing

Building Paper or Felt if Required

1/2"

PANEL SIDING

Panel Siding Nailing Detail Over Sheathing

Stud Spacing 16" O.C.

Sheathing If Required

Batten Over Butt Joint

Butt Joint

Calk

8" or 12" Depending on Siding Used

Fig. 9-1 Hardboard Siding

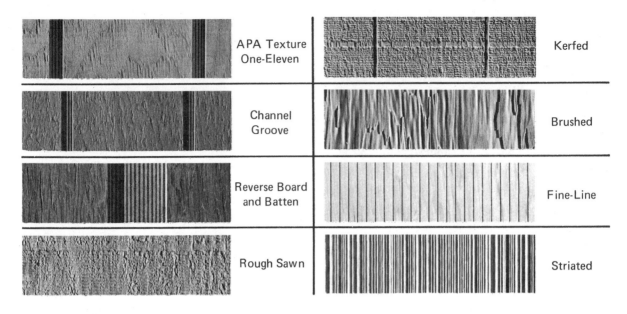

Fig. 9-2 Surface Textures of Plywood

HORIZONTAL SIDING

Horizontal wood siding, figure 9-4, is a traditional building material emphasizing horizontal lines. Horizontal siding is usually placed over solid sheathing. It may, however, be placed over rigid insulation or over an asphalt-saturated underlayment. Some of the typical types of horizontal siding are bevel siding and drop siding.

The thickness of the top edge of bevel siding varies from 15/32 inch to 3/4 inch; the bottom edge varies from 3/16 inch to 3/4 inch. The lower edge of one board overlaps the upper edge of the board underneath it, figure 9-5. The lap may vary according to the spacing of the siding, but should never be less than 3/4 inch.

Drop siding is usually 3/4 inch thick with the upper and lower edges aligned, figure 9-6. Drop siding is machined so that the back has a straight surface, thus allowing it to be nailed directly to the studs without the use of sheathing. If sheathing is not used, sidewalls should be adequately braced.

MINERAL FIBER SIDING

Mineral fiber siding, sometimes referred to as asbestos cement siding, is made from asbestos fiber and portlant cement. It is fire resistant, does not

CERTIGROOVE GROOVED RED CEDAR SIDEWALL SHAKES

Grade	Length	Thickness (at Butt)	No. of Courses Per Bdl/Carton	Bdls/Cartons Per Square		Description
No. 1	16″ (Fivex) 18″ (Perfections) 24″ (Royals)	.40″ .45″ .50″	33/33 28/28 13/14	1 carton 1 carton 4 bdls.	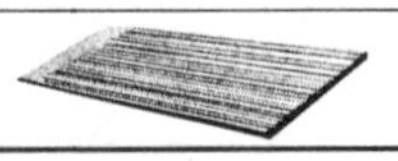	Same specifications as rebutted-rejointed shingles, except that shingle face has been given grain-like grooves. Natural color, or variety of factory-applied colors. Also in 4-ft. and 8-ft. panels.

LENGTH AND THICKNESS	Approximate coverage of one square (4 bundles) of shingles based on following weather exposures																									
	3½″	4″	4½″	5″	5½″	6″	6½″	7″	7½″	8″	8½″	9″	9½″	10″	10½″	11″	11½″	12″	12½″	13″	13½″	14″	14½″	15″	15½″	16″
16″ x 5/2″	70	80	90	100*	110	120	130	140	150x	160	170	180	190	200	210	220	230	240†	....	....	....	....	....	....	....	....
18″ x 5/2¼″	....	72½	81½	90½	100*	109	118	127	136	145½	154½x	163½	172½	181½	191	200	209	218	227	236	245½	254½†	....	....	....	....
24″ x 4/2″	....	....	....	....	....	80	86½	93	100*	106½	113	120	126½	133	140	146½	153x	160	166½	173	180	186½	193	200	206½	213†

NOTES: * Maximum exposure recommended for roofs.   x Maximum exposure recommended for single-coursing on sidewalls.   † Maximum exposure recommended for double-coursing on sidewalls.

Fig. 9-3 Sidewall Shingles

Standard Patterns*

TONGUE AND GROOVE	Size (nom.)	A	B	C	Pattern No.
Square Edges	1 x 3	25/32	2 1/2	2 1/4	131
	1 x 4	25/32	3 1/2	3 1/4	132
	1 x 6	25/32	5 1/2	5 1/4	133
	1 1/4 x 4	1 1/16	3 1/2	3 1/4	134
	1 1/4 x 6	1 1/16	5 1/2	5 1/4	135
Eased Edges	1 x 4	25/32	3 1/2	3 1/4	132EE
	1 x 6	25/32	5 1/2	5 1/4	133EE
V1S	1 x 4	3/4	3 1/2	3 1/4	207
	1 x 6	3/4	5 1/2	5 1/4	208
	1 x 8	3/4	7 1/2	7 1/2	215
	1 x 10	3/4	9 1/2	9 1/4	216
	1 x 12	3/4	11 1/2	11 1/4	217
V1S	1 x 4	3/4	3 1/2	3 1/4	209
	1 x 6	3/4	5 1/2	5 1/4	211
	1 x 8	3/4	7 1/2	7 1/4	212
	1 x 10	3/4	9 1/2	9 1/4	213
	1 x 12	3/4	11 1/2	11 1/4	214
V & CV	1 x 6	3/4	5 1/2	5 1/4	116
	1 x 8	3/4	7 1/2	7 1/4	116A
Drop Siding	1 x 6	3/4	5 1/2	5 1/4	106

BEVEL SIDING	Size (nom.)	A	B	C	Pattern No.
Plain Bevel	1/2 x 4	15/32 x 3/16	3 1/2	2 1/2	320
	1/2 x 5	15/32 x 3/16	4 1/2	3 1/2	321
	1/2 x 6	15/32 x 3/16	5 1/2	4 1/2	322
	1/2 x 8	15/32 x 3/16	7 1/2	6 1/2	323
	5/8 x 6	9/16 x 3/16	5 1/2	4 1/2	325
	5/8 x 8	9/16 x 3/16	7 1/2	6 1/2	326
	5/8 x 10	9/16 x 3/16	9 1/2	8 1/2	327
	3/4 x 6	3/4 x 3/16	5 1/2	4 1/2	329
	3/4 x 8	3/4 x 3/16	7 1/2	6 1/2	330
	3/4 x 10	3/4 x 3/16	9 1/2	8 1/2	331
	3/4 x 12	3/4 x 3/16	11 1/2	10 1/2	332
Rabbeted Bevel	5/8 x 4	9/16 x 3/16	3 1/2	3	350
	5/8 x 6	9/16 x 3/16	5 1/2	5	352
	5/8 x 8	9/16 x 3/16	7 1/2	7	353
	1/2 x 4	1/2 x 3/16	3 1/2	3	360
	1/2 x 6	1/2 x 3/16	5 1/2	5	362
	1/2 x 8	1/2 x 3/16	7 1/2	7	363
	3/4 x 6	11/16 x 9/32	5 1/2	5	371
	3/4 x 8	11/16 x 9/32	7 1/2	7	372
	3/4 x 10	11/16 x 9/32	9 1/2	9	373
	3/4 x 12	11/16 x 9/32	11 1/2	11	374
	5/8 x 6	9/16 x 3/16	5 1/2	5	382‡
	5/8 x 8	9/16 x 3/16	7 1/2	7	383‡
	3/4 x 6	3/4 x 9/32	5 1/2	5	391‡
	3/4 x 8	3/4 x 9/32	7 1/2	7	392‡
	3/4 x 10	3/4 x 9/32	9 1/2	9	393‡
	3/4 x 12	3/4 x 9/32	11 1/2	11	394‡
	1/2 x 4	1/2 x 3/16	3 1/2	3	400 §
Anzac	1 x 8	25/32 x 3/8	7 1/2	7 1/2	440
	1 x 10	25/32 x 3/8	9 1/2	8 1/4	441
	1 x 12	25/32 x 3/8	11 1/2	10 1/4	442

Fig. 9-4   Horizontal Wood Siding

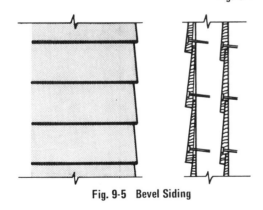

Fig. 9-5   Bevel Siding

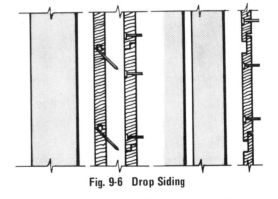

Fig. 9-6   Drop Siding

decay, and is not affected by salt, air, wind, rain, and ice. The siding units vary in size from 8 to 16 inches in width and from 24 to 48 inches in length. The shingles are available in a multitude of colors and textures. The units are available with nailholes which have already been aligned and punched. Mineral fiber shingles may be applied by the direct application method, wood nailing strip method, figure 9-7, shingle backer method, figure 9-8, or channel method, figure 9-9.

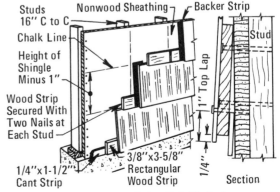

Fig. 9-7   Wood Nailing Strip Method

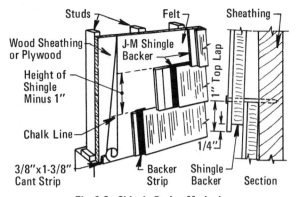

Fig. 9-8 Shingle-Backer Method

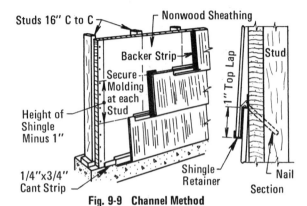

Fig. 9-9 Channel Method

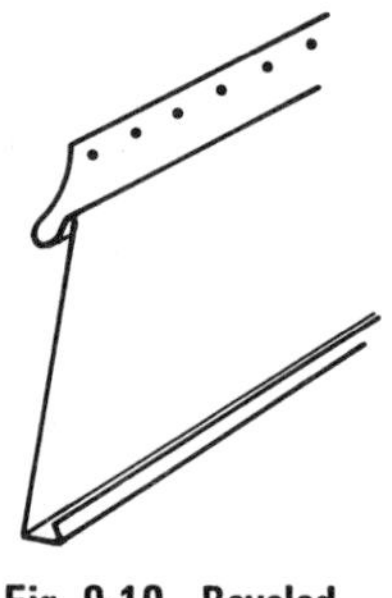

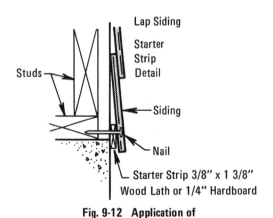

Fig. 9-10 Beveled Vinyl Siding

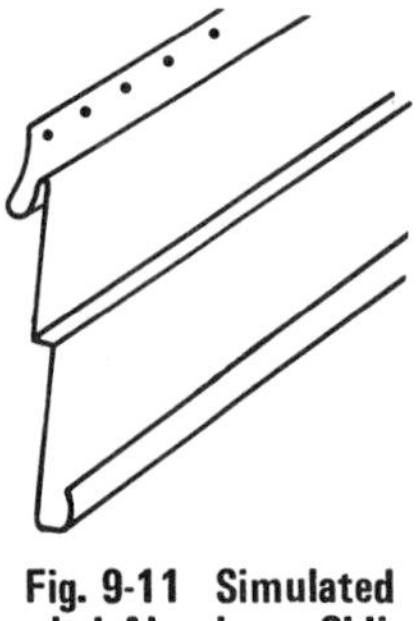

Fig. 9-11 Simulated Beveled Aluminum Siding

Fig. 9-12 Application of Hardboard Siding

VINYL SIDING

Vinyl is molded and machined into various shapes and textures to make vinyl siding. One popular version of vinyl siding is the beveled type with an 8-inch weather exposure, figure 9-10.

Vinyl siding, a product of modern chemistry, has distinct advantages over other types of siding: it never requires painting; it will not dent because of the built-in resiliency which provides high impact resistance; scratches and scars are not as visible because of its constant color; and it can be cleaned easily with soap and water.

There are, however, some disadvantages to using vinyl siding in construction; it becomes brittle in cold weather, and the siding may lose some of its shape if it is exposed to very hot weather.

ALUMINUM SIDING

Aluminum siding is available in various textures, patterns, and colors. The most popular type of aluminum siding is the pattern which simulates bevel siding, figure 9-11. It is also obtainable in vertical V-groove and board and batten siding. The finish applied to this siding is very similar to that which is applied to automobiles; the paint is baked on, a factor which lends the siding great durability.

Aluminum siding has disadvantages in that it is a good conductor of electricity and noise. However, these problems can be overcome by grounding the siding and by placing insulating boards behind the siding.

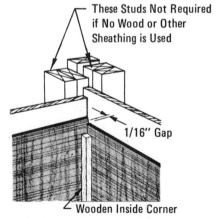

Fig. 9-13 Wooden Inside Corner

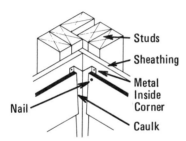

Fig. 9-14 Metal Inside Corner

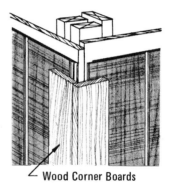

Fig. 9-15 Wooden Corner Boards

HOW TO APPLY HARDBOARD SIDING

1. Snap a chalk line 1 1/2 inches from the bottom of the sheathing.

2. Using the chalk line as a guide, nail a 3/8" x 1 3/8" starter strip to the sheathing, figure 9-12. A *starter strip*, or *cant strip*, is simply a thin strip of wood.

   Note: The inside corners should be covered by a wood corner member, figure 9-13, or butted against a metal inside corner, figure 9-14. Outside corners may be wooden corner boards, figure 9-15, or metal lap siding corners, figure 9-16.

3. Level and nail the first course, leaving 1/8 inch of siding below the starter strip.

   Note: To cut hardboard, use a fine crosscut-toothed handsaw or a power saw with a combination blade.

4. Secure the siding by applying a nail to each stud. The nail should be no less than 1/2 inch from the bottom edge and should be nailed through both siding units, figure 9-17.

   Note: Each siding unit should be nailed at the top and bottom, figure 9-18. Joints should occur only on studs.

HOW TO APPLY PLYWOOD SIDING WITH BATTENS

1. Install a continuous inside corner. Be sure that it is plumb, figure 9-19.

2. Install a continuous outside corner. Be sure that it is also plumb, figure 9-20.

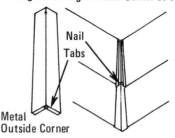

Fig. 9-16 Metal Siding Corners

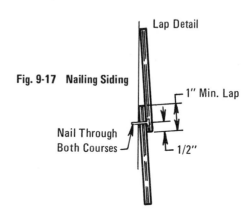

Fig. 9-17 Nailing Siding

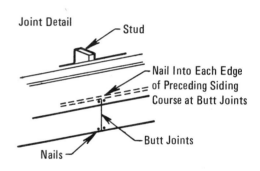

Fig. 9-18 Joint Placement on Lap Siding

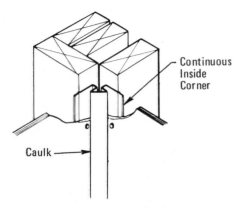

Fig. 9-19 Continuous Inside Corner

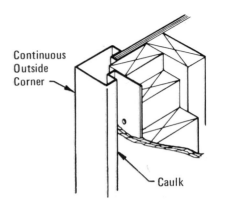

Fig. 9-20 Continous Outside Corner

3. Mark a point 1/2 inch below the bottom sill.

4. Starting at either the inside or outside corner, position the plywood siding against the frame wall with the bottom of the plywood resting on the mark below the bottom sill.

5. Secure the plywood to the wall frame with nails. The nails should be spaced 6 inches on center on all panel edges and 12 inches on center on intermediate studs. The nails used should be noncorrosive, figure 9-21.

6. Place another piece of plywood siding adjacent to the first and secure it.

Note: Avoid driving panel joints tight. Be sure that all bottom edges are flush with each other. Figure 9-22 shows American Plywood Association single-wall siding joint details.

7. Proceed down the exterior wall securing the plywood siding.

8. Nail 3/4" x 1 5/8" strips or milled battens, figure 9-23, over all joints and stud locations. Aluminum batten covers are available, but are usually used only with coated siding, figure 9-24.

HOW TO APPLY WOOD SHINGLES

1. Snap a chalk line 1 inch below the bottom sill.

PLYWOOD SIDING AND SOFFITS (direct to framing) (Applies to all species groups)						
Plywood siding type	Minimum thickness (inch)	Max. support spacing c. to c. (inches)	Nail (a) size	Nail type	Nail spacing (inches)	
					panel edges	intermediate
Panel siding	3/8	16	6d	non-corrosive siding or casing	6	12
	1/2	24	6d		6	12
	5/8	24	8d		6	12
	T 1-11 (5/8)	16	8d		6 (b)	12
Lap siding (c) (d)	3/8, 1/2,	16, 20	6d, 8d	non-corrosive siding or casing	one nail each stud along bottom edge	4" at vertical joint; 8" at studs if siding wider than 12"
	5/8	24	8d			
Bevel siding (c) (d)	9/16 min. butt	16	6d	non-corrosive siding or casing	one nail each stud along bottom edge	4" at vertical joint; 8" at studs if siding wider than 12"
Closed soffits	3/8	24	6d	non-corrosive box or casing	6 (or one nail each support)	12
	5/8	48	8d			12

(a) Nails through battens must penetrate studs at least 1".
(b) Use single nail on shiplap edges slant-driven to catch both edges. Can be nailed to within 3/8" of panel edge. Do not set nails. Nails may be set if placed on both sides of joint instead of slant-driven.
(c) Minimum head-lap 3/4".
(d) Typical widths are 12", 16", and 24".

Fig. 9-21 Plywood Siding Nailing Chart

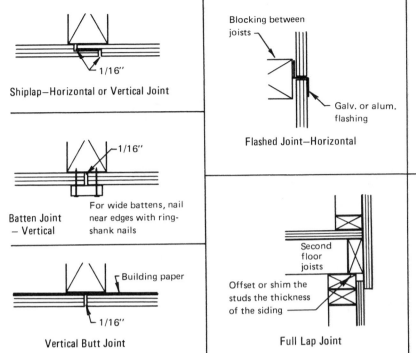

Fig. 9-22 Single Wall Siding Joint Details

For plywood over sheathing: Building paper may be omitted under lapped and bevelled siding with plywood sheathing. Joints may occur away from studs with either plywood or board sheathing.

Textured and overlaid plywood sidings make unusual, attractive soffits. Regular Exterior A-C panels provide smooth soffits with few joints at low cost. Soffit installation recommendations shown below.

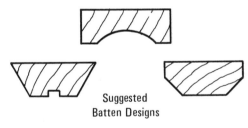

Suggested
Batten Designs

Fig. 9-23 Milled Battens

Lay a course of shingles 1/4 inch apart with the butt end on the chalk line.

3. Lay another course of shingles over the first staggering the vertical joints.

4. Snap a chalk line on the double course. The distance will vary, depending on the shingle size. The desired exposure for an 18-inch shingle is 8 1/2 inches. Therefore, the chalk line would be located 8 1/2 inches from the butt of the double course.

5. Continue laying courses of shingles up the sidewall.

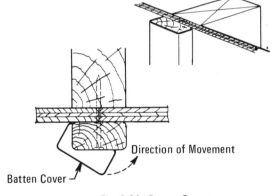

Fig. 9-24 Batten Covers

Note: The outside corners should either have mitered corners or be lapped alternately with every other course protruding past the corner and butting the shake on the other side. The inside corners may be either woven or jointed, figure 9-25.

HOW TO APPLY BEVEL SIDING

1. Measuring upward from the bottom of the sheathing, snap a chalk line. The distance will

Fig. 9-25 Inside and Outside Corners of Wood Shingles

vary, depending on the type of siding and amount of exposure of each course. The line should be parallel to the bottom of the sheathing.

2. Nail starter strips along the bottom edge of the sheathing.

3. Secure continous wood inside and outside corners.

4. Square the ends of the first board and place one end against the left corner board with the top

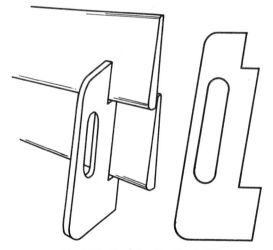

Fig. 9-26 Template For Bevel Siding

edge on the chalk line. Secure the top and bottom edges.

Note: Vertical joints in the siding should be staggered and centered over studs.

5. Continue the siding across to the right corner board.

6. Snap a chalk line for the second course and lay it.

Note: Some contractors prefer to use a story pole in laying the courses which follow. A *story pole* is a 1 x 2, with the butt end of each siding course marked on the pole. Once the first course is in place the story pole is used to determine the height of the next course of siding. A template can be used to serve the same purpose, figure 9-26.

HOW TO APPLY DROP OR MATCHED SIDING

1. Measure upward from the bottom of the sheathing and snap a chalk line. The distance will vary depending on the width of the siding. Allow the siding to extend 1 inch below the lower edge of the bottom sill.

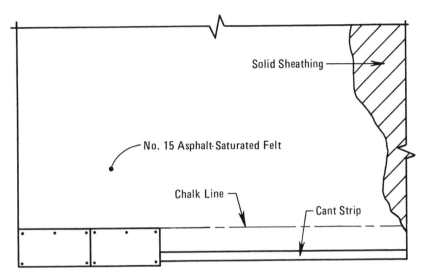

Fig. 9-27 Direct Application of Mineral-Fiber Siding

Note: This type of siding is usually applied directly to the studs.

2. Place the end flush with the corner and mark the other end on the center of a stud.

3. Cut the siding to the proper length.

4. Nail the siding in place. The tongue should face up and be flush with the chalk line.

   Note: When siding is applied directly to the studs, corner boards should be applied over the siding.

5. Continue across the building, keeping the first board straight and level.

6. Continue up the building, keeping all of the siding matched and the butt joints tight.

HOW TO APPLY MINERAL-FIBER SIDING BY THE DIRECT APPLICATION METHOD

Note: This technique is used on a solid nailing base, such as plywood or solid sheathing.

1. Place a 1/4" x 1 1/2" cant strip along the bottom edge of the sheathing; 3/4 inch of the cant strip should overhang the top of the foundation wall.

2. Assuming that 12" x 24" units are used, measure 11 inches up from the bottom of the cant strip and snap a chalk line.

3. Secure inside and outside wood or metal corner units.

4. Nail a full-sized unit on the lower left-hand corner of the wall using the chalk line as a guide, figure 9-27.

5. Before driving a nail in the upper right-hand unit, place a flashing strip behind the vertical joint.

6. Continue the first course, placing a flashing strip behind each vertical joint and keeping each unit aligned with the chalk line.

7. Snap a chalk line 11 inches above the top of the first course of shingles.

8. Start the second course with half a unit, overlapping the first course by one inch.

9. Continue the siding across to the right corner board.

10. Lay the remaining courses in the same manner as the second course.

HOW TO APPLY MINERAL-FIBER SIDING BY THE SHINGLE-BACKING METHOD

1. Place a 1/4" x 1 1/2" cant strip at the base of the wall sheathing with 3/4 inch of the strip overhanging the foundation wall.

2. Secure inside and outside corner units.

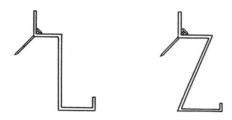

Fig. 9-28 Metal Channel Molding

3. Nail the shingle backing flush with the bottom of the cant strip.

   Note: The shingle backing should be rigid, water-resistant, insulating fiberboard with a minimum thickness of 5/16 inch. The shingle backing should also be a minimum of 4 feet long, and 1/4 inch narrower than the shingle unit. It should be placed with staggered joints.

4. Nail a full-sized unit flush with the left-hand corner board, keeping the top of the unit flush with the top of the shingle backing.

5. Continue to lay the first course of units.

6. Measure 11 inches upward from the top of the shingle unit and snap a chalk line.

7. Apply the shingle backing.

8. Start the second course of the fiber siding shingle units with a half unit and proceed to lay the courses.

9. The courses which follow are run in the same manner as is the second course.

HOW TO APPLY MINERAL-FIBER SIDING BY THE CHANNEL METHOD

1. Place a 1/4" x 1 1/2" cant strip at the base of the wall sheathing with 3/4 inch of the strip overhanging the foundation wall.

2. Secure inside and outside corner units.

3. Nail 1 5/8-inch metal channel molding to the cant strip, figure 9-28. *Channel molding* is a metal strip which aids in supporting the siding.

4. Place shingle units against the channel molding.

5. Place a channel mold unit on top of the shingle and nail the molding to the studs. The nails should be driven in at an angle with the molding to provide enough pressure to assure a tight assembly.

6. Start the course with a half unit and proceed to lay the course with full units.

7. The following courses are run by the same method.

HOW TO APPLY MINERAL-FIBER SIDING BY THE WOOD NAILING STRIP METHOD

1. Place a 1/4" x 1 1/2" cant strip at the bottom of the sheathing; 3/4 inch of the strip should overhang the foundation wall.

2. Measure 11 inches up from the bottom of the cant strip and snap a chalk line.

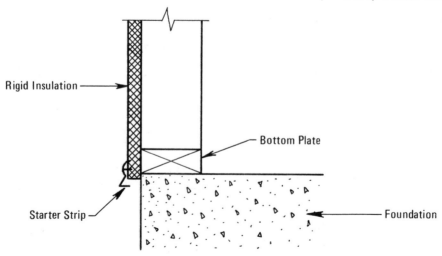

Fig. 9-29 Installation of Starter Strip

3. Secure the inside and outside corner units.

4. Nail a full-sized unit flush with the left-hand corner board, keeping the top of the unit flush with the chalk line. Place a flashing strip behind each vertical joint.

5. Continue to lay the units for the first course.

6. Measure 3/4 inch down on the first course and snap a chalk line.

7. . Nail a 3/8″ x 3 1/2″ wood nailing strip to the stud wall using the chalk line as a guide.

8. Measure 11 3/4 inches up from the bottom of the wood nailing strip and snap a chalk line.

9. Nail the second course of shingles, starting with half a unit.

10. The remaining courses are laid in the same manner as the second course.

HOW TO APPLY ALUMINUM OR VINYL SIDING

1. Install the starter strip, figure 9-29. The starter strip should be nailed to the bottom plate and project past the intersection of the bottom plate and finished floor.

2. Locate the top of the first course and snap a chalk line parallel to the starter strip. The distance measured is approximately 8 inches, but will vary depending on the brand name of the siding.

3. Install the inside corner post.

4. The corner post should be plumbed and nailed every 12 inches.

5. Install the outside corner post.

   Note: In some cases an outside corner post is not used and siding corners are placed over the siding.

6. Lock the first course of siding to the starter strip and nail the siding to the building, using the chalk line as a guide.

7. Mark and snap a chalk line for the second course and lay the course.

   Note: Vertical joints in the siding should be staggered and centered over the studs.

REVIEW

A. Choose the best answer or answers to complete each statement.

1. Plywood siding which is nailed directly to the studs should be _____ inch thick.

   a. 1/4 c. 3/8
   b. 5/16 d. 7/16

2. The highest grade of plywood siding is _____ .

   a. Z c. B
   b. A d. N

3. The shortest sidewall shingle is _____ inches long.

   a. 12 c. 18
   b. 10 d. 16

4. The lap on bevel siding should not be less than _____ inch in size.

   a. 1/4 c. 3/4
   b. 1/2 d. 1

5. The nails on the edges of plywood siding should be spaced _____ inches on center.

   a. 2   c. 6
   b. 4   d. 8

6. The exposure for 18-inch sidewall shingles is _____ inches.

   a. 6   c. 10
   b. 8 1/2   d. 11 1/2

7. Inside corners for sidewall shingles may be _____ .

   a. woven   c. butted
   b. jointed   d. mitered

8. To keep the course of bevel siding straight, some carpenters use _____ .

   a. a ruler   c. a template
   b. nylon string   d. a hammer

9. A cant strip is sometimes called a _____ .

   a. starter strip   c. kicker strip
   b. purlin   d. fiber siding strip

10. Shingle backing should be _____ inch thick.

    a. 3/8   c. 1/2
    b. 5/16   d. 3/4

B. Place the correct answer in the space provided.

1. The inside corners of hardboard siding are covered by _____ or _____ .

2. A _____ or _____ is used to cut hardboard siding.

3. Plywood siding projects _____ inch below the bottom sill.

4. Panel joints should be _____ inch wide.

5. An 18-inch sidewall shingle has an exposure of _____ inches.

6. The inside corners of wood shingles may be either _____ or _____ .

7. The tongue on matched siding is placed with the tongue _____ .

8. Mineral-fiber siding is applied with _____ joints.

9. The second course of mineral-fiber siding is started with a _____ unit .

10. Mineral-fiber siding is sometimes referred to as _____ .

C.   In the space provided sketch

   1.   bevel siding.

   2.   metal inside corner.

   3.   channel mold.

   4.   batten cover.

Section II *INTERIOR TRIM*

Unit 10 Gypsum Wallboard Construction

Gypsum wallboard is a sheet of gypsum which has been covered with some type of surface material such as specially treated paper. It has become quite popular in the past few years and has virtually replaced plaster as a means of interior wall finish. Drywall construction, or gypsum wallboard construction involves securing gypsum wallboard to a wood or metal frame, concealing joints and fasteners, and finishing the surface. Gypsum wallboard construction is commonly referred to as drywall construction because of the absence of water in the actual finishing process.

Gypsum, or hydrous calcium sulfate, is mined in great quantities. Gypsum undergoes a process known as *calcining*, which extracts the water from the mineral and leaves a powder, often called *plaster of paris*. In order to produce the core of gypsum board, as many as fourteen ingredients may be added to the powdery calcined materials. A nine-ply paper is then placed on top and the bottom of the core to sandwich the gypsum.

Gypsum wallboard is now found on most job sites for several reasons. The material is fire-resistant, crack-resistant, economical to use, and easily positioned. The wallboard is fire-resistant because its core is constructed of a mineral which does not burn. It is crack-resistant because extremes in temperature and humidity have little effect on the size of the panels, thus eliminating great expansion and contraction. Gypsum wallboard can receive many types of surface decoration such as paint, wallpaper, or fabric.

Gypsum wallboard varies in thickness, but most panels measure 4' x 8', 4' x 12', or 4' x 14', figure 10-1. Due to the size and ease in cutting, wallboard may be erected very quickly. In many cases, a worker can average 650 square feet of completed surface a day.

TYPES OF GYPSUM WALLBOARD

The five main classifications of wallboard are: regular, predecorated, insulating, fire-resistant, and

Thickness	Approx. Weight lbs. per sq. ft.	Size	Location	Application Method	Max. Spacing of Framing Members
1/4"	1.1	4' x 8' to 12'	Over Existing Walls & Ceilings	Horizontal or Vertical	
3/8"	1.5	4' x 8' to 14'	Ceilings	Horizontal	16"
3/8"	1.5	4' x 8' to 14'	Sidewalls	Horizontal or Vertical	16"
1/2"	2.0	4' x 8' to 14'	Ceilings	Vertical / Horizontal	16" / 24"
1/2"	2.0	4' x 8' to 14'	Sidewalls	Horizontal or Vertical	24"
5/8"	2.5	4' x 8' to 14'	ceilings	Vertical / Horizontal	16" / 24"
5/8"	2.5	4' x 8' to 14'	Sidewalls	Horizontal or Vertical	24"
1"	4.0	2' x 8' to 12'		For Laminated Partitions	

Fig. 10-1 Gypsum Wallboard Size and Application Method

Fastening Applications	Fastener Description	Nail Spacing C. to C. (1)	Approx. Lbs. Nails Req'd per MSF SHEETROCK
½", ⅜" and ¼" SHEETROCK Wallboard; ½" and ⅜" BAXBORD Gypsum Backing Board to wood frame (2) (3)	1¼" GWB-54 Annular Ring Nail 12½ ga.; ¼" dia. head with a slight taper to a small fillet at shank; bright finish; medium diamond point; meets ASTM C380 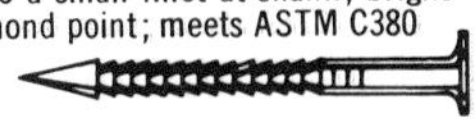	7" ceiling 8" walls	5¼
⅝" SHEETROCK Wallboard to wood frame (3)	1⅜" Annular Ring Nail (Same as GWB-54 except for length) 	7" ceiling 8" walls	5¼
⅝" SHEETROCK FIRECODE Wallboard face layers to staggered wood studs over ½" USG Wood Fiber Sound Deadening Board	2¼" 7d Gypsum Wallboard Nail Cement Coated, 13 ga., ¼" dia. head 	7" walls (face layer)	9
⅜" and ¼" SHEETROCK Wallboard over existing surface, wood frame	1⅞" 6d Gypsum Wallboard Nail Cement Coated, 13 ga., ¼" dia. head 	7" ceiling 8" walls	6¼
⅝" SHEETROCK FIRECODE Wallboard to wood frame	1⅞" 6d Gypsum Wallboard Nail Cement Coated, 13 ga., ¼" dia. head 	6" ceiling 7" walls	6¾
½" SHEETROCK FIRECODE "C" Wallboard to wood frame	1⅝" 5d Gypsum Wallboard Nail Cement Coated, 13½ ga., 15⁄16" dia. head 	6" ceiling 7" walls	5¼
⅜" ULTRAWALL Panels —to wood frame (3) —over existing surface, wood frame (3)	1⅛" USG Matching Color Nail (Steel)	8" walls	1½
	1⅞" USG Matching Color Nail (Steel) 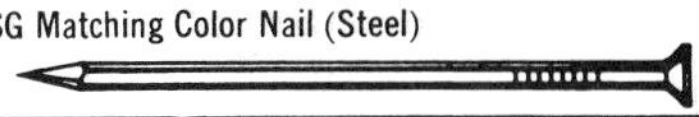	8" walls	4½
TEXTONE Vinyl Panels (17 finishes) to wood frame (3)	1⅜" USG Matching Color Nail (Brass) 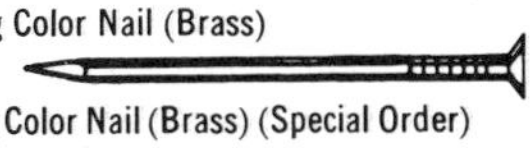	8" walls	2½
	1⅞" USG Matching Color Nail (Brass) (Special Order) 	8" walls	4½

NOTES:
(1) Spacing shown are for single layer application without adhesive. (2) See Wood Framing Requirements and Heating Recommendations, Chapter 1. (3) Nails shown for this application are also the proper size for use with adhesive.

Fig. 10-2 Selector Guide for Wallboard Nails

water-resistant. The edges of regular wallboard are usually tapered so that a smooth and even surface exists at the joint edges after the finishing process. The back of regular wallboard is surfaced with gray lining paper, with a smooth manila paper attached to the surface.

Predecorated wallboard is equipped with a factory-applied decorative finish. The decorative finish includes paper and vinyl coverings in a multitude of colors and patterns. The joints created when two predecorated wallboards meet can be concealed by batten or moldings. Sometimes the joint is not treated at all, but is beveled. This effect is known as a *shadowline*. Predecorated wallboard is secured to framing members by an adhesive bond or matching prefinished nails.

Insulating wallboard is very similar to regular wallboard with the exception that the back is bonded with aluminum foil. The foil back on the wallboard acts as a vapor barrier and thermal insulator.

The only major difference between fire-resistant wallboard and regular wallboard is in the composition of the core. To increase the fire resistance of the gypsum core, glass fibers and specially formulated additives are mixed with the gypsum. Water-resistant wallboard is manufactured with a gypsum core, asphaltic adhesives, and chemically-treated paper. Wallboards of this type are usually used in areas that have

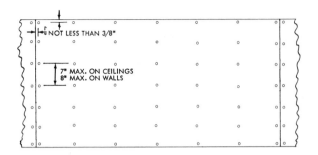

Fig. 10-3 Single-Nailing System

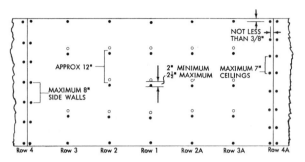

Fig. 10-4 Double-Nailing System

a high moisture content, such as kitchens, baths, or washrooms.

Although there are numerous advantages in using gypsum wallboard, there are certain limitations in its use. It should not be used in an area which receives an excessive amount of moisture unless water-resistant backing board is used. The wallboard should not be used as a plaster base. Also, if 1/4 inch thick gypsum wallboard is used, it should be placed only on solid surfaces. If 3/8 inch thick wallboard is used, the maximum spacing of the studs or framing members is 16 inches on center and 24 inches on center for 1/2 inch or 5/8 inch thick wallboards.

TYPES OF WALLBOARD FASTENERS

Nails

The two basic types of nails used in the application of gypsum wallboard are the annular ring type and a cement-coated type. It has been found that the annular ring nail has 20 percent greater holding power than the cement-coated nail. Whether the annular ring or the cement-coated type is used, the nail should comply with performance standards set by the Gypsum Drywall Contractors International Gypsum Association. Figure 10-2 is an approved selector guide for wallboard nails.

If a single layer of 1/4 inch thick gypsum wallboard is used, a nail not less than 1 inch long is used. The spacing of the nails along the edges and at support intervals is the same for all thicknesses of wallboard. In the single nailing system, the nails should be spaced not less than 3/8 inch from the edges, figure 10-3, and the nails driven into the studs are placed no more than

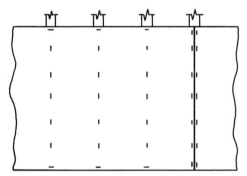

Fig. 10-5 Staple Application

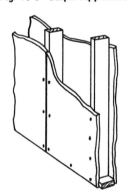

Fig. 10-6 Wood Framing

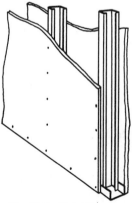

Fig. 10-7 Metal Framing

Fastening Application	Fastener Used
GYPSUM BOARD TO INTERIOR METAL FRAMING (1)	
½" single layer wallboard to interior studs, runners, channels	⅞" HI-LO Type S Bugle Head
⅝" single layer wallboard to interior studs, runners, channels	1" HI-LO Type S Bugle Head
½" double layer wallboard to interior studs, runners, channels	1⁵⁄₁₆" HI-LO Type S Bugle Head
⅝" double layer wallboard to interior studs, runners, channels	1⅝" HI-LO Type S Bugle Head
1" coreboard to metal angle runners in solid partitions	1¼" HI-LO Type S Bugle Head
½" wallboard through coreboard to metal angle runners in solid partitions	1⅞" HI-LO Type S Bugle Head
⅝" wallboard through coreboard to metal angle runners in solid partitions	2¼" HI-LO Type S Bugle Head
GYPSUM BOARD TO 12-GA. (MAX.) METAL FRAMING	
½" and ⅝" wallboard and gypsum sheathing to 20-ga. studs and runners	1" Type S-12 Bugle Head
USG Self-Furring Metal Lath through gypsum sheathing to 20-ga. studs and runners / E-Z WALL Panels to studs and runners	1¼" Type S-12 Bugle Head
½" and ⅝" double layer gypsum wallboard to 20-ga. studs and runners	1⅝" Type S-12 Bugle Head
Multi-layer gypsum board to 20-ga. studs and runners	1⅞" Type S-12 Bugle Head
WOOD TRIM TO INTERIOR METAL FRAMING	
Wood trim over single layer wallboard to interior studs, runners	1⅝" HI-LO Type S Trim Head
Wood trim over double layer wallboard to interior studs, runners	2¼" HI-LO Type S Trim Head

Fastening Application	Fastener Used
METAL STUDS TO DOOR FRAMES, RUNNERS	
Interior metal studs to runners	⅜" Type S Pan Head
Interior metal studs to door frame jamb anchor clips 20-ga. studs to runner Other metal-to-metal attachment (12-ga. max.)	⅜" Type S-12 Pan Head
Interior metal studs to door frame jamb anchor clips (heavier shank assures entry in clips of hard steel)	½" Type S-12 Pan Head
Strut studs to door frame clips, rails and other attachments in E-Z WALL partitions	½" Type S-16 Pan Head Cadmium Plated
TRIM AND ACCESSORIES TO METAL FRAMING	
Door hinges and trim to door frame Aluminum trim to metal framing (screw matches hardware and trim)	⅞" Finishing Screw Type S-18 Oval Head Cadmium Plated
Metal base splice plates through wallboard and runner	1¼" HI-LO Type S Bugle Head
Batten strips to interior metal studs in demountable partitions	1⅛" HI-LO Type S Bugle Head
Aluminum trim to interior metal framing in Demountable and E-Z WALL partitions	1¼" HI-LO Finishing Screw Type S Bugle Head Cadmium Plated
GYPSUM BOARD TO WOOD FRAMING	
⅜", ½" and ⅝" single layer wallboard to wood framing	1¼" Type W Bugle Head
RC-1 RESILIENT CHANNEL TO WOOD FRAMING	
Screw attachment required for ceilings, recommended for partitions	1¼" Type W, ⅞" or 1" HI-LO Type S Bugle Head (see details above)
For fire rated construction	1¼" HI-LO Type S Bugle Head (see details above)
GYPSUM BOARD TO GYPSUM BOARD	
Multi-layer adhesively laminated gypsum to gypsum partitions (not recommended for double layer ⅜" wallboard)	1½" Type G Bugle Head

Notes: (1) Includes USG Interior Metal Studs, Metal Runners, Metal Angle Runners, Metal Furring Channels, RC-1 Resilient Channels. For 20-ga. Metal Studs and Runners, always use Type S-12 screws. For steel applications not shown, select a screw length which is at least ⅜" longer than total thickness of materials to be fastened. USG Brand Screws are manufactured under U.S. Patent Nos. 2,871,752; 3,056,234; 3,125,923; 3,207,023; 3,221,588.

Fig. 10-8   Selector Guide for Wallboard Screws

8 inches apart. For gypsum board with a thickness of 3/8 inch to 5/8 inch, annular ringed nails are used.

In addition to the single nailing system, a double nailing system is sometimes used, figure 10-4. In this system, the nails are spaced 12 inches on center with an additional nail spaced 2 inches from the first. The head of the nail should be driven below the surface of

the wallboard, creating a dimple. However, the paper should not be broken in the process.

Staples

Power-driven staples are often used to fasten the first ply of a two-ply system. If staples are used, they should be 16 gage, flattened and galvanized. The staple

legs should have a minimum penetration of 5/8 inch and have a 7/16-inch crown. The crown of the staples should run parallel to the edge, figure 10-5. The staples should be spaced 3/8 inch from the edge and spaced 7 inches on center for intermediate supports.

Screws

In addition to nails and staples to secure gypsum wallboard, there are self-drilling and self-tapping gypsum wallboard screws. The screws are designed to secure the wallboard to either wood framing, figure 10-6, or metal framing, figure 10-7. They are available in various lengths and gages, figure 10-8. The spacing requirements for screws is 16 inches on center where the framing members are 16 inches on center and 12 inches on center in cases when framing members are 24 inches on center.

Adhesives and Nails

An adhesive is used in conjunction with nails to provide a continuous area of support for gypsum wallboard. When this technique is used, nailing is reduced approximately 50 percent. The concealment of screw or nailheads is also reduced. The framing members are covered with a continuous bead of adhesive about 1/4 to 3/8 inch wide. To provide a bond for two adjacent pieces, the adhesive should be applied in a zigzag or serpentine pattern, figure 10-9. If the joint of two adjacent pieces is not treated, two parallel beads of adhesive should be used. If the wallboard can be braced until the adhesive develops the required bond strength, no nailing is necessary. However, if nails must be used, they should be placed no further than 24 inches on center.

CUTTING OF GYPSUM WALLBOARD

Gypsum wallboard can be sawed or cut. If the wallboard is cut, the face side should be scored with a knife, figure 10-10, and then bent back. The paper on the back side can then be easily cut or broken. Cutouts for electrical outlets, air-conditioning ducts, pipes, and other small openings can be made by several different techniques. One technique involves covering the opening with *keel*, a chalklike substance which usually comes in crayon form. Once the keel is applied, the wallboard is placed in position and struck with the heel of the hand near the outlet. The blow forces the wallboard to make contact with the outlet, leaving the impression of the outlet on the back of the wallboard. A saw or other suitable tool is then used to cut along the outline.

HOW TO APPLY SINGLE-PLY GYPSUM WALLBOARD

Note: Single-ply application involves the use of 3/8-inch, 1/2-inch, or 5/8-inch gypsum wallboard applied directly to wood or metal framing members.

1. Position the wallboard against the ceiling; the edges should lap over the framing members.

2. Place the nails or screws at the center of the wallboard and work toward the edges. While the fasteners are being placed, the wallboard is held in firm contact with the framing members.

3. Apply wallboard to the sidewalls using the horizontal or vertical application, figure 10-11.

   Note: If the wallboard is applied horizontally, the long edges of the board are at right angles to the framing members; in the vertical application,

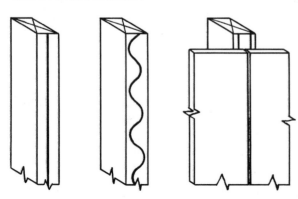

Fig. 10-9 Adhesive Application

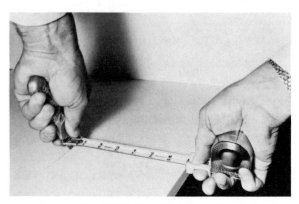

Fig. 10-10 Scoring Wallboard

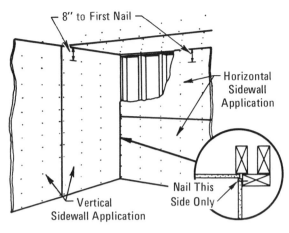

Fig. 10-11 Horizontal and Vertical
Sidewall Application

Fig. 10-12 Floor Jack

Fig. 10-13 Two-Ply Adhesive Application

the long edges are parallel to the framing members. If the ceiling height is 8 feet 2 inches or less, horizontal application of the wallboard will result in less cutting, fewer joints, joints at more convenient heights, and easier handling. If the ceiling height is more than 8 feet 2 inches, the vertical application is more practical.

4. The wallboard should be butted against the ceiling and secured with nails or screws. If the vertical application technique is used, a floor-jack, figure 10-12, is helpful in getting a tight fit.

   Note: No vertical joints should occur within 8 inches of the corner of any opening.

5. Pound on the walls and ceiling to detect any loose nails or screws.

6. Pull the nails that were not driven into the framing members and drive any other loose fasteners tight.

7. If a fastener has punctured the paper, place an additional fastener 1 1/2 inches from the fracture and remove the faulty fastener.

HOW TO APPLY TWO-PLY GYPSUM WALLBOARD

Note: Two-ply gypsum wallboard is used to produce a high-quality finished appearance.

1. Check for proper alignment of the framing members. If the framing members are not aligned or

are twisted, the wallboards may become loose or the paper may be punctured.

2. Secure the base layer to the framing members with nails, screws, or staples.

   Note: In this particular type of construction, two layers of 3/8-inch gypsum wallboard are normally used.

3. Apply an adhesive to the back of the finished layer, figure 10-13. The adhesive can be applied with notched trowels or mastic spreaders, figure 10-14. There should always be a space between the ribbons of adhesive.

4. Apply the face layer either vertically or horizontally, depending on which technique results in the least waste and least number of joints. The face layer should be placed so that the joint of the base layer and the face layer are offset 10 inches.

5. Secure the face layer to the base layer. If temporary support is desired, the nails used should penetrate 3/4 inch into the nailing members. If predecorated panels are to be permanently attached, use nails of a matching color.

Fig. 10-14 Mastic Spreader

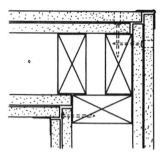

Fig. 10-15 Floating Corner

Note: Only the overlapping base layer panel is nailed to the framing on the inside corner. This corner is commonly referred to as a *floating corner*, figure 10-15. Both base layers are nailed to the framing members on the outside corner; however, the finish layer is not nailed.

HOW TO APPLY PREDECORATED VINYL-COVERED PANELS

Note: Predecorated panels with vinyl facing have a vinyl flap at each long edge.

1. Cut the panels to the desired size and tape the vinyl flaps back, figure 10-16.

2. Run a bead of adhesive along the face of the framing members. Do not apply adhesive at joint locations.

3. Secure the panels vertically to the framing member with nails spaced 8 inches on center and screws 12 inches on center.

    Note: The edges of the panels should be centered on the framing member.

4. Fill the vertical joints with a joint compound. Two or three coats may be necessary for a level joint; if so, the base coat should be hard before applying the next coat.

    Note: Do not allow any compound to touch the vinyl.

5. Apply an adhesive to the back of each vinyl flap. Lay one flap down and smooth with a broad knife, figure 10-17. The broad knife presses out the excess adhesive and rids the flap of air pockets.

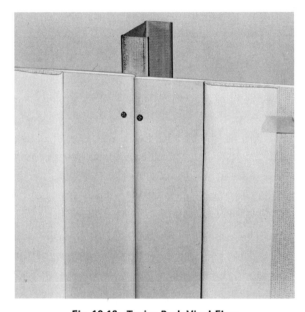

Fig. 10-16 Taping Back Vinyl Flaps

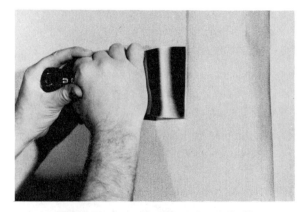

Fig. 10-17 Smoothing With a Broad Knife

6. Place the second flap over the one that has been smoothed and press it in place. Use a broad knife to smooth the flap.

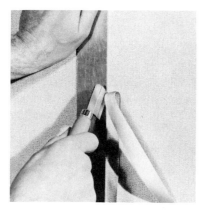

Fig. 10-18   Trimming Edge Strips

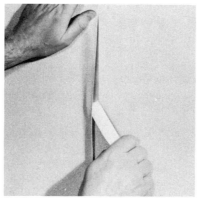

Fig. 10-19   Removing Trim Strips

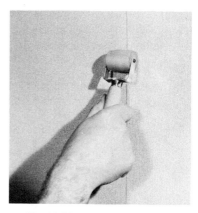

Fig. 10-20   Rolling Edges Flat

7. Using a straightedge and a knife, cut both vinyl flaps about 2 inches from the second flap, figure 10-18.

8. Remove the cut strips of vinyl which are on the finished surface and beneath the vinyl flap, figure 10-19.

9. Smooth the joint with a broad knife and sponge off any excess adhesive.

10. Roll the two edges flat, figure 10-20.

HOW TO CONCEAL JOINTS

1. Spread a bedding coat of joint compound into the depression formed by the two panels of wallboard.   A broad knife with a 4-inch or 5-inch blade should be used, figure 10-21.

2. Place reinforcing tape over the joint compound and draw the broad knife down the seam, figure 10-22.

Fig. 10-21   Applying Bedding Coat

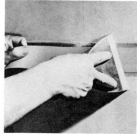

Fig. 10-22   Placing Reinforcing Tape

Fig. 10-23   Applying Second Coat

3. After the bedding coat is dry, apply a second coat, feathering out the edges. *Feathering* is a

Fig. 10-24   Applying Third Coat

Fig. 10-25   Finishing Inside Corners

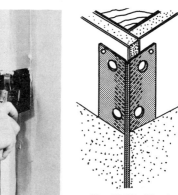

Fig. 10-26   Metal Corner Bead

process in which the second coat of the joint compound is spread past the edges of the first coat, figure 10-23.

4. After the second coat is dry, place a third coat over the first two coats, feathering the edges of the third coat two inches past the edge of the second coat, figure 10-24.

5. If needed, sand the joint compound lightly.

Note: Interior corners are sometimes finished with reinforcing tape and a joint compound, figure 10-25. Exterior corners are reinforced with a metal corner bead fastened to the framing, figure 10-26.

REVIEW

A. Choose the best answer or answers to complete each statement.

1. The average worker will install _____ square feet of gypsum wallboard a day.

    a. 650 c. 500
    b. 975 d. 300

2. Gypsum wallboard which is _____ inch thick should be placed only on solid surfaces.

    a. 5/8 c. 1/4
    b. 1/2 d. 3/8

3. Nails should not be spaced less than _____ inch from the edges of wallboard.

    a. 1/2 c. 5/8
    b. 3/8 d. 3/4

4. In the single nailing system, the nails at support intervals should be placed _____ inches on center.

    a. 2 c. 6
    b. 4 d. 8

5. In the double nailing system, the nails are spaced 12 inches on center with additional nail spaced _____ inches from the first.

    a. 2 c. 3
    b. 4 d. 1

6. Staple legs should have a penetration of _____ inch.

    a. 1/8 c. 3/4
    b. 1/4 d. 5/8

7. A bead of adhesive is about _____ inch wide.

    a. 1/4 c. 5/8
    b. 1/2 d. 3/4

8. No vertical joint should occur within _____ inches of the corner of any opening.

    a. 4 c. 8
    b. 6 d. 10

9. The vertical joint of a predecorated panel is filled with _____ .

    a. joint compound   c. glue

    b. tape   d. adhesive

10. Exterior corners are reinforced with _____ .

    a. adhesive   c. metal corner beads

    b. reinforcing tape   d. joint compound

B. Place the correct answer in the space provided.

1. Interior corners are finished with _____ .

2. Adhesive can be applied with a _____ or a _____ .

3. If the ceiling height is more than 8 feet 2 inches, the_____ application of wallboard is more practical.

4. A single-ply application involves the use of _____ , _____ , or _____ sized gypsum wallboard.

5. The _____ process extracts water from mineral gypsum.

6. If framing members are spaced 16 inches on center, screws should be spaced _____ .

7. The two basic types of nails used in gypsum wallboard construction are _____ and _____ .

8. The five main classifications of wallboard are _____ , _____ , _____ , _____ , and _____ .

9. The foil backing on insulating wallboard acts as a_____ and _____ .

Unit 11 Paneling

Paneling can provide an increase in the structural strength of a room besides being decorative. The three basic types of paneling are hardboard, plywood, and solid wood.

HARDBOARD PANELING

Wood fibers are subjected to heat and pressure and then shaped to form hardboard paneling. The paneling is smoother, harder, and denser than most other types of paneling and is highly resistant to moisture and dents. The paneling is usually 1/8 or 1/4 inch thick and is available in sizes of 4' x 7', 4' x 8', 4' x 9', and 4' x 10'.

The panels have varying surface finishes to complement the decor of any room. They are available in simulated wood-grain patterns of walnut, pecan, chestnut, teak, oak, cheery, and birch. Other panels have surfaces that are marbleized, burlapped, louvered, embossed and covered with lacy prints. The panels may also be purchased in a plain design and painted any color. If a particular building code requires a flame-retardant surface, there are hardboard panels that are impregnated with fire-retardant chemicals.

Most hand and power tools will easily cut hardboard paneling. Some carpenters prefer to keep a special blade for cutting hardboard, since hardboard is tougher than most natural woods and has a tendency to destroy the set of a blade. The *set* is the angle of the saw teeth. A crosscut saw is used for straight cuts, and a coping saw is used for curved cuts.

Conventional wood fasteners or adhesives may be used to secure the paneling to framing members. If plain finishing nails are used, they should be set and the holes filled with colored putty. Color-coordinated nails may be purchased to match paneling.

Inside corners of hardboard paneling are usually butted, but a special inside corner may be used, figure 11-1. Outside corners are sometimes mitered, but wood or metal corners are usually used, figure 11-2. The joints between the panels are usually butted, forming a V-groove, or covered with a batten, figure 11-3. Some joints have joint molding inserted between the panels, figure 11-4.

PLYWOOD PANELING

Plywood paneling is available in many different hardwood-faced veneers and designs. This paneling is constructed by gluing pieces of veneer, or thin wood, together. In the manufacture of plywood paneling, veneers are glued with the grain of each layer perpendicular to each adjacent layer. The panels are usually composed of an odd number of layers, such as three. The outside layer is called the *face*, and the center layer composes the core.

Some of the plywood paneling used in light construction has a factory-applied finish and can be used with matching prefinished trim and molding. The panels are usually 4' x 8' and have V-grooves

Fig. 11-1 Inside Corner   Fig. 11-2 Outside Corner

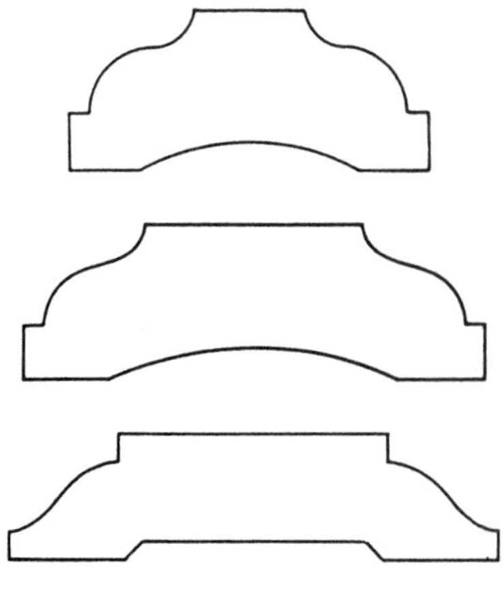

Fig. 11-3 Battens

Fig. 11-4 Joint Molding

16 inches on center; other V-grooves are randomly spaced. The grooves help to conceal the nails and give the appearance of solid wood paneling. Nailheads should be set, and the hole filled with matching colored putty. The joints of plywood paneling are treated in much the same manner as hardboard joints. In the installation of plywood paneling, a V-groove usually occurs where two panels meet. A butt joint is often used in an interior corner, and usually the outside corner is covered with a strip of corner molding.

Plywood panels should be removed from their cartons 48 hours prior to installation. One-inch stripping is placed under and between each face-to-face panel. The panels can then adjust to atmospheric conditions of the job site.

If the plywood panels are to be placed over old frame walls, masonry walls, or concrete, furring strips are used. The furring strips, usually 1 x 4s or 1 x 2s, are secured to old frame walls with 6d nails. Hardened steel nails, anchor nails, or adhesives should be used to fasten the strips to concrete and masonry walls. The furring strips should be placed horizontally on 16-inch centers with any low spots shimmed up, figure 11-5. Shimming a furring strip involves building the strip up so that it is level with the other furring strips; this is usually accomplished by placing small wedges under the low spots.

Before installation, the panels should be leaned against the walls and arranged for the most attractive match of color and grain.

SOLID WOOD PANELING

Solid wood paneling is made from hardwood and softwood and is available with a rough-sawed or planed finish. The rough-sawed has a rustic effect, while the planed paneling appears smooth. The panels are machine-molded to produce shadowlines and decorative edges. The boards usually have tongue-and-groove joints for assembling and are blind nailed, figure 11-6, thus eliminating the need for countersinking. *Countersinking* is the placing of a nailhead below the surface of the wood. The grading of solid wood paneling falls into two categories, knotty and clear. Knotty paneling is usually used for a casual

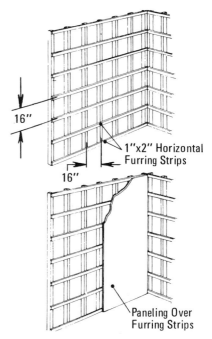

Fig. 11-5 Furring Strips

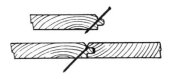

Fig. 11-6 Blind Nailing

effect; clear, solid wood paneling has a more formal appearance.

The paneling should be delivered to the job site several days prior to its installation. The panels should be stacked in a manner so that air can circulate around them, allowing the boards to adjust to the temperature and humidity of the room.

HOW TO INSTALL HARDBOARD PANELING WITH NAILS

Note: Before the installation of hardboard panels, the panels should be separated and stood on edge for a period of 48 hours. This allows the panels to adjust to atmospheric conditions.

1. Starting at one corner of a room, place a panel in position, plumb it, and attach it to the stud wall. It may be necessary to *scribe,* or mark

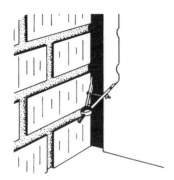

Fig. 11-7 Scribing a Panel

with a knife or scriber, figure 11-7. The scribing provides a pattern for the placement of the paneling.

Note: The intermediate spacing of studs should be no more than 16 inches on center.

2. Starting at the center of the panel, place 3d finishing nails or ring-grooved hardboard nails 12 inches on center at the intermediate supports, nailing in the panel grooves when possible.

    Note: The nails should be driven through predrilled holes if ordinary finishing nails are used.

3. Nail the edges and joints, spacing the nails 6 inches on center, figure 11-8.

    Note: Strike the nailheads vertically and drive the head flush with the face of the paneling. The nail should be placed at least 1/4 inch from the edge of the panel.

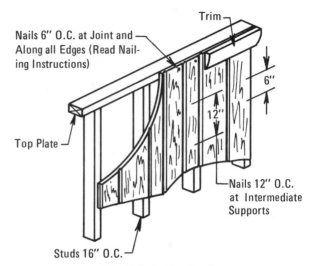

Fig. 11-8 Nailing Paneling

4. Set the nails with a 2/32-inch nail set. The head should be placed slightly below the hardboard surface.

5. Place and secure the remaining panels.

6. Fill the holes with putty of a matching color.

    Note: To eliminate the predrilling and dressing of holes, special color-matched, ring-grooved hardboard nails may be used.

HOW TO INSTALL PLYWOOD PANELING WITH AN ADHESIVE

Note: Clean all surfaces to which the adhesive will be applied. During the application of the adhesive, the room temperature should range between 60- and 100-degrees Fahrenheit.

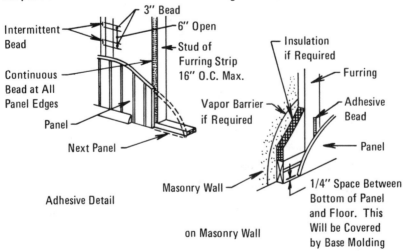

Fig. 11-9 Application of Adhesive

Fig. 11-10 Caulking Gun

1. Apply a 1/8-inch continuous bead of adhesive to the framing members where the panel edges will be placed, figure 11-9.

2. Apply a 1/8-inch intermittent bead (3-inch bead, 6 inches open) on the middle framing members.

3. Place the panel in position and secure it to the wall frame with two nails placed at the top of the panel.

4. Placing uniform pressure against the panel, press it against the beads of adhesive.

5. Place and secure the remaining panels in the same manner.

6. After a 20-minute interval, place a padded block of wood against each panel. Strike the padded block with a hammer at edges, joints, and intermediate supports.

7. Remove the excess adhesive with a clean cloth dampened with white gasoline.

   Note: There are numerous panel adhesives available. Most are packed in cartridges for application with a caulking gun, figure 11-10. Because of the number of available adhesives, it is advisable to follow the specific manufacturer's instructions.

HOW TO INSTALL SOLID WOOD PANELING

Note: The wall must be prepared to receive paneling before it is installed. If the paneling is installed vertically, furring or blocking must be used. Two rows of blocking should be provided if it is used, figure 11-11. If it is necessary to use furring strips, a strip is placed at the top and bottom of the wall with strips spaced between them, figure 11-12.

1. If the wall is not plumb, shim the furring strips sufficiently.

2. Starting at one corner, place the first panel in position. Check to be sure it is plumb.

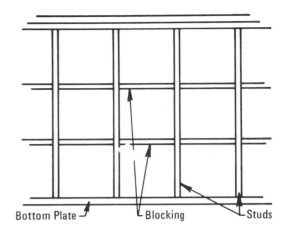

Bottom Plate — ⌐ ⌐Blocking ⌐Studs

Fig. 11-11 Blocking for Solid Wood Paneling

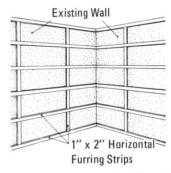

Existing Wall

1" x 2" Horizontal Furring Strips

Fig. 11-12 Furring Strips for Solid Wood Paneling

3. Secure the position of the panel by face nailing with 6d finishing nails. The rest of the nails are blind nailed, eliminating the need for countersinking and filling. Only the first and last panels are face nailed.

4. Place the second board in position and blind nail it.

5. Install the remainder of the panels in the same manner.

   Note: Avoid ending with a molded edge in a corner.

6. Interior corners are butted together to form a tight joint. Exterior corners may be either fitted with corner moldings or mitered to form a finished corner.

   Note: The joint between the paneling and the ceiling and the joint between the paneling and the floor are usually covered by molding.

REVIEW

A.   Choose the best answer or answers to complete each statement.

1.   A _____ saw is used to form curved cuts on hardboard paneling.

a. coping   c. crosscut

b. rip   d. keyhole

2.   Plywood paneling is usually composed of _____ layers.

.a. 3   c. 5

b. 4   d. 6

3.   Plywood paneling is usually _____ in size.

a. 5′ x 10′   c. 4′ x 8′

b. 4′ x 9′   d. 6′ x 12′

4.   Furring strips used in the installation of plywood paneling are usually _____ or _____ in size and are secured with 6d nails.

a. 2″ x 6″   c. 1″ x 2″

b. 2″ x 4″   d. 1″ x 4″

5.   Hardboard paneling is nailed with _____ finishing nails.

a. 6d   c. 5d

b. 3d   d. 2d

6.   Nails should be placed _____ inch from the edge of the panel.

a. 1/8   c. 1/2

b. 1/4   d. 3/4

7.   A _____ inch continuous bead of adhesive is applied on panel edges.

a. 1/8   c. 1/2

b. 1/4   d. 3/4

8.   Excess adhesive is removed from paneling with _____ .

a. water   c. a knife

b. white gasoline   d. sandpaper

9.   The first panel of solid wood paneling is _____ .

a. face nailed   c. toenailed

b. blind nailed   d. leg nailed

10. The second panel of solid wood paneling is _____ .

a. face nailed   c. toenailed

b. blind nailed   d. leg nailed

B.   Place the correct answer in the space provided.

1.   The joint between paneling and ceiling is usually covered by _____ .

2.   Solid wood paneling is secured with _____ .

3.   During the application of an adhesive the room temperature should range from _____ to _____ .

4.   The grading of solid wood paneling falls into two categories, _____ and _____ .

5.   Solid wood paneling is made from _____ and _____ .

6.   Plywood panels have V-grooves spaced _____ inches on center.

7.   Inside corners of hardboard paneling are usually _____ .

8.   Hardboard paneling is made from _____ .

9.   Outside corners can be mitered but in most cases _____ or _____ is used.

10. Plywood panels should be removed from their cartons _____ prior to installation.

C.   In the space provided sketch

1.   an inside corner.

2.   an outside corner.

3.   a stud that has been blind nailed.

Unit 12 Acoustical Ceilings

Acoustical ceilings combine great sound-absorption properties with decorative appeal. The units are available in a variety of colors and patterns, such as circles, swirls, and surfaces which are embossed or studded with metallic flakes, figure 12-1. The panels have uniform or random pattern openings which help develop the pattern and reduce noise level. The openings can be drilled or punched holes, slots, striations, or fissures.

Most acoustical ceiling tiles are manufactured from mineral fibers, cane fibers, or asbestos fibers. The fibers are bonded and matted together to form a single unit. The unit thickness ranges from 3/16 inch to 1 1/4 inches; sizes range from 12" x 12" to 4' x 4'. One of the more inexpensive types of ceilings is made from *bagasse*, a substance derived from sugarcane fiber. The fibers are molded into units with small spaces or voids existing between the fibers. The voids in the tile provide the noise absorption quality. A disadvantage of cane-fiber tiles is that the tile loses its strength and changes dimensions when subjected to an excessive amount of moisture.

Mineral-fiber ceiling tile is largely made from mineral wool, a product of blast-furnace slag. Binders are added for strength. The ceiling tiles are then produced in a variety of shapes and sizes with most of the units perforated or fissured to aid in noise reduction.

Cement-asbestos tiles are made largely from asbestos fibers, portland cement, and water. Outstanding features of cement-asbestos tiles are compression strength, fire resistance, and resistance to alkalies and acids.

INSTALLATION METHODS

The three common methods of installing acoustical ceilings are the *cementing, nailing,* and *suspension* systems. Almost half of the acoustical ceiling tile installed today is cemented to a solid surface. If 12" x 12" tile is used, half-dollar sized spots of adhesive are placed in each corner and the tile is pressed into place over a clean, solid surface.

If cement is not used, the tiles are usually secured with nails, screws or staples; staples are pre-

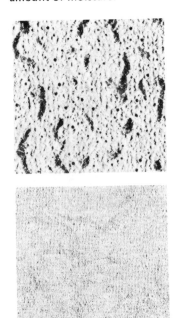
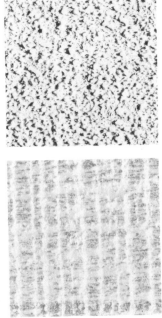
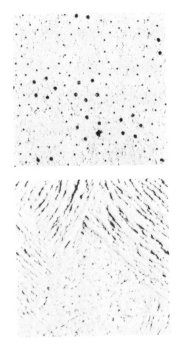

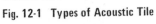

Fig. 12-1 Types of Acoustic Tile

ferred. If staples are used, one staple should be driven directly over the other, figure 12-2. The first staple is driven; and, without moving the staple gun, a second staple is driven in. The legs of the second staple are forced to flare out. The flared legs of the second staple secure the tile to the furring strips.

Suspension systems are useful in concealing flush lighting fixtures and heating or air-conditioning ducts. The ceiling panels fit into a metal framework grid which is supported by hanger wires, figure 12-3. The suspension system is popular in basements or other places where it is necessary to conceal plumbing lines and heating ducts.

Fig. 12-2 Stapling Procedure

To condition acoustical tile to the atmospheric conditions of a room, the cartons are opened and allowed to stand 24 hours prior to its installation.

HOW TO INSTALL ACOUSTICAL TILE WITH NAILS OR STAPLES

Note: Assume that the acoustical tile is 12″ x 12″ and that it is to be placed over furring strips.

1. Determine the correct location of the furring strips.

2. Locate the center of the room and snap a chalk line perpendicular to the ceiling joist.

3. Measure the distance from the chalk line to the wall. If the dimension does not measure an exact foot, the remaining inches are included in the trimmed border row tile. If the border row is 6 inches or larger, nail a furring strip, usually a 1 x 4, over the chalk line and space the remaining strips 12 inches on center, figure 12-4.

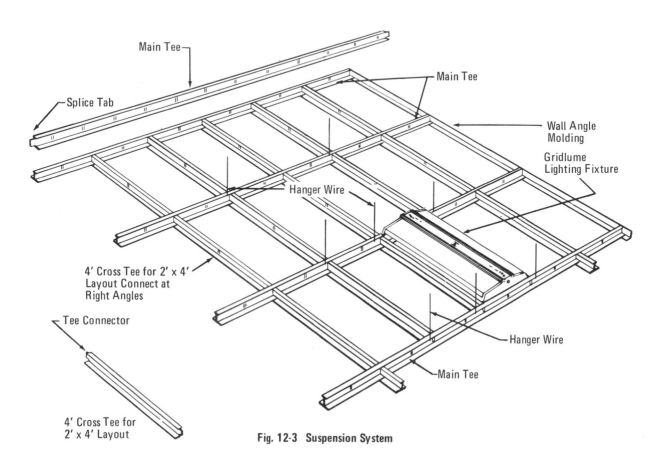

Fig. 12-3 Suspension System

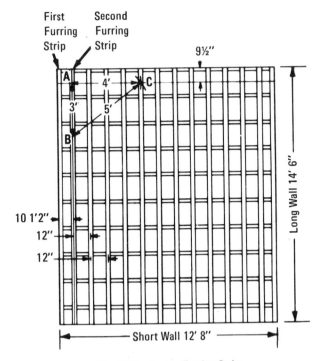

Fig. 12-4 Placing Furring Strips

Note: If the border tiles are smaller than 6 inches, the ceiling has an unfinished appearance and the ceiling tiles are difficult to trim. If the distance from the chalk line to the edge of the ceiling indicates that the border tiles are smaller than 6 inches, adjust their width by installing a furring strip 6 inches on either side of the chalk line, figure 12-5.

4. Secure the furring strips to the ceiling joist with 8d nails, figure 12-6.

   Note: If the furring strips are placed across an old ceiling, the nails should be long enough to penetrate the existing ceiling as well as 1 inch of the joist.

5. Place a straightedge across the furring strips to determine if they are even; if there are any low spots, shim them with small wedges placed between the strips and joist.

6. Trim the border tile to its correct width. The ceiling tile should be trimmed from the finished side with a sharp knife or fiberboard cutter. If a knife is used, a carpenter's square should be used as a guide, figure 12-7.

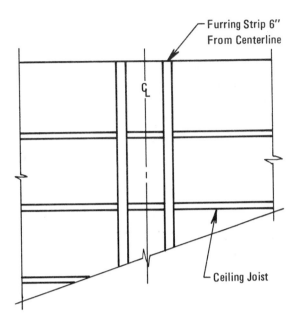

Fig. 12-5 Adjustment of Furring Strips

Fig. 12-6 Nailing Furring Strips

7. Snap a chalk line along the first furring strip.

   Note: The distance from the wall to the chalk line equals the width of the border tile.

8. Place the first ceiling tile in the corner with the beveled edge directly over the chalk line.

9. Secure border tiles by face nailing with 1 1/4-inch brads at the joint where the wall and ceiling meet, figure 12.8. The brads will be covered with a molding later. The flanges of the ceiling tile are secured with 9/16-inch staples or Number 17 flathead nails, figure 12-9.

Fig. 12-7   Trimming Ceiling Tile

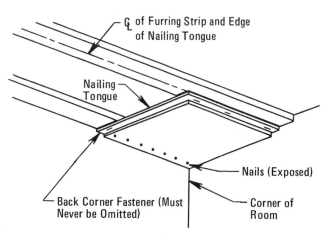

Fig. 12-8   Securing Ceiling Tile

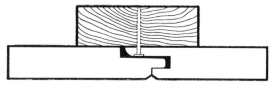

Fig. 12-9   Nailing Flanges

10. Continue to place and secure the border tile by sliding the tongue of one unit into the groove of the unit next to it.

    Note: Each row of tiles should be started with a trimmed border tile.

11. Place molding around the perimeter of the ceiling to cover the joint created by the ceiling tile and wall, figure 12-10.

    Note: The molding should be painted before it is installed to avoid brush marks on the ceiling tile.

HOW TO INSTALL A SUSPENDED CEILING SYSTEM

1. Determine the ceiling height. The ceiling should be located above the highest window or door casing and 3 inches below any overhead obstruction, such as air-conditioning ducts or water pipes. If concealed fluorescent lighting is used, the ceiling should be suspended 6 inches below the fluorescent tubes.

2. Snap a chalk line on the walls around the perimeter of the room. This line will indicate the ceiling height.

3. Secure wall molding to the walls, using the chalk line as a guide. Screws, nails, or masonry fasteners may be used to attach the molding to the wall, figure 12-11.

4. Attach main tee hanger wires to the existing ceiling joist or to the ceiling itself with nails, screw eyes, or screw hooks, figure 12-12. If the

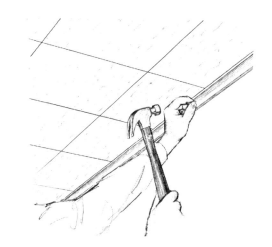

Fig. 12-10   Placing Molding

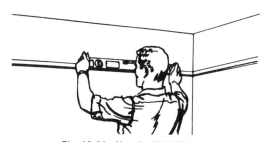

Fig. 12-11   Hanging Wall Molding

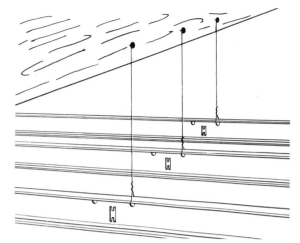

Fig. 12-12   Hanging Main Tees

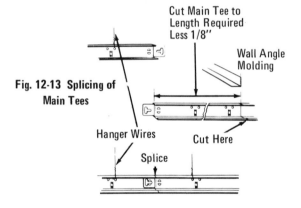

Fig. 12-13   Splicing of Main Tees

Cut Main Tee to Length Required Less 1/8''

Wall Angle Molding

Hanger Wires

Cut Here

Splice

Fig. 12-14   Cross Tees

Cut Cross Tee to Length Less 1/8''

Wall Angle Molding

Main Tee or Cross Tee

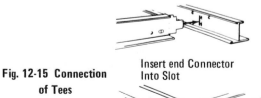

Fig. 12-15   Connection of Tees

Insert end Connector Into Slot

wire is attached to the joist, 8d nails or screw eyes are used. If the eyes or hooks are screwed through the actual ceiling, the screws should penetrate the bottom of the joist at least 1 inch.

Note: The hanger wire should be Number 14-gage or Number 12-gage wire.

5.   Stretch a series of strings from one wall molding to the opposite wall molding. The strings serve as a guide in the placing of the main tees.

6.   Cut the main tees the length of the room minus 1/8 inch.

7.   Place the end of the main tee on the wall molding and attach the hanger wire in the perforations of the main tee.

8.   Level the main tees using the stretched string as a guide.

Note: If the main tees need to be spliced, there is an engaging end and a splicing tab which join the two pieces. A hanger wire is then placed on each side of the tab, figure 12-13.

9.   Cut the cross tees to the required length minus 1/8 inch, figure 12-14.

10.   Place the cut end of the cross tee on the wall molding and insert the end connector into the slot of the main tee, figure 12-15.

11.   Continue to cut, place, and secure the cross tees to the main tees.

12.   Position the panels by placing one end of the panel on the flange of a tee and then lowering the panel to rest on the other flanges, figure 12-16.

Fig. 12-16   Placing Panels

REVIEW

A. Choose the best answer or answers to complete each statement.

1. Most mineral-fiber ceiling tile is made from _____ .

   a. asbestos fibers   c. mineral wool
   b. bagasse   d. cane fiber

2. One of the most inexpensive ceiling tiles is made from _____ .

   a. asbestos fibers   c. mineral wool
   b. bagasse   d. cane fiber

3. The preferred method of securing ceiling tile is with _____ .

   a. wire   c. staples
   b. adhesive   d. screws

4. Acoustical tile cartons should be opened _____ hours before installation of the tile.

   a. 12   c. 24
   b. 18   d. 36

5. The border tile should be no smaller than _____ inches wide.

   a. 6   c. 10
   b. 8   d. 12

6. If 12″ x 12″ ceiling tile is used, furring strips should be placed _____ inches on center.

   a. 12   c. 18
   b. 16   d. 22

7. Furring strips should be secured to the ceiling joist with _____ nails.

   a. 6d   c. 10d
   b. 8d   d. 12d

8. Ceiling tile should be face nailed with _____ .

   a. 1 1/4-inch brads   c. 6d nails
   b. staples   d. 16d nails

9. Hanger wire should be Number _____ or Number 12-gage wire.

   a. 2   c. 8
   b. 14   d. 24

10. A main tee equals the length of the room minus _____ inch.

    a. 1/8   c. 5/8
    b. 1/2   d. 3/4

B. Place the correct answer in the space provided.

1. To help reduce the noise level in a room, acoustical tile has _____ .

2. Most acoustical ceiling tiles are made from _____ , _____ , or _____ .

3. The **three** most common methods of installing acoustical ceilings are _____ _____ , and _____ .

4. The spots of adhesive that are placed on ceiling tile are about the size of _____ .

5. Furring strips used on acoustical ceilings are usually _____ , or _____ in size.

6. Furring strips are leveled by _____ .

7. Ceiling tile is trimmed with a _____ or _____ .

8. The first ceiling tile is placed in the _____ .

9. Main tees are hung with _____ .

10. Wall molding for suspended ceilings is fastened to the wall with _____ , _____ , or _____ .

C. In the space provided sketch

1. a main tee.

2. a tongue-and-groove tile.

3. a cross tee.

Unit 13 Base, Ceiling, and Wall Molding

Moldings are thin strips of wood or metal which are shaped and used for finishing and decorative purposes. Moldings are essential in the development of a particular architectural style since they define the style of a room. They may also cover unsightly joints and reduce maintenance.

Moldings are available in lengths ranging from 3 to 16 feet. When buying molding, the length should be rounded off to the next highest foot. Add the width of the molding to the length for each miter that is to be cut when measuring molding. If the molding is 2 1/2 inches wide and has two miters, add 5 inches to the total length and round off the length to the next highest foot.

Prefinished wood moldings are used primarily to complement prefinished paneling. Prefinished wood molding should be purchased with the paneling. The factory-applied finish eliminates the need for finishing on the job and provides a tough surface which resists abrasions. To fill nail holes and deep scratches, a color-coordinated putty stick may be used.

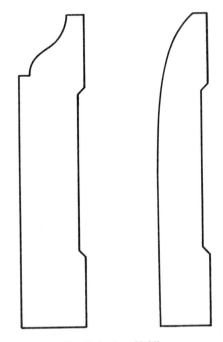

Fig. 13-1 Base Molding

BASE MOLDINGS

Base molding, figure 13-1, is used at the intersection of a vertical wall and finished floor. The molding protects the wall covering from damage and provides a finished look to the room. The typical 8-foot ceiling should have a 3- to 4-inch base. As the ceiling height increases, the base should also increase. In addition to the base, a base shoe is sometimes added to conform to uneven floor lines.

CEILING MOLDINGS

Ceiling molding is used at the intersection of a vertical wall and the ceiling. The most common type of ceiling moldings are *common crown*, figure 13-2, and *cove,* figure 13-3. Moldings can be mixed and matched to produce a variety of effects. The most common type of joint used for an outside corner is a 45-degree miter. The inside corners are usually *coped*, which means that a portion of one piece is removed to receive another.

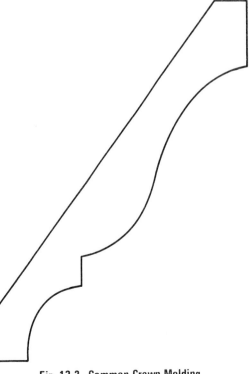

Fig. 13-2 Common Crown Molding

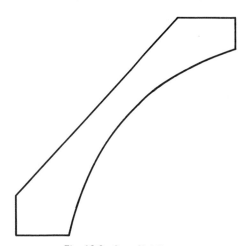

Fig. 13-3 Cove Molding

WALL MOLDINGS

Wall molding, figure 13-4, usually emphasizes the decorative theme of a room. The molding can be used by itself or in combination with other molding.

CHAIR RAILS

Chair rails, figure 13-5, are used to protect the walls from the damaging effects sometimes caused by furniture.   The moldings are usually placed one-third the distance from the floor to the ceiling and may be one piece of molding, or several pieces of

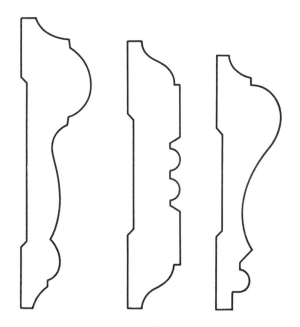

Fig. 13-5 Chair Rails

Fig. 13-4 Wall Molding

moldings which are combined to give a heavy, massive appearance.

TOOLS

The basic tools needed for the installation of wood molding are a miter box and saw, figure 13-6, coping saw, figure 13-7, a 12-foot tape, hammer, glue, and nails. The *miter box* is usually a wooden box or metal frame which guides a handsaw to achieve the proper angle. The most common cuts are 90 degrees and 45 degrees. The *coping saw* has a narrow blade set in a steel bow frame and is used for cutting curves and hollowing out moldings.

Fig. 13-6 Miter Box

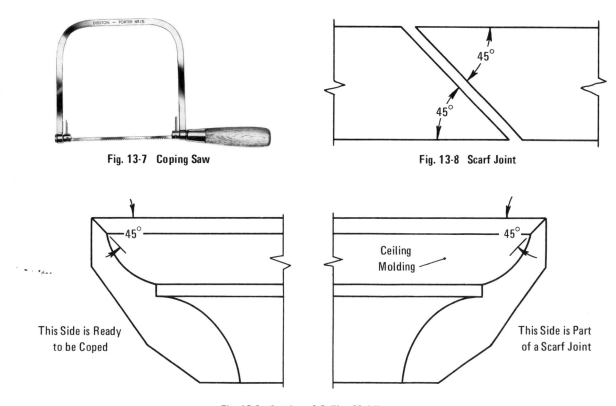

Fig. 13-7 Coping Saw

Fig. 13-8 Scarf Joint

Fig. 13-9 Cutting of Ceiling Molding

HOW TO INSTALL CEILING MOLDING

1. Assuming that the molding does not reach the entire length of the room, square one end of the molding and cut a 45-degree angle at the other end.

2. Cut the next piece of molding with one mitered end and one square end.

   Note: When cutting the miter, hold the molding in the same position it will have in the finished installation.

3. Butt the square end into the corner and nail the molding in place with 6d finishing nails. The two mitered joints should fit together forming a *scarf joint*, figure 13-8.

   Note: At this point, the molding has been placed against one wall with a butt joint in each corner.

4. Cut a piece of molding with two 45-degree angles opposite from one another, figure 13-9.

5. Trim one angle with a coping saw, cutting back from the miter. The profile of the 45-degree cut serves as a guide for the coping saw.

   Note: Some carpenters prefer to outline the profile with a pencil and then cut along the penciled line.

6. The cut profile is then positioned against the molding and nailed into place.

7. The remainder of the ceiling molding is placed in the same manner for all interior corners; one piece of molding is squared on one end and butted against an adjacent wall and the adjoining piece of molding is cut on a 45-degree angle and coped to fit.

8. If an exterior corner receives ceiling molding, the two ends of the molding are mitered at a 45-degree angle and joined together.

   Note: Interior corners may be fitted with two 45-degree miter joints; however, this is not the best means of finishing an interior corner.

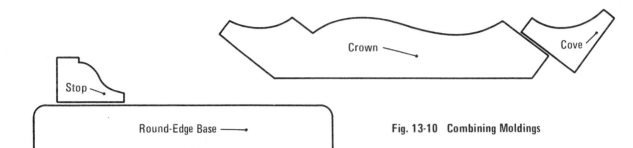

Fig. 13-10 Combining Moldings

HOW TO MAKE AND INSTALL WALL MOLDING

Note: Wall molding can be made from a variety of moldings or molding combinations, figure 13-10.

Fig. 13-11 Cutting Molding on a 45-Degree Angle

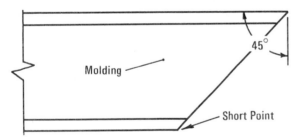

Fig. 13-12 Miter Cut Measured From the Short Point

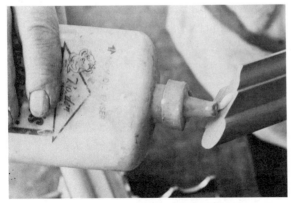

Fig. 13-13 Adding Glue to the Miter

1. Using a miter box, saw off at a 45-degree angle, one end of the molding, figure 13-11.

2. Determine the desired length of the molding and mark it accordingly.

    Note: Most measurements are taken from the short point, figure 13-12.

3. Place the molding in the miter box and cut it to its proper length.

4. Measure a second piece of molding from the cut piece so that the two pieces are the same length.

5. Determine the width of the wall molding, mark it and cut it to its proper length. Using the cut piece, measure a second piece and cut it to its proper length.

6. Take a side piece and a top or bottom piece and place a small amount of glue on one end of each piece, figure 13-13.

7. Place the two pieces in a corner clamp, figure 13-14. The two pieces should be clamped tightly. The excess glue must be wiped off.

8. Drive two brads in each side, locking the two pieces together, figure 13-15.

9. Set the brad heads 1/16 inch below the surface of the wood.

10. Follow the same procedure with the other three corners.

11. Fill the nail holes. There are several products available that can be used to fill the holes. Mixing fine sawdust and glue is one popular method.

12. Dry sand the frame lightly with fine sandpaper.

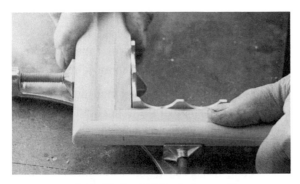

Fig. 13-14 Placing Molding in Corner Clamp

Fig. 13-15 Nailing Molding From Both Ends

13. If a series of wall moldings are to be placed on the same wall, snap a chalk line the length of the wall. The lines, located at the bottom of the wall moldings, serve as a guide for the placement of the moldings.

14. Secure the moldings to the wall with 6d finishing nails, using the chalk line as a guide.

15. Fill the nail holes.

   Note: It is usually advantageous to finish the wall molding before placing it on the wall, especially if the molding is a different color than the wall.

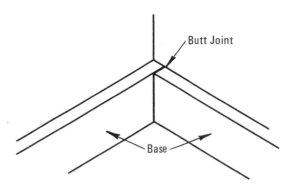

Fig. 13-16 Butt Joint of Plain Baseboards

HOW TO INSTALL A CHAIR RAIL

Note: Assume that the ceiling height is 8 feet.

1. Measure 2 feet 8 inches from the floor and snap a chalk line parallel to the floor.

2. Select the chair rail. Square one end of the rail and cut a 45-degree miter on the other end.

3. Place the molding along the chalk line and secure it to the wall with 6d finishing nails.

4. To finish the corner, cut two 45-degree miters opposite from one another and cope one end.

5. Fit the coped end against the chair rail and nail it in place.

6. Proceed placing the chair rail using a coped joint where the interior corners meet, two 45-degree miters for exterior corners, and a scarf joint where the two pieces along the wall meet.

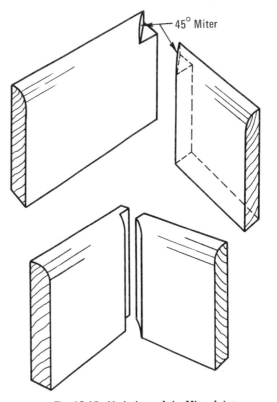

Fig. 13-17 Variations of the Miter Joint

7. Set the nails 1/16 inch below the surface of the molding.

8. Fill the nail holes and sand lightly.

HOW TO INSTALL BASEBOARD

1. Select clear baseboard free from imperfections. If it is molded baseboard, inspect the molded edges for imperfections such as chipped edges or poorly machined surfaces.

2. Measure the distance along one wall with an extension rule or tape measure.

3. Transfer this length to a length of baseboard. Mark these points on the top edge of the baseboard and square from these points.

   Note: Some carpenters add 1/8 inch to the overall length of the baseboard to assure a tight fit.

4. Place the baseboard in position and nail it in place with 8d finishing nails.

5. Measure and cut another baseboard adjacent to the baseboard that has been placed. One end of the baseboard should be coped; therefore, allow enough stock to form the joint.

   Note: If the baseboard is not long enough to reach the length of the wall, a scarf joint is used to join the two pieces together.

6. Continue placing the baseboard around the room, using coped joints for interior corners and 45-degree miters for exterior corners.

   Note: There are other acceptable joints which may be used for interior corners in addition to coped joints. The butt joint, figure 13-16, is a common joint and is used primarily on plain baseboards. A miter joint and variations of the joint, figure 13-17, are also common means of joining bases at interior corners.

7. If a base shoe is used, lay it in the same manner as the base is laid. A *base shoe* is a quarter round mold located between baseboard and flooring.

REVIEW

A. Choose the best answer or answers to complete each statement.

1. The most common type of joint used for an outside corner is a _____.

   a. miter   c. scarf
   b. dado   d. coped

2. Most cuts made in a miter box are cuts of 90 degrees and _____ degrees.

   a. 60   c. 45
   b. 30   d. 50

3. Ceiling molding is secured with _____ nails.

   a. 6d   c. 4d
   b. 16d   d. 3d

4. Nailheads should be set _____ inch below the surface of the molding.

   a. 1/8   c. 1/4
   b. 1/16   d. 3/8

5. To assure a tight fit for base molding, some carpenters add _____ inch to the total length of the molding.

   a. 1/4   c. 1/32
   b. 1/2   d. 1/8

B.   Place the correct answer in the space provided.

1.   Moldings are available in lengths from _____ to _____ .

2.   Deep scratches on prefinished wood molding may be filled with _____ .

3.   The most common types of ceiling moldings are _____ and
_____ .

4.   The joint used for interior corners is the _____ .

5.   An 8-foot ceiling should have a base _____ inches wide.

6.   If a room has a ceiling height of 9 feet, a chair rail should be placed _____ feet
from the floor.

7.   The _____ is a metal frame which guides a handsaw.

8.   The first step in installing ceiling molding is to _____ .

9.   The various pieces of wall moldings are held together with brads and
_____ .

10. Wall molding is nailed to the wall with _____ nails.

C.   In the space provided sketch

1.   crown molding.

2.   cove molding.

3.   base molding.

4.   a chair rail.

Unit 14 Wood Flooring

Wood flooring is a highly desirable product for many reasons. Wood offers durability, beauty, ease of maintenance, high resistance to wear, and low heat conductivity. It is widely used since its grain structure, texture, and color can be made to blend with the surrounding environment.

WOODS USED IN FLOORING

Wood flooring is manufactured from two broad classifications of trees, hardwoods and softwoods. The groups are distinguished by the broad leaves of hardwood trees and the needles of softwood trees. The names hardwood and softwood in no way indicate a degree of hardness, but rather a general classification. Of the hardwoods, oak and maple are the most popular, but beech, birch, and pecan are used extensively. The two most popular softwoods used in wood flooring are southern pine and Douglas fir. Other softwoods used for wood flooring are western hemlock, ponderosa pine, redwood, and cypress.

GRADING WOOD FLOORING

The grading of wood flooring is primarily based on the appearance of the stock, with no regard to color. While the lower grades permit some knots and wormholes, higher grades are free of such defects. Oak flooring is subject to grading rules set forth by the National Oak Flooring Manufacturers' Association, figure 14-1, and Maple, Beech and Birch are under the auspices of the Maple Flooring Manufacturers' Association, figure 14-2.

TYPES OF WOOD FLOORING

At one time, the only wood flooring available was the random width plank type. However, with advancements in technology and seasoning techniques, hardwood strip, plank flooring, and block flooring have become popular.

Hardwood Strip Flooring

Strip flooring is available in lengths from 1 to 16 feet and has a face width of 2 1/4 inches. One type of strip flooring is tongued and grooved, in which one edge of the flooring strip has a tongue and the other edge has a groove, figure 14-3. The ends are also matched with a tongue and groove to assure a tight fit. The top face of strip flooring is narrower than the bottom face, thus allowing the face edges to

TABLE 1.—*Grade, description, and dimensions* [1] *of oak flooring* [2]

Kind of flooring	Grade		Standard length
	Name	Description	
			Feet
Quartersawed	Clear	The face shall be practically clear, admitting an average of ⅜ inch of bright sap. The question of color shall not be considered.	2 and up; av., 4¼.
Do	Select	The face may contain burls, small streaks, pinworm holes, slight imperfections in working, and small tight knots that do not average more than 1 to every 3 feet.	2 and up; av., 3¾.
Plainsawed	Clear	The face shall be practically clear, admitting an average of ⅜ inch of bright sap. The question of color shall not be considered.	2 and up; av., 4¼.
Do	Select	The face may contain burls, small streaks, pinworm holes, slight imperfections in working, and small tight knots that do not average more than 1 to every 3 feet.	2 and up; av., 3¾.
Do	No. 1 Common.	Shall be of such nature as will lay a good residential floor and may contain varying wood characteristics, such as flags, heavy streaks and checks, wormholes, knots, and minor imperfections in working.	2 and up; av., 3.

[1] All grades are made in the following combinations of thickness and width: 25/32-inch thickness, 3¼-, 2¼-, 2-, and 1½-inch widths; ½- and ⅜-inch thicknesses, 2- and 1½-inch widths.

[2] Data are from rules of the National Oak Flooring Association in effect June 17, 1957. All flooring listed is kiln-dried, grade-marked, trade-marked, hollow backed, and side and end matched. For lower grades than those listed above and for square-edge strip flooring, see the latest issue of the grading rules of the National Oak Flooring Manufacturers' Association, 814 Sterick Bldg., Memphis, Tenn.

Fig. 14-1 Grades, Descriptions, and Dimensions of Oak Flooring

TABLE 2.—*Grades, description, and dimensions* [1] *of northern hard maple, beech, and birch flooring* [2]

Kind of wood	Grade		Standard length
	Name	Description	
Beech, birch, and maple.	First grade_____	Shall have the face practically free from all defects, but the varying natural color of the wood shall not be considered a defect.	*Feet* 2 and up. Not over 30 percent under 4 feet.
Do_____	Second grade_____	Will admit tight sound knots and slight imperfections in dressing, but must lay without waste.	2 and up. Not over 45 percent under 4 feet.
Maple_____	Selected first grade, light northern hard maple.[3]	Special stock selected for uniformity of color. It is almost ivory white and is the finest grade.	2 and up. Not over 30 percent under 4 feet.
Do_____	Selected first grade, amber northern hard maple.[3]	Special stock selected for uniform brown color. It has more grain pattern than other types.	Do.
Beech and birch__	Selected first grade, red.[3]	Made from all-red-faced stock especially selected for color.	Do.

[1] All grades are made in the following combinations of thickness and width: $^{25}/_{32}$-inch thickness, $3\frac{1}{4}$-, $2\frac{1}{4}$-, 2-, and $1\frac{1}{2}$-inch widths; $\frac{5}{8}$-, $\frac{1}{2}$-, and $\frac{3}{8}$-inch thicknesses, $2\frac{1}{4}$-, 2-, and $1\frac{1}{2}$-inch widths.
[2] Data are from grading rules of the Maple Flooring Manufacturers' Association in effect December 4, 1956. All flooring listed is kiln-dried, grade-marked, trade-marked, and side and end matched. The hollow back is optional. For lower grades than those listed above and for jointed (square-edge) flooring, see the latest issue of the grading rules of the Maple Flooring Manufacturers' Association, 35 East Wacker Drive, Chicago, Ill.
[3] Special grade.

Fig. 14-2 Grades, Descriptions, and Dimensions of Northern Hard Maple, Beech, and Birch Flooring

make contact with each other while the bottom edges are slightly separated. Another type of strip flooring has square edges and ends, figure 14-4, and is usually face nailed rather than blind nailed.

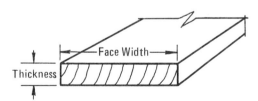

Fig. 14-3 Strip Flooring With Tongue-and-Groove Construction

Fig. 14-4 Square Edge Strip Flooring

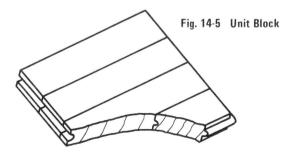

Fig. 14-5 Unit Block

Strip flooring is available in both hardwood and softwood. The most popular hardwoods used are oak and maple; Douglas fir and southern pine are the most common softwoods.

Plank Flooring

Plank flooring is similar to strip flooring except that the strips are wider. The planks are usually more than 3 1/4 inches in width and are sometimes cross-laminated for greater strength. Most plank floors are made of red or white oak and are end- or side-matched. Plank flooring is used to reproduce floors which were popular during colonial times. To achieve this effect, wooden plugs of a contrasting color are set into the edges of the flooring.

Block Flooring

Block flooring is manufactured in two basic types: unit block, figure 14-5; and laminated or plywood block, figure 14-6. Block flooring is made of pieces of strip flooring bonded together edgewise to form a square unit. Most of the units are tongue and grooved and laid in mastic on a concrete slab. They may, however, be nailed to a subfloor. In most cases, the blocks are laid with the grain running parallel to each adjacent block. Numerous patterns can be achieved by changing the grain patterns.

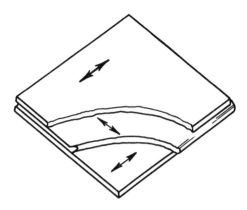

Fig. 14-6 Laminated Block

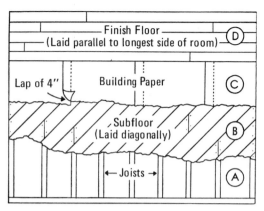

Fig. 14-7 Cutaway View of Floor, Showing Details of Construction: (a) Joists, (b) Subfloor, (c) Building Paper, (d) Finish Floor

The laminated blocks are available in various sizes, but most of the units are manufactured in 9-inch squares. The laminated block has three or more plys bonded by phenol resin, resorcinol resin, melamine resin, or any water-resistant adhesive. This type of floor is good to use on a structure that may be exposed to an excessive amount of moisture, since blocks which are warped may be replaced much easier than planks.

FINISHING

The process of finishing a wood floor usually involves sanding and application of a filler, stain, and finish.

The flooring is usually sanded with a machine in progressive stages. Number 2 sandpaper is used first to eliminate any surface irregularities, and a finer sandpaper, Number 00, is used to remove scratches and imperfections.

Wood fillers are used to fill the pores of open-grained woods. The filler helps prevent the entrance or exit of moisture and level the surface of the wood flooring. There are three basic types of wood fillers: a transparent filler, such as linseed oil, which is used on woods having small cell openings that are invisible to the naked eye; a liquid filler, consisting of varnish and silica, which is used to fill nonporous or diffuse porous woods having small pore openings; and paste wood filler, made from a ground-rock base and used to fill wood with large cell openings, such as red oak and white oak.

Stain is applied to change the tone of wood flooring and, in some cases, to give the flooring an aged effect. The most common types of stains used for wood flooring are oil stains, spirit stains, or non-grain raising stains. These stains penetrate only the top surface of the wood. For that reason, care should be taken to protect the finish.

There are many types of finishes for floors, all used primarily to protect and enhance the beauty of wood. Traditional types of finishes include varnish, lacquer, and shellac. In the past few years, however, synthetic resin finishes have gained popularity. All of these finishes should be applied according to manufacturers' specifications.

HOW TO INSTALL STRIP FLOORING OVER A SUBFLOOR

Note: Wood flooring should arrive at the job site five days prior to its installation. The flooring should first be placed loosely through the building, allowing the moisture content of the flooring to equalize with that of the building.

1. Cover the subfloor with 15-pound, asphalt-saturated felt. Use 4-inch side and end laps, figure 14-7. Red resin paper is sometimes used.

2. Snap a chalk line over the center of each floor joist. The chalk lines will aid in nailing the flooring to the floor joist correctly. This procedure is especially necessary if plywood is used as subflooring.

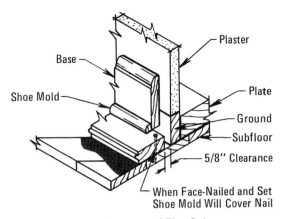

Fig. 14-8 Placement of First Strip

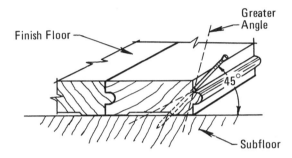

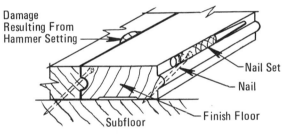

Fig. 14-9 Nailing and Setting Tecnique

3. Snap a chalk line parallel to a sidewall for the first course. The distance of the chalk line from the wall will vary, depending on the width of the flooring.

4. Place the first strip along the chalk line with the tongue out. Leave a 1/2- to 5/8-inch space between the wall and flooring for expansion, figure 14-8.

Note: Strip flooring should be laid perpendicular to the floor joist.

5. Face nail the first strip to the floor joist. The nails should be close enough to the wall to be covered by the base shoe.

Note: Different sizes of nails are used for different thicknesses of flooring. Size 8d nails are recommended for 25/32-inch flooring and 6d flooring nails are recommended for 3/8-inch flooring.

6. Install the second course, staggering the joints in end-matched flooring.

7. Drive the second course tight against the first and blind nail it.

Note: The nails should be driven at an approximate angle of 45 degrees. Do not drive the nail all the way in. If the nailhead is driven too far down, the flooring may be damaged. Use a nail set to finish driving the nail, figure 14-9.

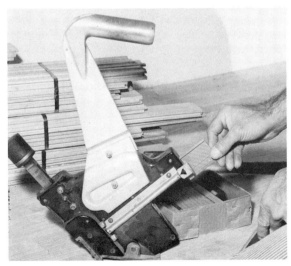

Fig. 14-10 Portable Nailing Machine

Fig. 14-11 Applying Mastic

Fig. 14-12 Installing Bottom Sleepers

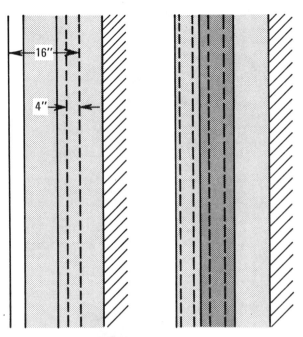

Portable nailers rather than hammers are sometimes used, figure 14-10.

8. Proceed laying the courses, discarding any uneven pieces.

HOW TO INSTALL STRIP FLOORS OVER CONCRETE SLABS

1. Be sure the concrete slab is free of dirt and litter.

2. Snap chalk lines 16 inches apart.

3. Cover the chalk lines with a 2-inch strip of mastic, figure 14-11.

4. Place 1" x 2" sleepers over the mastic and nail them in place with 1 1/2-inch concrete nails, figure 14-12. A *sleeper* is a strip of wood to which the finished floor is nailed.

5. Place a strip of .004 polyethylene film against the wall and extending 4 inches beyond the first sleeper, figure 14-13A. Lay the second strip so that it overlaps the first sleeper by 8 inches and extends 4 inches beyond the second sleeper, figure 14-13B. Repeat the process until all sleepers are covered.

6. Place another sleeper over the polyethylene film, figure 14-14.

7. Secure the top sleeper to the bottom sleeper with 4d nails spaced 16 to 24 inches apart.

Fig. 14-13 Installing Polyethylene Film

Fig. 14-14 Securing Top Sleeper

Fig. 14-15 Installing Strip Flooring

8. To lay the strip flooring over the sleepers, follow the same procedure used in installing strip flooring over floor joists, figure 14-15.

HOW TO INSTALL WOOD BLOCK FLOORING

1. Locate the center of the room and snap two chalk lines. The lines should be parallel to the walls and form right angles to each other.

2. Clean the area and apply mastic to one-quarter of the space. Apply the mastic up the chalk line but do not cover the line.

   Note: Spread the mastic with a notched trowel. Care should be taken in the selection of a trowel since the notches determine how much mastic is applied to the subfloor.

3. Begin laying the blocks in the center of the room using the chalk line as a guide.

Fig. 14-16 Applying Mastic and Block Flooring

Note: Individual blocks can be placed to establish certain patterns.

4. Continue laying the blocks to the sidewalls. Leave a 1-inch space between the blocks and the wall.

   Note: The mechanic should leave a space between each block to allow for expansion. Rubber strips are sometimes inserted to eliminate the small cracks between each joint.

5. Apply mastic to another portion of the room and lay the wood blocks as previously described, figure 14-16.

REVIEW

A. Choose the best answer or answers to complete each statement.

    1. Strip flooring is available in lengths ranging from _____ .

        a. 4 to 12 feet   c. 2 to 8 feet

        b. 1 to 16 feet   d. 3 to 9 feet

    2. Strip flooring is made from _____ .

        a. hardwood   c. sawdust

        b. sapwood   d. hardboard

3. The wood most often used for plank floors is _____.

    a. pine   a. walnut

    b. oak   b. cypress

4. The distinguishing characteristic of a hardwood tree is its _____ .

    a. needles   c. broad leaves

    b. bark   d. density of wood

5. One of the most popular softwoods used for wood flooring is _____.

    a. Douglas fir   c. beech

    b. cypress   d. birch

6. Wood filler is used to _____.

    a. clean floors   c. fill the pores of wood

    b. fill cracks between strip   d. fill scratches
       flooring

7. The subfloor should be covered with _____ .

    a. rigid insulation   c. glue

    b. asphalt-saturated felt   d. mastic

8. The size nail recommended for 1/2-inch flooring is _____ .

    a. 4d   c. 5d

    b. 8d   d. 12d

9. Sleepers are attached to the concrete slab with _____.

    a. mastic and concrete nails   c. mastic

    b. concrete nails   d. staples

10. Wood block flooring should be laid _____ .

    a. from the center of the room   c. parallel to the joist

    b. from the side of the room   d. perpendicular to the joist

B. Place the correct answer in the space provided.

1. Two types of strip flooring are _____ and _____ .

2. The most popular hardwoods used for flooring are _____ and

    _____ .

3. Block flooring is manufactured in two basic types, _____ and

    _____ .

4. Wood flooring should arrive at the job site five days prior to installation so
    that the _____ can equalize with that of the building.

5. The chalk lines used in the installation of strip flooring are used to

    _____ .

6. Strip flooring should be laid _____ to the floor joist.

7. The top sleeper is secured to the bottom sleeper with _____ .

8. The starting point for laying wood block flooring is _____.

C. Find the center of the room in the illustration below. Draw lines parallel to the sidewalls, shade one-quarter of the area which will represent application of mastic, and sketch in seven blocks of wood block flooring.

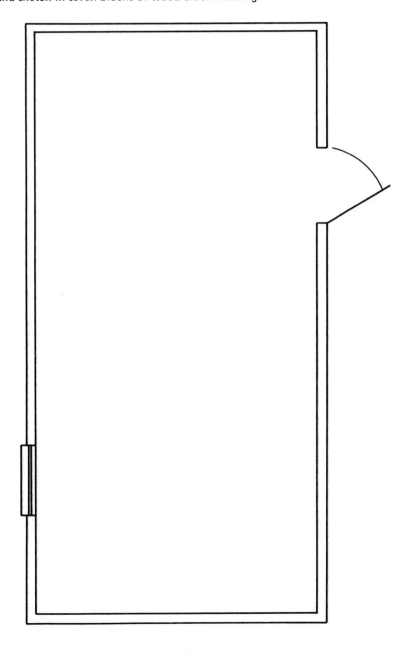

Unit 15 Joints in Cabinet Construction

The joints used in the construction of cabinets are of vital importance. There are over 100 types of joints, but they may be subdivided into twelve basic categories.

A *joint* is formed when two pieces of wood are fastened together. Most joints are fastened with glue. nails, or screws. In special cases, the joints are held in place with splines, dowels, or corrugated fasteners. If the joints are exposed, nails, screws, or corrugated fasteners are seldom used. Metal fasteners are used primarily in hidden areas, such as drawer guides, drawer bottoms, and at the backs of cabinets.

The strength of a particular joint depends on many factors, such as the type of wood used, moisture content of the wood, and the effectiveness of the fasteners. The craftsman's skill in constructing the joint is also important. Remember that a joint is as strong as its weakest part.

TYPES OF JOINTS

Butt Joints

In the construction of a *butt* joint, a squared end of a board is fitted against the end or edge of another board, figure 15-1. If two edge grains are being fitted together, an adhesive is usually an adequate fastener. However, if an edge grain and an end grain or two end grains are being fitted together, another type of fastener should be used in conjunction with the adhesive. Butt joints are often strengthened by dowels or glue blocks.

Rabbet Joints

The *rabbet* joint, figure 15-2, consists of a grooved board recessed into the end of another board. The end grain of one member of the joint is hidden, and two surfaces of the joint are covered with ad-

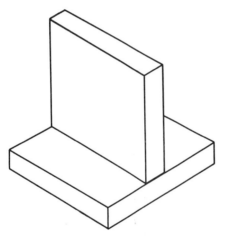

Fig. 15-1 Butt Joint

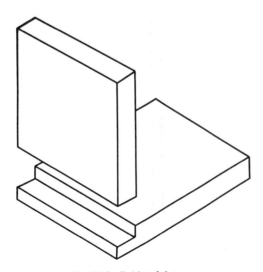

Fig. 15-2 Rabbet Joint

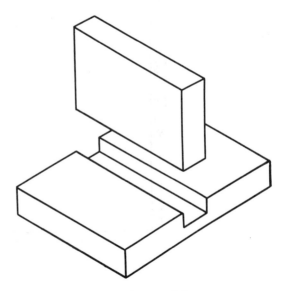

Fig. 15-3 Dado Joint

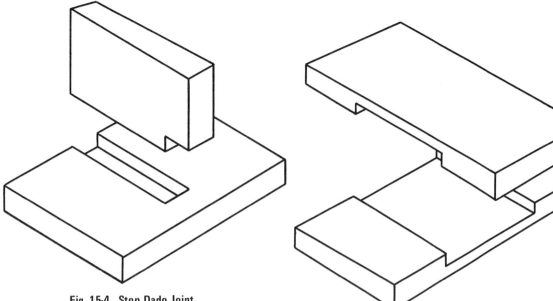

Fig. 15-4   Stop Dado Joint

hesive.   To further strengthen the joint, nails or screws are usually used.   The nails and screws reduce the tendency of the joint to twist besides adding an extra element of strength.   The rabbet joint is used extensively in drawer construction.

Dado Joints

In a *simple dado* joint, figure 15-3, the end of one board is recessed into the surface of another board a certain distance from the end.   A *stop dado*, or *gain*, joint is used where a simple dado joint would show on the front of a case.   In the construction of stop dado, the groove ends about 1 inch from the edge of the board and the board fitting into the groove has a notch cut out of the end so that the two members fit tightly.   Dado joints are used in the construction of bookracks and stepladders.

Lap Joints

A *lap* joint is formed when two boards lap, figure 15-5.   Half the thickness of each board is removed so that when the two boards are placed together, a thickness equal to one board is achieved.   The joints cut are actually two dado joints; placing them together forms the cross lap joint.   The *end lap* joint, figure 15-6, is constructed by forming a dado joint on one member and a rabbet joint on the other with the

Fig. 15-5   Lap Joint

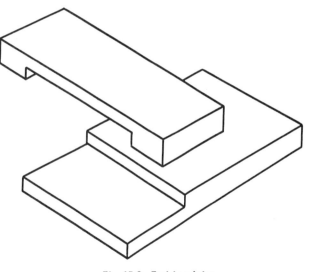

Fig. 15-6   End Lap Joint

two members joining, usually at a right angle.   The lap joint is a relatively simple joint and is used extensively in the construction of frames.   A combination of glue, nails, and screws are usually used to reinforce this joint.

Miter Joints

A *miter* joint, figure 15-7, is formed by the intersection of two boards cut at an angle of less than 90 degrees. To compensate for its structural weakness,

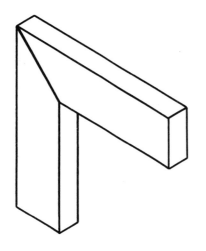

Fig. 15-7   Miter Joint

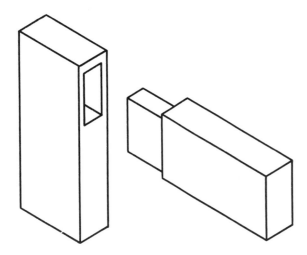

Fig. 15-8   Mortise and Tenon Joint

this joint is usually reinforced with nails, dowels, splines, or corrugated fasteners. Miter joints are found on most door casings, window casings, ceiling molding, and picture frames.

Mortise and Tenon Joints

The *mortise and tenon* joint, figure 15-8, is one of the most popular joints used in cabinet construction. This joint has several variations, including the *blind*, *pinned*, *open*, and *keyed* joints, figure 15-9.

The *tenon* is the protruding part of a structural member; the *mortise* is recessed into another member to form the socket. The tenon fits into the mortise, adding structural strength to the joint without giving the appearance of a reinforced joint.

Dowel Joints

A *dowel* joint, figure 15-10, is used to increase the strength of a butted joint and is often used in place of the mortise and tenon joint. A dowel is usually a round piece of birch or maple wood with a diameter ranging from 1/4 inch to 1 1/2 inches. Some dowels have spiral rings cut around them which allow glue and air to escape when the dowels are placed in the drilled holes. In cabinet construction, dowels are sometimes used to fasten rails to stiles and to reinforce boards which are glued edge to edge.

HOW TO MAKE A BUTT JOINT

Note: There are various types of butt joints; for illustrative purposes, an edge-to-edge joint is described here.

1. Run the edges of the stock through a jointer. A *jointer* is a machine used to square edges of boards and to plane surfaces on wood.

    Note: To minimize shrinkage and the opening of the joint at the end, a slight arch should exist in the center of the board, figure 15-11. When the two boards are clamped, the opening disappears and compression at the end of the joint keeps the end of the joint from opening up. To achieve the arch, apply more pressure in the center of the stock when running it through the jointer.

2. Place the boards in bar clamps alternating the direction of the annual rings, figure 15-12. In alternating the annual rings, the possibility of *cupping*, or *warping*, is reduced. A *bar clamp* is a long clamp that is used for holding large sections of wood which are glued together.

3. Place a thin line of glue on the two edges of the stock. Spread the glue evenly along the edge of the board.

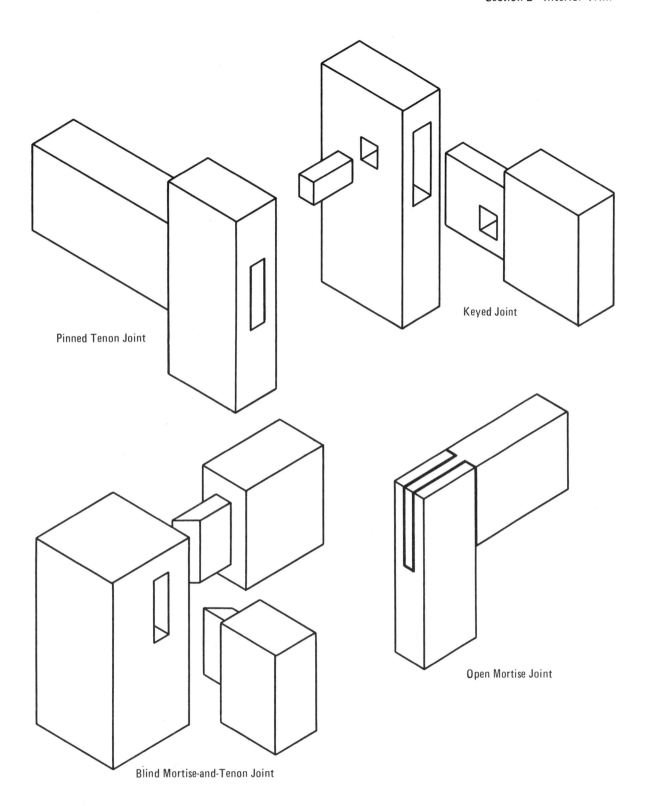

Pinned Tenon Joint

Keyed Joint

Blind Mortise-and-Tenon Joint

Open Mortise Joint

Fig. 15-9 Variations of the Mortise and Tenon Joint

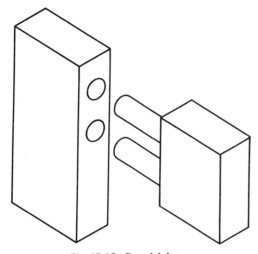

Fig. 15-10 Dowel Joint

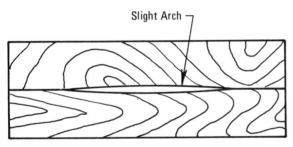

Fig. 15-11 Spring Joint

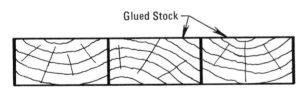

Fig. 15-12 Alternating Annual Ring Direction

4. Apply pressure with the bar clamps. When a moderate amount of pressure is achieved, tap the glued boards with a small block of wood. Tapping with the block prevents the boards from buckling up.

   Note: The bar clamps should be spaced 12 inches on center and should be no further than 2 inches from the end of the stock.

5. Wipe off any excess glue with a damp cloth. If the glue is allowed to harden, it must be removed with a scraper.

   Note: A properly glued joint has no space between the two joined surfaces.

HOW TO MAKE A RABBET JOINT

1. Square the ends of the stock that are to be joined.

2. Lay out the width of the rabbet joint. This is usually accomplished by placing the edge of one piece of stock over the edge of another piece of stock and marking it.

3. Lay out the depth of the rabbet joint. The depth is usually equal to half the thickness of the stock.

4. Remove the marked portion of the stock with a circular saw, radial arm saw, portable electric saw, or router.

   • If the rabbet joint is made with the circular saw, two cuts are required, figure 15-13. On

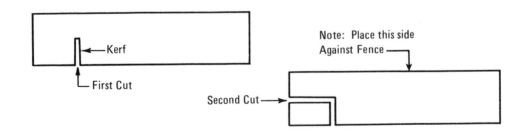

Fig. 15-13 Cutting a Rabbet

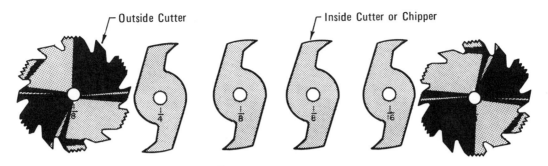

Fig. 15-14   Parts of a Dado Head

the first cut, the blade is lowered to the depth of the joint and the fence is adjusted to the width of the joint. The board is then placed on its edge; the fence and blade are adjusted and the strip is removed, completing the rabbet joint.

• If a dado head is used, the rabbet may be made with a single cut. A *dado head* is a series of knife blades placed together to form one blade, figure 15-14. The number of blades can be adjusted to regulate the width of the cut.

Note: Cut on the inside of the line; if the cut is made on the line or outside of the line, the joint will be too large.

   CAUTION: When using any power equipment, wear safety goggles and follow all safety rules.

HOW TO MAKE A DADO JOINT

1. Locate one edge of the dado and mark a line across the stock.

2. Place the other member next to the line and mark a second line parallel to the first.

3. Cut the dado with a radial arm saw or circular saw. A dado head can be used, or a series of cuts can be made with a single blade. Always cut the dado in *waste stock*, that part of the board which will be removed. A joint can be easily enlarged, but it is difficult to decrease its size.

Note: If a stop dado is desired, the dado head or circular saw blade is stopped about 1 inch from the edge. The end of the cut has a concave surface and must be chiseled out. The board placed in the stop dado must be notched on the front edge, the notched edge equaling the depth of the dado and the distance from the edge of the board to the dado.

4. Place a bead of glue in the dado and join the two pieces, reinforcing the joint with nails or screws where necessary.

HOW TO MAKE A LAP JOINT

1. Square the ends of the stock that are to be joined.

2. Locate the edge of the lap joint and mark a line across the stock. Place the second member next to the line and mark a second line parallel to the first line. Follow the same procedure to locate the lap joint on the second member.

3. Locate the depth of the joints. The joint depth should equal half the thickness of the stock.

4. Remove the stock from between the two parallel lines.

Note: When the two pieces are fitted, the upper and lower surfaces should be flush. It is sometimes necessary to clean the joint with a 1 1/2-inch chisel, especially if a single blade was used to cut the joint.

5. Cover the faces of the stock with glue and join the two pieces together, reinforcing the joint with nails or screws where necessary.

HOW TO MAKE A MORTISE AND TENON JOINT

1. Square the stock and mark its face side.

2. Lay out the tenon, figure 15-15. The length of the tenon is usually marked first and should not exceed two-thirds the width of the member into which it is fitted.

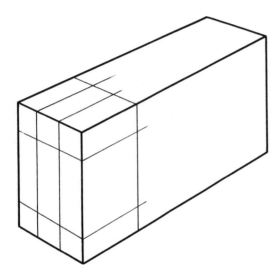

Fig. 15-15   Layout of a Tenon

Fig. 15-16   Layout of a Mortise

3. Measure 1/2 inch from the bottom and top of the tenon and draw a line perpendicular to the line previously drawn.

4. Determine the thickness of the tenon and draw parallel lines on the ends and edges to depict its size. The thickness of the tenon is usually equal to half the thickness of the stock.

5. Cut along the lines with a back saw or a circular saw. Be certain that the cut is on the waste side of the line.

   It is sometimes necessary to pare the cheeks and shoulders with a chisel, especially if the joint is cut with a back saw. The ends of the tenon are sometimes beveled for easier insertion into the mortise.

6. Lay out the mortise, figure 15-16. The length and width of the mortise is determined by the length and width of the tenon.

7. Drill a series of holes 1/16 inch smaller in diameter than the width of the mortise. The holes should be drilled 1/8 inch deeper than the length of the tenon.

8. Using a 1 1/2-inch chisel, pare the sides of the mortise. Use a smaller chisel to cut the ends of the mortise.

9. Cover the cheeks of the tenon with glue and insert the tenon into the mortise.

   Note: The joint should be snug but not excessively tight. A tight joint may cause the joint to bulge or the wood around the mortise to split. In some cases the shoulders can be beveled to assure a good ·fit, figure 15-17. The opposite shoulders should be parallel whether they are beveled or square.

HOW TO MAKE A DOWEL JOINT

1. Draw a centerline on the two edges of the stock that are to be fastened together.

2. Draw a line perpendicular to the centerline to indicate the dowel position, figure 15-18.

3. Using an awl, make a small hole at the intersection of the two lines. An *awl* is a small tool

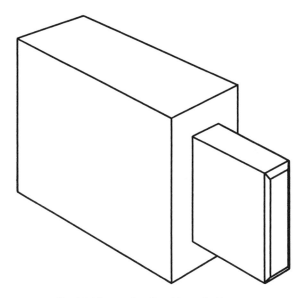

Fig. 15-17   Beveled Shoulders of a Tenon

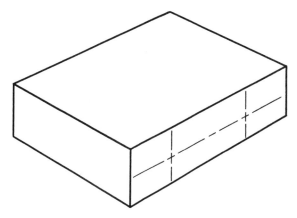

Fig. 15-18   Location of Dowel Holes

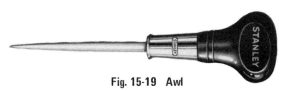

Fig. 15-19   Awl

with a wooden handle and a long, round metal shank with a pointed end, figure 15-19.

Note: The diameter of the dowel should equal half the thickness of the stock.

4. Select the dowel and the bit. Place the bit at the intersection of the two lines and drill the hole to the required depth. The dowels should be no longer than 3 inches; the holes should be drilled 1/8 inch deeper than the length of the dowel.

Note: To help keep the bit at a 90-degree angle with the stock, a doweling jig can be used, figure 15-20. The jig can be adjusted to fit different bits and different sizes of stock.

5. Place glue in the dowel holes and along the edges of the stock that are to be fastened together.

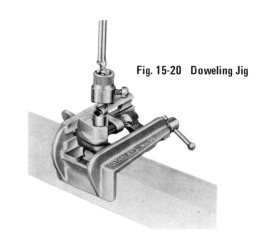

Fig. 15-20   Doweling Jig

6. Cover the dowels with glue and insert them in the drilled holes. The dowel ends are sometimes beveled for easier insertion.

7. Apply pressure to the joint and wipe off any excess glue with a damp cloth.

REVIEW

A.   Choose the best answer or answers to complete each statement.

1. A squared end of a board is fitted against the end or edge of another board to form the _____ joint.

   a. butt   c. dowel
   b. mortise and tenon   d. dado

2.   One acceptable method of strengthening a butt joint is to use_____ .

    a. screws   c. dowels

    b. brads   d. nails

3.   The _____ joint consists of a grooved board placed next to the edge of another board.

    a. dado   c. rabbet

    b. butt   d. dowel

4.   A _____ joint is very close in construction to the rabbet joint.

    a. dado   c. miter

    b. dowel   d. tenon

5.   A _____ joint is actually a combination of two dado joints.

    a. gain   c. blind dado

    b. lap   d. rabbet

6.   A _____ joint is formed by the intersection of two boards cut at an angle of less than 90 degrees.

    a. miter   c. dowel

    b. dado   d. mortise and tenon

7.   A _____ joint is often substituted for a mortise and tenon joint.

    a. lap   c. dado

    b. dowel   d. gain

8.   Bar clamps should be spaced _____ inches on center.

    a. 12   c. 16

    b. 18   d. 9

9.   A rabbet joint should be about _____ inch deep if the stock used is 3/4 inch thick.

    a. 1/8   c. 3/8

    b. 5/8   d. 1/2

10. If a stop dado is used the dado should stop _____ inch(es) from the edge of the board.

    a. 1   c. 3

    b. 2   d. 4

B.   Place the correct answer in the space provided.

    1.   The depth of a lap joint should be _____ .

    2.   A dado head is a _____ .

    3.   The length of a tenon usually measures _____ .

4. The width of a mortise is determined by the width of the _____ .

5. A _____ is used to keep a bit at a 90-degree angle.

6. The strength of a joint depends on _____ , _____ and
    _____ .

7. Most joints are fastened together with _____ , _____ ,
    or _____ .

8. Another name for a gain joint is _____ .

9. Variations of the mortise and tenon joint include the _____ .
    _____ , _____ , and _____ joints.

10. To minimize shrinkage and the opening of an edge-to-edge joint, a(an) _____
    should exist in the center of the board.

C. In the space provided sketch

    1. a dowel joint.

    2. a miter joint.

    3. a mortise and tenon joint.

    4. a lap joint.

    5. a stop dado joint.

Unit 16 Kitchen Cabinets

The modern kitchen cabinet, figure 16-1, is one of the most frequently used built-in features of a home. The kitchen cabinet should be carefully planned to allow a properly-sized working area and adequate storage space.

Most kitchen cabinets are built to the same basic dimensions, figure 16-2. The countertop is usually 36 inches high and 25 inches deep. These dimensions provide adequate working space at a most convenient height for the average person. A countertop 36 inches high is level with most stoves; a built-in sink at this height is convenient. Drawers are provided directly under the countertop for frequently used utensils. There are large cupboards underneath the countertop with shelves concealed by doors. At the bottom of the cabinet, a 3 1/2" x 3 1/2" recess provides extra room for a person working at the counter.

The wall cabinet is usually a separate unit fastened to the wall. The cabinet is usually 12 inches deep and 30 to 36 inches high. In most cases, the wall cabinet contains two shelves spaced 12 inches apart and hinged doors arranged to correspond to the doors of the lower cabinet.

In a typical home, there is a 12-inch space from the top of the wall cabinet to the ceiling. To fill the void, the ceiling is furred down to the top of the wall cabinet. This section is sometimes used for the installation of a light over the sink or electric outlets for a clock or exhaust fan.

The space between the countertop and the bottom of the wall cabinet should be no less than 18 inches. Special attention should be paid to this feature if the wall cabinet is over 12 inches deep, since there is a possibility of an individual striking his head against the cabinet while working at the counter shelf.

Materials Used in Kitchen Cabinets

Framing materials for cabinets are usually a good grade of soft pine or plywood. Both base and wall cabinets are sometimes constructed entirely of plywood. In other instances, the rails and stiles are of solid stock while shelves, doors, drawers, and sides of the cabinet are plywood.

Countertops are usually constructed of stainless steel, plastic laminates, vinyl plastic, linoleum, ceramic tile or hardwood. Countertops should be moisture-proof and resistant to heat, scratching, staining, and fading. Most of the materials used for kitchen countertops are available in a variety of colors, textures, and patterns.

PREFABRICATED CABINETS

Most kitchen cabinets used today are prefabricated. Prefabricated cabinets are often superior to cabinets built on the job site. They are available in three basic types: disassembled (knocked down); assembled but not finished (in-the-white); and assembled and finished. The disassembled cabinet consists of precut units which are assembled on the job. In-the-white cabinets are ready for finishing and installation. The assembled and finished unit is ready to be hung.

Prefabricated cabinets some in standard-sized units and may be arranged to fit almost any kitchen layout, figure 16-3. It is necessary to decide before the house plans are drawn whether the units are to be obtained from the factory or built in by the carpenter.

HOW TO BUILD THE BOTTOM PLATFORM FOR BASE CABINETS

Note: The *bottom platform* is that portion of the base cabinet which is secured to the subfloor, figure 16-4. It is constructed of 2 x 4s.

1. Lay out a complete floor plan of the cabinet.

2. Determine the length of the base cabinet and cut two 2 x 4s to the required length. These 2 x 4s are known as *stringers*.

3. Lay out the 2 x 4 stringer to receive the 2 x 4 lookouts spaced 24 inches on center.

4. Lay out and cut the 2 x 4 to 17 1/2 inches.

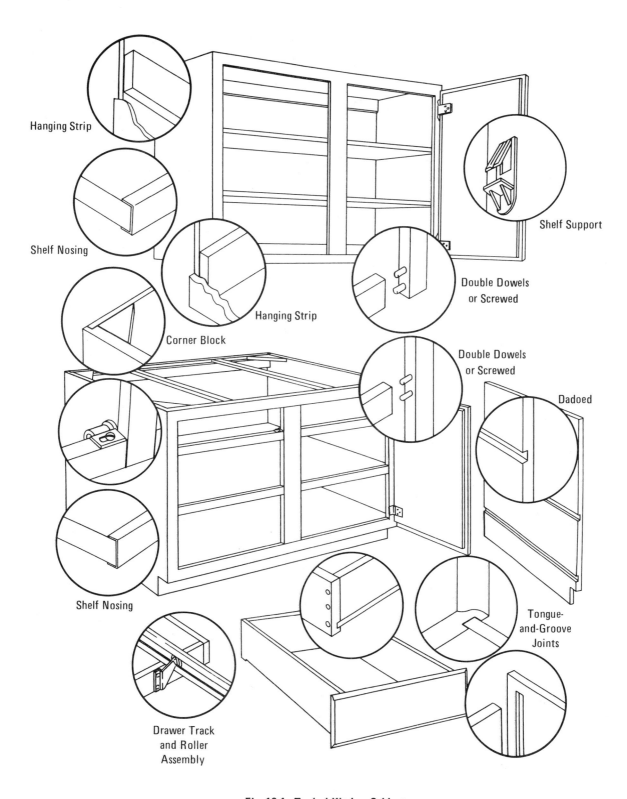

Hanging Strip

Shelf Nosing

Corner Block

Hanging Strip

Shelf Support

Double Dowels
or Screwed

Double Dowels
or Screwed

Dadoed

Shelf Nosing

Drawer Track
and Roller
Assembly

Tongue-
and-Groove
Joints

Fig. 16-1   Typical Kitchen Cabinet

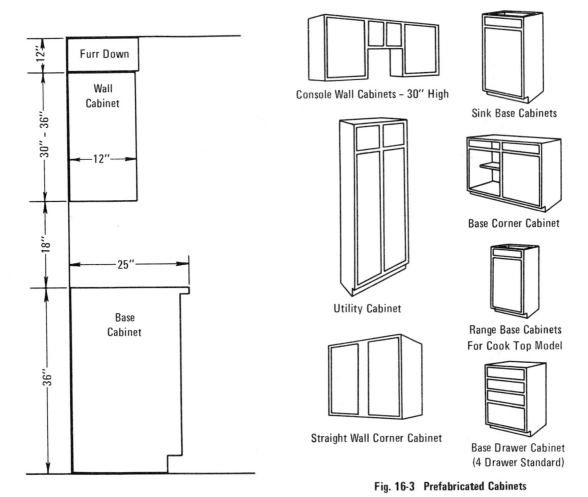

Fig. 16-2   Typical Cabinet Dimensions

Furr Down

Wall Cabinet

12"

30" – 36"

18"

36"

25"

Base Cabinet

Console Wall Cabinets – 30" High

Sink Base Cabinets

Utility Cabinet

Base Corner Cabinet

Range Base Cabinets For Cook Top Model

Straight Wall Corner Cabinet

Base Drawer Cabinet (4 Drawer Standard)

Fig. 16-3   Prefabricated Cabinets

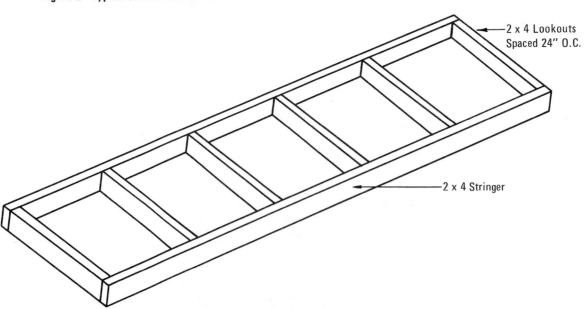

2 x 4 Lookouts Spaced 24" O.C.

2 x 4 Stringer

Fig. 16-4   Bottom Platform

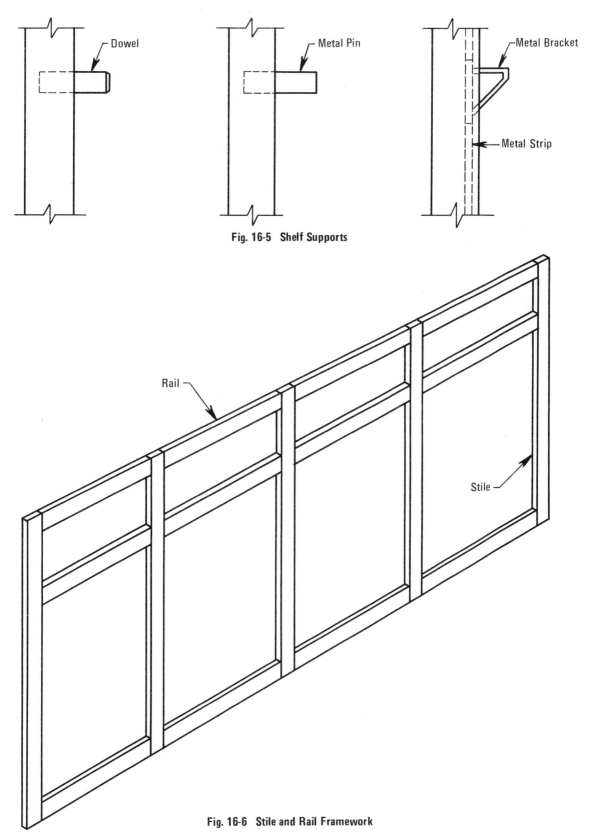

Fig. 16-5 Shelf Supports

Fig. 16-6 Stile and Rail Framework

5. Nail the 2 x 4 lookouts to the two stringers, spacing them 24 inches on center.

    Note: The 2 x 4 frame should be nailed with 12d or 16d nails.

6. Square the frame and place it on the floor against the back and end walls.

Fig. 16-7   Trimming the Plastic Laminate

7. Level the bottom platform frame and toenail it to the floor.

8. Cover the frame with 1/2 inch thick plywood, allowing it to project 3 inches over the front edge of the platform frame.

HOW TO BUILD THE BASE CABINET

1. Lay out the elevation on the back wall and end wall or walls.

2. Cut and install the end panels. Typical end panels are cut to measure 24″ x 32″.

    Note: If the base cabinet is to be shelved, dado the end panels and install the shelf after the end panels are in position. Adjustable shelves may be more suited to the cabinet. There are several methods used for supporting adjustable shelves, such as wooden dowels, metal shelf pins, and

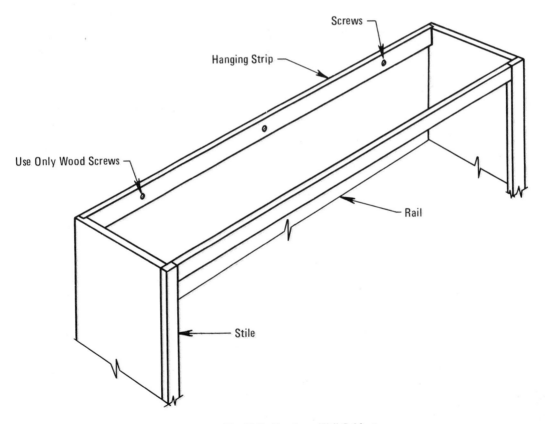

Fig. 16-8   Hanging a Wall Cabinet

metal shelf brackets fitted into a perforated metal strip, figure 16-5.

3. Snap a chalk line along the wall, using the top edge of the two end panels as a reference point.

4. Nail a 1 x 2 strip along the wall, using the chalk line as a guide.

5. Rip a piece of stock to form the three front rails. *Ripping* is the sawing or splitting of wood with the grain. Most rails are 1 1/2 inches wide; stiles are usually 2 inches wide. However, the dimensions may vary.

   Note: The front stile and rail framework may be laid out from the floor plan and then assembled. All connecting joints should be assembled with half lap, mortise and tenon, or dowel joints. The joints should be glued and clamped together from the back of the frame.

6. Secure the front stile and rail framework, figure 16-6.

   Note: A rail should be placed against the back wall to correspond with each front rail. If the rails and stiles are installed separately, the stiles are usually placed first, with the rails inserted afterwards.

7. Cut and fit the countertop base, allowing a 1-inch projection past the edge of the rail.

8. Install the countertop material, usually a plastic laminate or a vinyl plastic.

HOW TO INSTALL A PLASTIC-LAMINATED COUNTERTOP

1. Cut a piece of plastic laminate to the approximate size. The countertop should be allowed to project at least 1/4 inch pass the edge of the countertop base.

   Note: The large sheets of plastic laminate should be handled very carefully, since it can be very brittle before installation.

2. Apply contact bond cement to the underside of the plastic laminate and to the top side of the countertop base.

Note: Follow the manufacturer's recommendations in the application of the contact bond cement.

3. Allow the contact bond cement to set or dry; when a piece of brown paper can be pressed against the coated surface with no adhesive sticking to the paper, the plastic laminate is ready to be bonded.

4. Lay a sheet of brown wrapping paper, or *slipsheet,* across the countertop. The paper allows the countertop to be adjusted without permanent bonding.

5. Gradually slide the paper out; as the paper is withdrawn, the plastic laminate is bonded to the countertop base.

6. Apply pressure to the countertop with a 2-inch hand roller.

7. Trim the edges of the countertop. Most carpenters prefer to use a router with a special guide, figure 16-7; however, a small block plane is satisfactory.

8. If a bevel is desired along the countertop edge, use a mill file to cut a bevel of 20 to 30 degrees.

HOW TO CONSTRUCT WALL CABINETS

1. Cut the two end pieces to the desired length and width.

2. Determine the location of the shelves and cut the dado joints accordingly.

   Note: At an internal corner, the end pieces may be nailed directly to a wall. If the wall cabinet does not fit between two internal corners, a hanging strip must be secured to the wall cabinet, figure 16-8.

3. Lay out the shelves and cut them to the proper length and width.

4. Insert the shelves in the dadoes and nail them in place with 6d finishing nails.

5. Cut and position the stiles and rails. Half-lap the joints and glue them together.

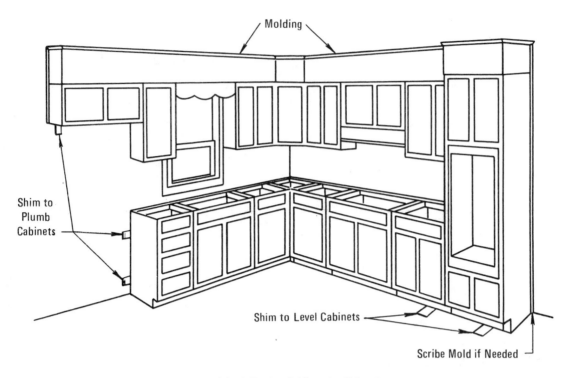

Fig. 16-9   Adjusting Cabinets by Shimming

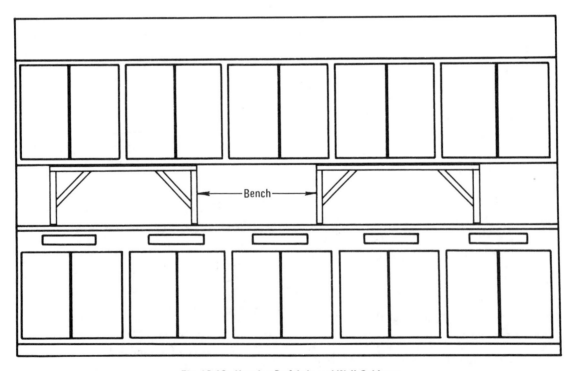

Fig. 16-10   Hanging Prefabricated Wall Cabinets

6. Hang the wall cabinets using one of the following two methods. If there are two interior corners, nail the sides of the wall cabinet to the sidewall; if there are no interior corners, or only one, the hanging strip should be secured to the studs.

HOW TO INSTALL PREFABRICATED CABINETS

1. Mark the location of each unit on the kitchen wall.

2. Mark the location of the studs on the wall frame where the cabinets are to be fastened.

3. Temporarily place the cabinet units, beginning with the corner cabinets.

4. Level and plumb the base cabinets, scribing them to the wall and floor if necessary. Use shims to adjust the cabinets to an uneven wall or floor, figure 16-9.

5. Screw the base units into the studs through the back frame.

6. Place the wall cabinets in position and secure them to the studs with screws. If the wall is not plumb, place shims behind the wall cabinet.

Note: To position the wall cabinet, it is sometimes helpful to build a bench to rest the wall cabinets on, figure 16-10. The bench is placed on the base cabinets, and the wall units are placed on the bench and secured to the wall.

REVIEW

A.   Choose the best answer or answers to complete each statement.

1. The kitchen countertop is usually _____ inches high.

   a. 36
   b. 24
   c. 48
   d. 30

2. The wall cabinet is usually _____ inches deep.

   a. 48
   b. 36
   c. 24
   d. 12

3. The countertop is usually _____ inches deep.

   a. 12
   b. 18
   c. 25
   d. 36

4. The bottom platform is constructed from _____ .

   a. 1 x 4s
   b. 2 x 4s
   c. 2 x 6s
   d. 1 x 6s

5. The bottom platform should be secured with _____ .

   a. 16d nails
   b. 8d nails
   c. staples
   d. wire brads

6. Most rails are about _____ inches wide.

   a. 1 1/2
   b. 3
   c. 3 1/2
   d. 4

7. The countertop base should project _____ inch(es) past the edge of the rail.

   a. 5   c. 3
   b. 1   d. 4

8. The countertop base should be constructed of _____ .

   a. plywood   c. particleboard
   b. shiplap   d. plastic

9. A slip-sheet is _____ .

   a. brown paper   c. plastic laminate
   b. 1 x 4s   d. particle board

10. After the plastic laminate is in position, pressure is applied with _____

    _____ .

    a. the palm of the hand   c. a 2 x 4
    b. a 2-inch roller   d. a 12-inch roller

B. Place the correct answer in the space provided.

   1. A prefabricated cabinet is secured with _____ .

   2. If the wall is not plumb, it may be necessary to place _____ behind the cabinet.

   3. The wall cabinet is usually _____ inches deep and _____ inches high.

   4. Kitchen cabinets are usually made from _____ or _____ .

   5. The three basic types of prefabricated cabinets are _____ , _____ , and _____ .

   6. Cabinet shelves may be supported by _____ , _____ , _____ , and _____ .

   7. Contact bond cement should be applied to the _____ and _____ .

   8. A slip-sheet is placed between the _____ and _____ .

   9. A_____ is used to bevel a countertop.

   10. Wall cabinets are sometimes temporarily supported by a _____ .

C. In the space provided make a sketch of the end section of a typical kitchen cabinet, including appropriate dimensions and notes.

Unit 17 Cabinet Drawers and Doors

CABINET DRAWERS

The construction of cabinet drawers is one of the most difficult operations performed in cabinet-making. Drawers must fit prescribed dimensions and withstand years of handling. If the drawers are not properly constructed, they may bind, stick, or fall apart under normal use.

Most kitchen drawers are either lip or flush drawers, figure 17-1. The *lip* drawer has a rabbet cut around the four sides of the drawer front and fits over the rails and stiles, thereby allowing a margin for error. The *flush* drawer fits into the stile and rail framework. The flush drawer is difficult to construct because there is no room for error in the space between the sides of the drawer front and the stile and rail framework. Very few flush drawer fronts are constructed for use in kitchen cabinets for this reason.

Drawer fronts are usually made of 3/4-inch plywood. They should be designed to complement the decor of the kitchen. Several techniques can be used to add a decorative flare. A routered edge is an inexpensive way of decorating draw fronts, figure 17-2. The router may also be used to cut a particular design

in a drawer front. Molding can also be used to create a decorative design, such as special corner molding placed around the edge of the drawer front. If corner molding is used, it is not necessary to rabbet the drawer front.

The sides and back of a drawer are usually made from 1/2-inch plywood, although 3/8-inch and 3/4-inch plywood can be used. To receive the drawer bottom, the sides are grooved or rabbeted along the bottom. In quality drawer construction, the drawer sides are dadoed to receive the drawer back. The bottom of the drawer is usually 1/4-inch plywood or hardboard and fits into the grooves of the front, back, and sides of the drawer.

Drawer Guides

Drawer guides are used to assure a smoothly operating drawer. Three basic types of drawer guides can be made on the job site: side guides, center guides, and corner guides, figure 17-3. A *corner guide* is constructed by placing a rail on either side of the drawer, allowing 1/16-inch clearance on either side of the drawer. In addition to the drawer guide, a *kicker* is

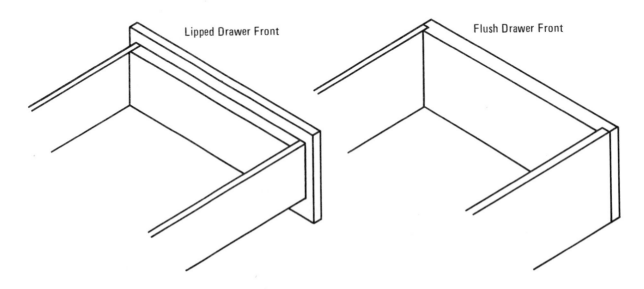

Lipped Drawer Front

Flush Drawer Front

Fig. 17-1 Lipped and Flush Drawers

Fig. 17-2 Routered Drawer Fronts

sometimes added above the drawer to eliminate the tilting of the drawer after it has been pulled out. *Side guides* may be either built into the drawer side, with a strip nailed to the cabinet side; or a strip may be nailed on the drawer side and then fitted into a dado. A *center guide* is attached to the bottom of a drawer and operates along a wooden runner.

In addition to drawer guides that can be made on the job site, there are numerous types of commercial drawer guides available. Some of the drawer guides consist of single tracks running under the drawers. These guides fit drawers of any length or width, figure 17-4. Other drawer guides are comprised of two parallel extension slides operating on nylon rollers, figure 17-5. The channels are mounted flush with the cabinet front, while the roller plate is flush with the bottom of the drawer.

CABINET DOORS

The cabinet door usually falls under one of two classifications, swinging or sliding. The *swinging* door,

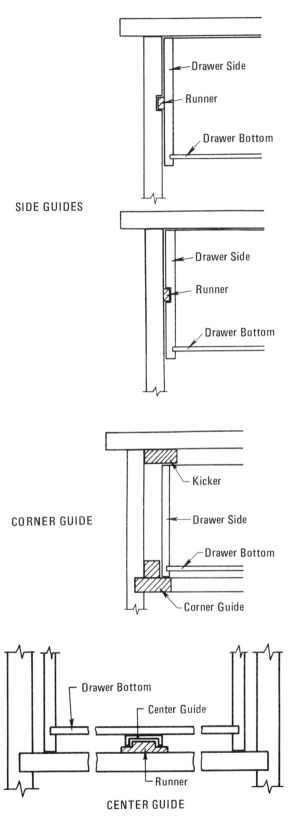

Fig. 17-3 Drawer Guides

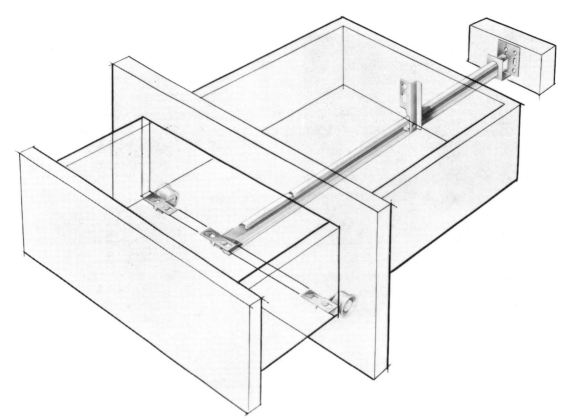

Fig. 17-4   Single Track Drawer Slide

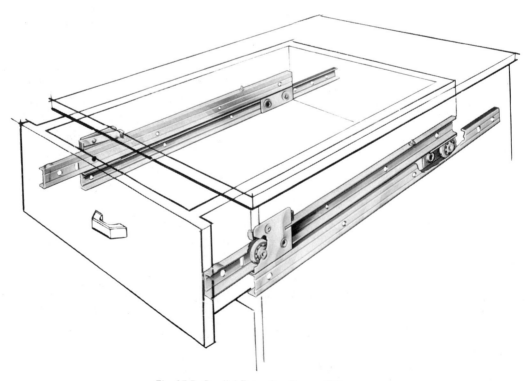

Fig. 17-5   Parallel Extension Drawer Slide

Fig. 17-6 Cabinet Door Frames With Inserted Panel

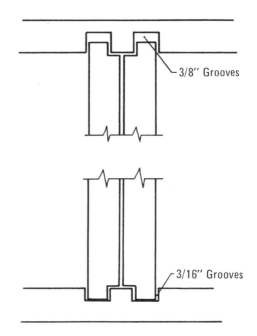

Fig. 17-7 Sliding Door Detail

3/8″ Grooves

3/16″ Grooves

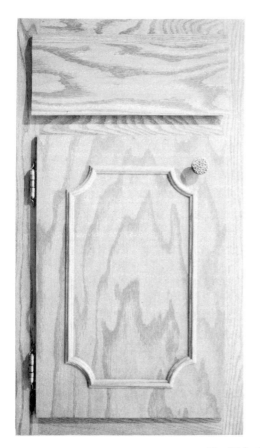

Fig. 17-8 Cabinet Doors With Molding

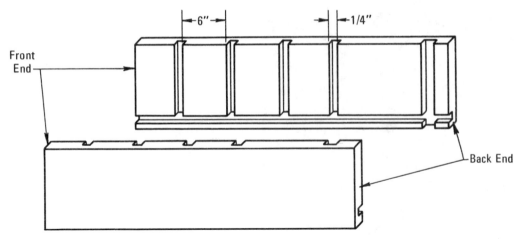

Fig. 17-9 Drawer Sides

a popular type of cabinet door, usually has a 3/8-inch lip encircling three or four of the sides. Most swinging doors are constructed of a 3/4-inch lumber core, plywood frame with an inserted panel, figure 17-6.

Sliding doors should be tight enough to prevent the infiltration of dust. To make a tight-fitting sliding door, the back side of the front door and the front side of the back door should be rabbeted, figure 17-7. Two grooves are cut in the top and bottom of the cabinet to receive the rabbeted edges. If 3/8-inch doors are used, the grooves should be 1/2 inch apart. Placing the grooves 1/2 inch apart provides sufficient room for the doors to pass.

Precut molding, routered edges, and special molding may be used to decorate cabinet doors, figure 17-8.

HOW TO CONSTRUCT CABINET DRAWERS

1. Square two pieces of 1/2-inch plywood. These will be used for the drawer sides. The sides should be 1/8 inch shorter than the height of the drawer opening and 2 inches less than the depth of the opening.

2. Lay out the two drawer sides, specifying one for the right side and one for the left side.

    Note: The groove in the bottom of the side pieces should be about 1/4 inch deep. The width should equal the thickness of the drawer bottom. The groove should be at least 1/2 inch

from the edge. The dado for the drawer back should be 1/4 inch deep. The width should be equal to the thickness of the back. The dado should also be at least 3/4 inch apart on both sides of the drawers so that partitions may be installed to form small compartments in the drawers, figure 17-9.

3. Cut the dadoes.

4. Lay out and square the drawer front using 3/4-inch stock.

    Note: The height of the drawer front should equal the height of the sides plus 3/4 inch for the two lips. The length of the drawer front is the same as the width of the opening plus 3/4 inch for the two lips.

5. Lay out and cut the rabbets around the sides of the drawer front.

    Note: The distance A should be the same as the distance from the top of the groove in the drawer side to the top edge of this side, figure 17-10. Note that the rabbet along the bottom edge of the drawer front is wider than the one along the top edge. The distance B, between the two end rabbets of the drawer front, should be such that the finished drawer will be 1/8 inch narrower than the opening.

6. Lay out and cut the drawer back from 1/2-inch plywood.

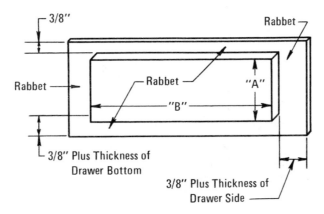

Fig. 17-10 Back View of Drawer Front

7. Cut a groove for the bottom. The groove should be about 1/4 inch deep; the width should equal the thickness of the bottom.

8. Lay out and cut the drawer bottom from 1/4-inch plywood.

    Note: If the drawer front is to be the flush type, it may be squared and fitted to the opening with a 1/16-inch allowance on all sides. The remainder of the drawer construction is the same as for the lipped drawer.

9. Glue and nail the sides to the front. Keep the top edges of the sides flush with the top rabbet of the drawer front.

10. Slide the bottom into the side grooves. Do not force it since the joints could spread.

11. Glue the back into the dadoes on the drawer sides. Keep the top edge of the back flush with the top edge of the sides. Drive 1 1/2-inch brads into the back through the sides.

12. Square the drawer and nail the bottom to the lower edge of the back and front.

13. Finish driving the nails into the back and front from the sides and sand the rough edges of the drawer. Set the nails.

14. Fit the drawer into the opening and adjust the guides so that the drawer will slide easily. Be sure the drawer front lips fit squarely against the front of the cabinet.

Note: Thumbtacks are sometimes inserted in the wearing surfaces of the drawer supports and guides so that the drawer operates smoothly.

HOW TO CONSTRUCT A SWINGING CABINET DOOR

1. Measure the height and width of the opening between the rails and stiles.

2. Add 5/8 inch to each dimension and lay out the cabinet door accordingly. Most cabinet doors are made from 3/4-inch stock.

3. Cut the cabinet door to the correct size with a handsaw, radial arm saw, table saw, or portable power saw.

    Note: If a handsaw, radial arm saw, or table saw it used, the better face of the plywood should be up. If a portable power saw is used, the better face of the plywood should be down. If the two cabinet doors are to be laid out side by side and cut from the same stock, be sure to allow for a *saw kerf,* the groove formed by a saw when cutting lumber.

4. Cut a rabbet around three or four sides of the door. The size of the rabbet may vary but it usually measures 3/8″ x 3/8″.

5. If accessories such as moldings or router edges are required, follow normal procedures for construction.

6. Lightly sand the cabinet door with the grain. If the door is sanded across the grain, deep scratches may be left.

HOW TO CONSTRUCT A SLIDING CABINET DOOR

1. Before assembling the cabinet, cut two parallel grooves in the top and bottom of the cabinet. The bottom groove should be 3/16 inch deep and the top groove should be 3/8 inch deep.

2. Measure the height of the cabinet opening and add 5/16 inch to get the height of the cabinet door.

3. Lay out and cut two doors.

4. Cut a rabbet in the back side of the front door; reverse the procedure for the back door.

5. Lightly sand the cabinet door and wax the grooves so that the doors will slide smoothly.

REVIEW

A.   Choose the best answer or answers to complete each statement.

1. Drawer fronts are usually made of _____ -inch plywood.

   a. 1/4   c. 1/2
   b. 3/8   d. 3/4

2. To receive the drawer bottom, the sides are grooved or _____ .

   a. mitered   c. dadoed
   b. rabbeted   d. doweled

3. A drawer should have a _____ -inch clearance on either side of the drawer.

   a. 1/16   c. 1/4
   b. 1/8   d. 1/2

4. The most popular cabinet door is the _____ type.

   a. swinging   c. revolving
   b. sliding   d. rolling

5. If 3/8-inch sliding doors are used, the bottom grooves should be _____ inch apart.

   a. 1/4   c. 1/2
   b. 3/8   d. 3/4

6. The drawer side should be _____ inch shorter than the height of the drawer opening.

   a. 1/16   c. 1/4
   b. 1/8   d. 3/8

7. The groove for the drawer bottom should be about _____ inch deep.

   a. 1/4   c. 1/2
   b. 3/8   d. 5/8

8. A flush drawer front should have a _____ -inch allowance on all four sides.

   a. 1/2   c. 1/8
   b. 1/4   d. 1/16

9. The size of the rabbet for a swinging door is usually _____ .

    a. 3/8 x 3/8   c. 3/4 x 3/4
    b. 1/2 x 1/2   d. 5/8 x 5/8

10. Most cabinet doors are made from _____ -inch stock.

    a. 1/4   c. 3/4
    b. 1/2   d. 1

B. Place the correct answer in the space provided.

    1. Most kitchen drawers are one of two types, _____ or
        _____ .

    2. Three ways to decorate a drawer front are with _____ ,
        _____ , and _____ .

    3. Drawer guides are used to assure a _____ .

    4. Three types of drawer guides are _____ , _____ ,
        and _____ .

    5. The height of a drawer front equals the height of the sides plus _____ .

    6. To make the drawer operate more smoothly _____ are
        sometimes inserted in the wearing surfaces.

    7. If a table saw is used to cut plywood the good face of the plywood should be
        _____ .

    8. The top groove for a sliding door should be _____ deep.

    9. The sides and back of a drawer are usually made from _____ .

    10. Drawer bottoms are usually made from _____.

C. In the space provided sketch an exploded (disassembled) view of a cabinet drawer.

Unit 18 Stairs Built on Open Stringers

A *stairs* is a series of steps leading from one level of a structure to another. Some aspects of stair construction apply not only to one type of stair, but to stairs in general.

GENERAL STAIR CONSTRUCTION

Parts of a Stairs

A stairs is composed of several parts with each performing a unique function, figure 18-1. The *stringer*, or *carriage*, stretches from one level to the next and supports the treads, risers, and loads imposed on the stairs.

A *riser* is a board placed in a vertical position on the stringer which helps to enclose the stairs. The *tread* is a board placed in a horizontal position on the stringer. It is the portion of the stairs that is actually stepped on. *Nosing* is that part of the tread which

extends past the riser. It may be finished in several different ways, figure 18-2.

The space above the stairs is called the *head-room*. It is the vertical distance measured from the top of one tread to the stairwell header. The *stairwell header*, usually a 2 x 10 or a 2 x 12, is the structural member which helps to frame the stairwell.

A *glue block* is a small triangular block which is glued and nailed to the back side of the tread and riser, increasing the rigidity of the joint, figure 18-3.

The *total rise* of a stairs is the distance from one finished floor to the next; the *total run* is a horizontal dimension measured from one end of the stringer to the other end of the stringer.

Treads and Risers. The treads for main stairs are usually made from 1 1/4-inch stock, while most service stairs are constructed from 2 x 12s. The risers are

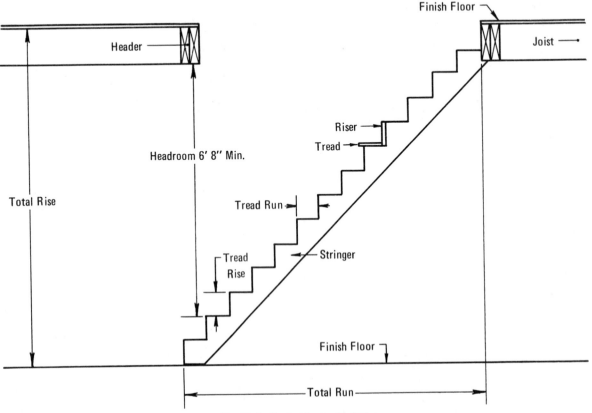

Fig. 18-1 Typical Parts of a Stairs

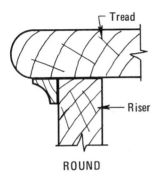

ROUND

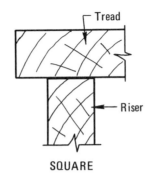

SQUARE

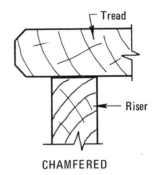

CHAMFERED

Fig. 18-2 Nosing Treatment

usually not as thick as the treads and are usually made from 3/4-inch stock. Common materials for main stairs include birch and oak, while southern pine is most often used for service stairs.

There are several methods used to connect treads to risers, or risers and treads to stringers, but the more common methods include butt joints, rabbet joints, and miter joints, figure 18-4. If a butt joint is used, the riser is butted into the tread. In some cases, the joint is covered with cove molding. If a rabbet joint is used, a groove is usually cut along the nosing of the tread and the joint is cut at the base of the tread. A mitered riser and tread make a tight joint and are sometimes used with a mitered stringer.

Rules

The three most accepted rules for calculating tread width and riser height are

- one riser + one riser + one tread = 25 inches.
- one riser + one tread = 17 to 18 inches.
- riser x tread = 75 inches (approximately).

If the rules are followed, a 7 1/2-inch riser would require a 10-inch tread (7 1/2" + 7 1/2" + 10" =

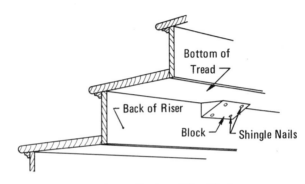

Fig. 18-3 Application of Glue Blocks

25"), a 7-inch riser could be complemented with a 10- to 11-inch tread (7" + 10 1/2" = 17 1/2") and the product of a 7 1/2-inch riser and a 10-inch tread equals 75 inches.

To calculate the number and size of risers needed, divide the total rise by 7. For example, if the total rise is 8 feet 6 inches, or 102 inches, the result would be 14.40 inches. Round off the result to the nearest whole number and divide that figure into the total rise (102 ÷ 14 = 7.35 or 7 3/8"). The stringer requires 14 risers, each being 7 3/8 inches in height. There is always one less tread than riser, so 13 treads are required; following one of the established rules, a

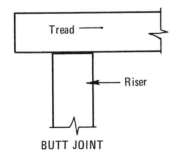

BUTT JOINT

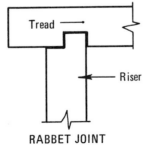

RABBET JOINT

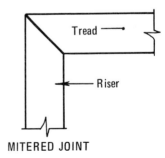

MITERED JOINT

Fig. 18-4 Connection of Tread to Riser

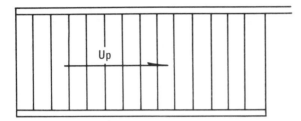

Fig. 18-5 Straight Flight Stairs

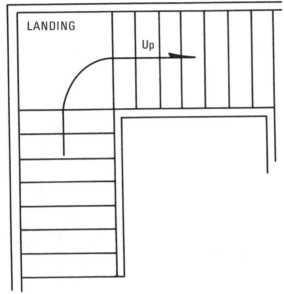

Fig. 18-6 Quarter-Turn Stairs

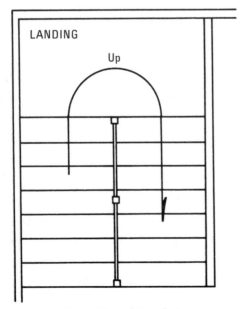

Fig. 18-7 Half-Turn Stairs

10-inch tread is sufficient. The total run is found by multiplying the number of treads by their width (13 x 10 = 130-inches total run).

Stair Dimensions

Stairs should meet basic minimum standards. Headroom for a main stairway should be 6' 8". Service stairs should be provided with minimum headroom of 6' 4". Main stairs should have a minimum 2' 8" clearance above the handrail. Service stairs should have a minimum clearance of 2' 6". Riser height should not exceed 8 inches and the maximum width of the tread should be 12 inches. Each stairway should be provided with a handrail on at least one side; if the stairway is equipped with a door at the top, a 3-foot landing should be built adjacent to the door. A stairway should be easy to ascend; in most cases, a stair built on an incline of about 30 degrees is easiest to climb.

TYPES OF STAIRS

There are many types of stairs, or variations of stair styles, that are used in light construction. Three of the most popular styles in design are the straight-flight, the quarter-turn, and the half-turn. The straight flight, figure 18-5, takes up a considerable amount of room and is usually located at the side of a room. However, the space below straight-flight stairs can be utilized for storage. The quarter-turn stair, figure 18-6, has a landing located approximately one-half the distance between floors and is used where space is restricted. The half-turn stair, figure 18-7, also has a landing located midway between the two floors and provides a complete change in direction.

Most stairs incorporate the use of risers and treads; however, for service stairs or for a special effect, the risers are sometimes omitted.

The *open stringer* is perhaps the most commonly used type of stringer for stairways, figure 18-8. Its best feature is the simplicity of its design. The open stringer is usually cut from 2 x 12s. The risers and treads are then attached, leaving the ends exposed.

Carpeted stairways usually require an open stringer, since the carpet hides cracks left by the intersection of the treads and risers.

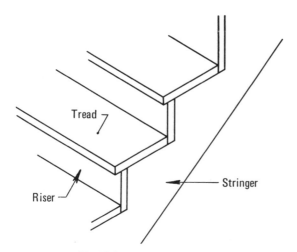

Fig. 18-8 Open Stringer

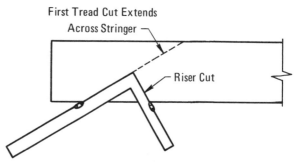

Fig. 18-9 Layout of a Stringer

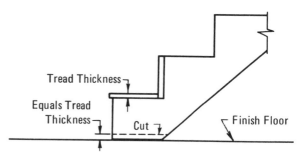

Fig. 18-10 Adjustment for Thread Thickness

HOW TO BUILD OPEN STRINGER STAIRS

1. Determine the total rise of the stair. To find the total rise, a story pole is placed in the well opening and the top of the story pole is marked flush with the top of the finished floor. A *story pole* is a rod or pole used to determine the distance between floors. A tape is then used to measure the distance from the end of the story pole to the mark, thereby determining the total rise.

2. Calculate the riser height. The plans should have the riser height noted, but it is good practice to recheck the plans to be certain that the information is correct.

3. Set a pair of dividers to show the desired riser height and measure the total rise on the story pole, riser by riser. Adjust the dividers and measure the distance again if the riser height is not exactly correct. Repeat the process until the story pole is divided into equal segments.

4. Transfer the riser height to the tongue of the framing square and place a stair gage at the proper location. A *stair gage* is a metal clamp that fits on a framing square and assures accurate layout work.

5. Locate the tread width on the blade of the framing square and place a stair gage at the proper location.

6. Place stock for the stringers, usually a 2 x 12, on two sawhorses.

7. Starting at one end of the stringer, place the framing square in position and mark the tread and riser cut. The first tread line should extend completely across the stringer, figure 18-9. This

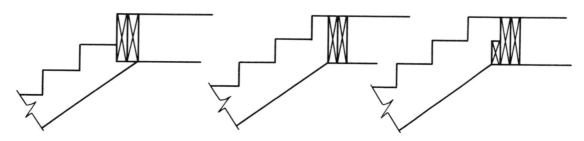

Fig. 18-11 Techniques Used to Secure the Stringer to the Header

line is that part of the stringer which will rest on the floor.

Note: A section of the stringer which is the thickness of the tread must be trimmed off, figure 18-10.

8. Move the square up the stringer, placing the stair gage against the top of the first riser. Mark the first tread and the second riser.

   Note: In layout work, a sharp pencil or knife should be used to mark the stringer.

9. Continue to mark the position of treads and risers on the stringer.

10. Cut the treads and risers with a handsaw or a portable electric saw. A sharp plane may be used to trim the tread and riser cuts.

11. Place the stringers in position and secure them to the header. Some of the more common methods of securing stringers to the header are shown in figure 18-11.

12. Place the risers in position and secure them with 8d finishing nails.

13. Place the treads in position and secure them with 8d finishing nails. Once the treads and risers are in place, the risers should be nailed to the tread from the backside of the stair. If a rabbet joint is used, the joint should be covered with glue before the tread is placed.

14. Place and secure glue blocks.

REVIEW

A. Choose the best answer or answers to complete each statement.

1. Another name for a stringer is a _____ .

   a. carriage
   b. purlin
   c. riser
   d. header

2. The space directly above the staircase is called the _____ .

   a. attic
   b. headroom
   c. trimmer
   d. header

3. The part of the tread that extends past the riser is the _____ .

   a. tread
   b. stringer
   c. nosing
   d. purlin

4. The headroom for a main stairs should be a minimum of _____ ,

   a. 6 feet 8 inches
   b. 6 feet 0 inches
   c. 5 feet 8 inches
   d. 7 feet 4 inches

5. The riser height should not exceed _____ inches.

   a. 6
   b. 8
   c. 10
   d. 12

6. The maximum width of a tread is _____ inches.

   a. 6
   b. 8
   c. 10
   d. 12

7. The width of the main stair should be a minimum of _____ .

   a. 2 feet 0 inches
   b. 3 feet 6 inches
   c. 3 feet 0 inches
   d. 2 feet 8 inches

8. Stairs should be built on an incline of _____ degrees.

   a. 30   c. 14
   b. 45   d. 60

9. The stairwell header is usually a 2 x 10 or a _____.

   a. 2 x 12   c. 1 x 6
   b. 2 x 4   d. 1 x 4

10. That part of the stairs which is stepped on is the _____.

   a. riser   c. step on
   b. tread   d. foot

B. Place the correct answer in the space provided.

   1. The three most popular styles of stairs in design are _____ .
      _____, and _____ .

   2. The three most common methods used to connect the tread to the riser are
      _____ , _____ , and _____ .

   3. The three most accepted rules for calculating the size of treads and risers are
      _____ , _____ , and _____ .

   4. If the total rise of a stair is 93 inches, what is the height of each riser?

      _____

   5. A story pole is a (an) _____ .

C. Identify the parts of the stair in the figure.

STRAIGHT FLIGHT STAIR

A. _____   D. _____

B. _____   E. _____

C. _____   F. _____

D. Complete the sketch of the stairs in the figure, calculating the size of treads and risers, determining the total run, and sketching necessary details.

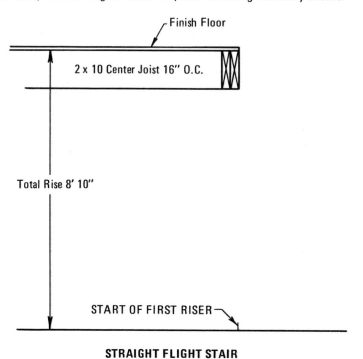

STRAIGHT FLIGHT STAIR

Unit 19 Stairs Built on Semihoused Stringers

The *semihoused stringer* consists of a rough stringer cut from 1-inch stock attached to a 2 inch solid-finish stringer, figure 19-1. The semihoused stringer construction is usually preferred in cases where the treads and risers must be nailed to the stringers. It is sometimes used where the rough stringers are fitted temporarily when the stair bridgework is framed.

In stairs built on semihoused stringers, the risers are nailed to the riser cuts of the rough stringer and are butted against each finish stringer. The treads are nailed to the tread cuts of the carriage and are also butted against the finish stringer. Semihoused stringers save time and labor in the installation of stairs but there are some disadvantages in their use. Many times this type of construction is subject to squeaking when the stairs are stepped on. Also, any shrinkage of the building frame may cause the joints to open, presenting an unsightly appearance.

The finish stringer, usually constructed from 2-inch stock, should be wide enough to cover the intersection of the tread and riser cut in the stringer and to reach about 2 inches beyond the tread nosing, usually 12 to 14 inches. The layout of the finish stringer is similar to that of the rough carriage but, unlike the rough stringer, the rough carriage is not cut out at the riser and tread marks. Only the level cut for the floor, the plumb cut for the header, and the plumb cuts at the top and bottom of the stringer are made.

CUTOUT STAIR STRINGERS

Another method of fitting the treads and risers is to use a cutout stair stringer, figure 19-2. These stringers are laid out with the same rise and run as the stair carriages, but are cut out in reverse direction. The risers are butted and nailed to the riser cuts of the wall stringers and the assembled stringers and risers are laid over the carriage. The assembly is then adjusted so that the tread cuts of the stringers fit against the tread cuts of the carriage. The treads are

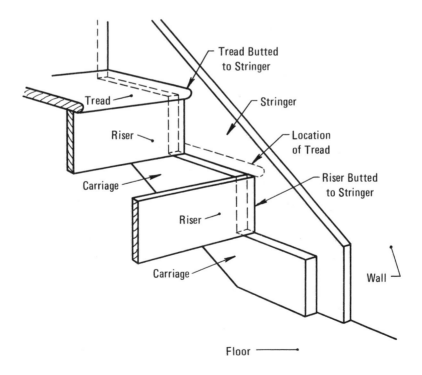

Fig. 19-1 Semihoused Stringers

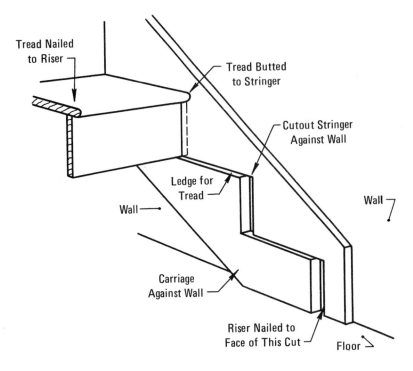

Fig. 19-2   Cutout Stringer

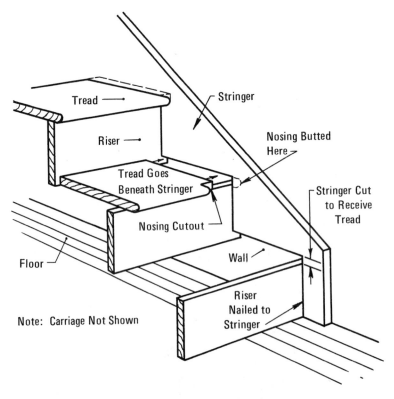

Fig. 19-3   Notched Threads

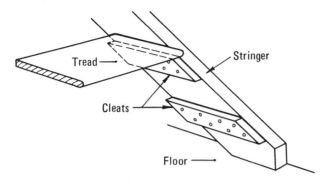

Fig. 19-4 Thread Fastened to Stringer With Cleat

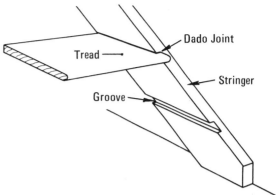

Fig. 19-5 Thread and Stringer Attached by Dado Joint

then nailed to the tread cuts of the carriage and butted against the stringers.

Cutout stair stringers have the same disadvantages as semihoused stringers. However, there is the advantage of having the two stringers connected by the risers. This prevents the side stringers from spreading and exposing open joints at the ends of the treads. Since the risers are nailed to the stringers, there is no need for face nailing the risers to the carriages. This type of stringer is sometimes used in cases where the carriages are fitted permanently to the bridgework when the building is framed.

Sometimes the treads are allowed to run underneath the tread cut of the stringer. In these cases the tread must be notched at the nosing so that it fits around the stringer, figure 19-3.

BASEMENT STAIRS

Basement stairs may be built with or without riser boards. The treads may be fastened to the stringers with cleats, figure 19-4, or dado joints, figure 19-5. *Cleats* are boards which are nailed to the stringer to support the treads. The stringers should be at least 1 1/2 inches thick and wide enough to give a full-width bearing for the tread. If cleats are used, they should be at least 3/4 inch thick, 3 inches wide, and as long as the tread is wide. The treads should be at least 1 1/16 inches thick; if the stairs are more than 3 feet wide, they should be thicker.

The dado joint method of fastening stringers to cleats is commonly used on steep stairs or ladders which lead to attic or scuttle openings. If dado joints are used, they should be one third as deep as the stringer is thick.

HOW TO BUILD STAIRS ON SEMIHOUSED STRINGERS

1. Lay out and cut the rough stringers using 1 1/2-inch stock.

2. Lay out and cut a right-hand and left-hand finish stringer.

3. Nail the right-hand finish stringer to the rough stringer, keeping the bottom of the pieces level and the top edge of the stringers at least 4 inches above the cutouts of the carriage, figure 19-6.

4. Nail the left-hand finish stringer to a rough stringer in the same manner.

5. Position the semihoused stringers against the header and sidewalls of the stair opening and nail them in place.

6. Select the required number of riser boards. The risers are usually 3/4 inch thick, 7 1/2 inches wide, and as long as the distance between the inside faces of the two stringers.

7. Rip a board for the first riser. The width of the board should be equal to the height of the first tread above the floor. *Ripping* is the cutting of wood lengthwise with the grain. Square the ends of the riser so that it fits tightly against the finish stringer on each side of the stairs.

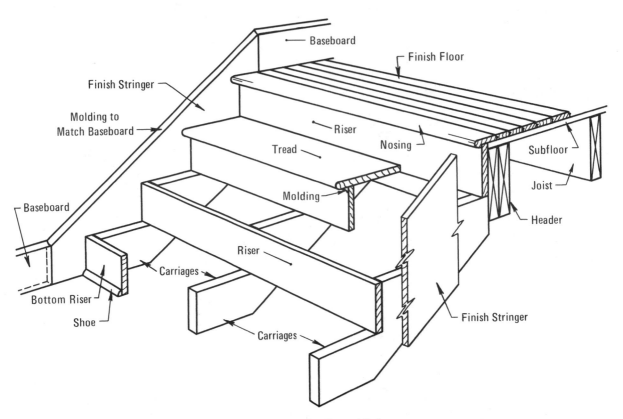

Fig. 19-6 Stairs on Semihoused Stringer

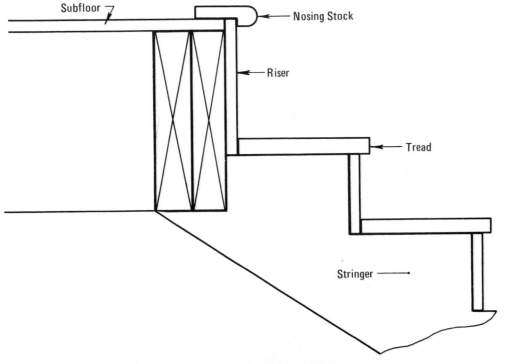

Fig. 19-7 Application of Nosing Stock

8. Facenail the riser boards to the riser cuts of the stringers with 8d finishing nails. Keep the nails about 1 inch from the top and bottom edges of the board.

   Note: The nails at the top will be covered by the molding that is to be placed underneath the tread nosing; the nails at the bottom of the riser will be covered by the floor shoe and by the thickness of the tread on the other risers.

9. Cut, fit, and nail the remaining riser boards in a similar manner.

10. Cut the treads to the same length as the riser boards and place them. Face nail the treads with three 8d finishing nails at each tread cut of each carriage.

    Note: After each tread is face nailed, drive 8d common nails through the back of each riser board into the back edge of each tread. Space the nails every 8 inches between the carriages.

11. Cut a piece of rabbeted nosing stock the same length as a tread and face nail it to the top edge of the top riser and to the subfloor, figure 19-7. Set all exposed nails and sand surfaces where necessary.

12. Fit and nail cover molding under each tread nose.

HOW TO BUILD STAIRS ON CUTOUT STRINGERS

1. Lay out right-hand and left-hand stringers.

2. Cut along the riser and tread marks. Be careful not to break the wood where the riser and tread cuts meet.

3. Temporarily nail a stringer to the wall on the left-hand side of the stair opening. Keep the riser cuts of the stringer approximately 1 1/4 inches from the riser cuts of the carriages; keep the tread cuts of the stringer above the tread cuts of the carriage.

4. Measure the distance between the walls at the top and bottom of the stairs to find the correct length of the riser boards. The riser boards should be 1/2 inch shorter than the distance between the walls. Cut the riser boards.

5. Place the top riser board between the riser cut of the left-hand stringer and the riser cut of the carriage.

6. Position the right-hand stringer on the right-hand wall of the opening.

7. Mark the face of the top riser board along the inside surface of both stringers. Be certain that there is a space of 1/4 inch on each side between the outside of the stringers and the plastered wall.

8. Follow the same procedure for the bottom and intermediate riser boards.

9. Remove the stringers and risers. Face nail the risers to the riser cuts of the stringer, keeping the tops of the risers set firmly against the tread cuts of the stringers and the face of the stringer in line with the marks on the faces of the risers. Nail the riser boards to both stringers in the same way.

10. Replace the assembled stringers on the carriages and adjust them so that the riser boards are firm against the riser cuts of the carriage and the tread cuts of the stringers are firm against the tread cuts of the carriages.

11. Nail the stringers to the walls.

12. Cut, fit, and nail the treads in the same manner as they were done for the semihoused stringer.

HOW TO BUILD BASEMENT STAIRS

1. Select clear, dressed stock free from defects.

2. Lay out the right-hand and left-hand stringers.

   Note: In cases where the treads are to be attached to the stringers with cleats, the tread marks on the stringers represent the top of the the finish treads. The top of the cleat should be the thickness of the tread below this line. If the treads are to be dadoed into the stringers, assume that the tread marks on the stringers represent the tops of the dado cuts.

3. Determine the length of the treads and cut the required number.

4. Cut the required number of cleats and chamfer edges that are exposed. To *chamfer* is to bevel the edge slightly.

5. Nail the cleats to the proper marks below the tread marks on the stringers. Use nails long enough to reach within 1/2 inch of the combined thickness of the stringers and cleat.

6. Assemble the treads on the cleats or in the dadoes; nail through the stringers into the ends of the treads. Use 16d common nails if the stringers are 1 1/2 inches thick and cleats are used; use 10d casing nails if dado joints are used.

7. Square the assembled stairs and secure them in place.

Note: If the lower floor and sidewall are a type of masonry, some means should be used to fasten the stringers firmly to the surfaces. Expansive shields with lag screws or wood blocks inserted into the masonry may be used.

REVIEW

A. Choose the best answer or answers to complete each statement.

1. A semihoused stringer has a rough stringer cut from _____ -inch stock.

   a. 1/2   c. 1
   b. 3/4   d. 2

2. The finished stringer is usually cut from _____ -inch stock.

   a. 1   c. 3
   b. 2   d. 4

3. The treads of basement stairs may be fastened to the stringer with cleats or _____ .

   a. nails   c. dado joints
   b. screws   d. dowels

4. The risers are usually _____ inch(es) thick.

   a. 1/2   c. 1
   b. 3/4   d. 2

5. The risers are face nailed to the riser cuts with _____ finishing nails.

   a. 8d   c. 16d
   b. 12d   d. 6d

B. Place the correct answer in the space provided.

1. The semihoused stringer saves _____ and _____ .

2. The disadvantages of a cutout stair stringer are _____ and _____ .

3. In most cases _____ is placed under the nose of each tread.

4. The treads are fastened to the risers with _____ .

C. Explain the difference between a cutout stringer and a semihoused stringer.

D. In the space provided sketch

1. a semihoused stringer.

2. a cutout stringer.

Unit 20 Stairs Built on Housed Stringers

A *housed stringer* staircase has dadoed stringers which receive the ends of the treads and risers. The treads and risers are wedged approximately 3/8 inch into the dado joints of the stringers, figure 20-1. Housed stair stringers are frequently constructed in mills but may be housed by the carpenter.

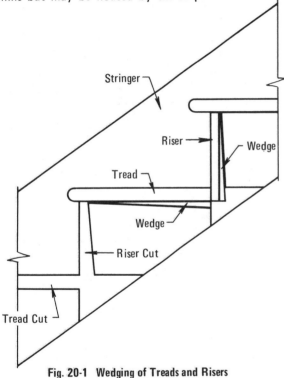

Fig. 20-1 Wedging of Treads and Risers

LAYOUT

Treads and Risers

The layout of the treads and risers is similar to that of the cutout stair stringer with this exception: before the stringer is laid out, a mark is gaged about 1 1/2 inches from the bottom edge of the face of each stringer. The gaged line acts as a measuring line. By using the line instead of the edge of the stringer, room is provided for the wedges which support the riser and tread boards. Figure 20-2 shows the position in which the framing square is used on the gaged line in laying out the stringer.

The marks of the individual risers and treads represent the outside faces of the tread and riser boards when they are placed in the stringers. To form the proper dado outlines for the risers, treads, and wedges, riser and tread templates are made and placed at the riser and tread marks on the stringers, figure 20-3.

Tread Templates

The tread template is laid out by drawing a straight line on the face of a board about 1/4" x 2" x

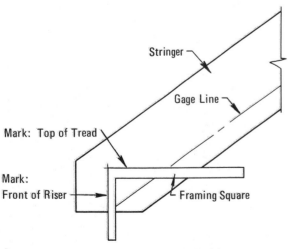

Fig. 20-2 Layout of Treads and Risers

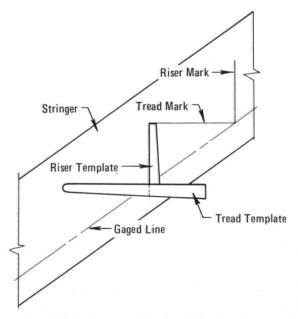

Fig. 20-3 Application of Tread and Riser Templates

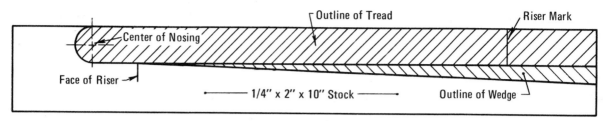

Fig. 20-4 Tread Template

14". On the straight line, draw the exact end section of the tread stock to be used; also draw the outline of the wedges to be used to tighten the tread boards in the dado joints of the stringer, figure 20-4. The exact width of the tread stock including the nosing is measured and marked on the template. This mark is also placed on the other face of the template so that the template may be used for both the right-hand and left-hand stringers. The center of the nosing profile is also located on the template, and is transferred to the other side by drilling a small hole through the template.

Riser Templates

The riser template, figure 20-5, is laid out in a similar manner by using the end section of a riser board and the wedge outline on a thin piece of board. The template is placed with its straight edge along the riser marks on the stringer. The outline of the tapered side of the template is then marked on the stringer face.

The tread template is placed with its straight edge on the tread mark of the stringer and the riser mark in line with the riser mark on the stringer. The location of the hole in the template is marked on the stringer with an awl. The marked point shows the center of the hole that is to be bored in the stringer to form the round end of the dado for the nosing of the tread.

The nosing at the floor line is laid out with the tread template to show the same nosing projection from the face of the riser as the other treads. The riser cut directly below the nosing is cut completely through the stringer and the top riser is nailed to the surface of the stringer.

The length of the treads is determined. They are then cut and inserted into the tread dadoes. They are wedged, glued, and nailed into the ends of the treads, from the outside of the stringers. All risers, except the highest one, are cut the same length as the treads. The top riser is about 1 1/4 inches longer. It does not fit into the dado cuts, but extends to the outside of the stringers. The other riser boards are inserted, wedged, glued, and nailed into the riser dadoes.

Joints

Some stairs are built with a rabbeted joint at the back of the tread and at the top of the riser. However, if the treads and risers are jointed, wedged, and nailed in the proper position, a butt joint is satisfactory.

STOCK

Stock for the various parts of stairs is usually obtained from a mill in a partially finished form.

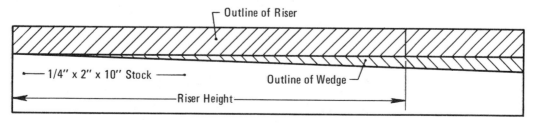

Fig. 20-5 Riser Template

Treads and risers may be obtained completely machined and sanded, but usually need to be cut down to size. Rabbeted nosing stock for the edge of the landing or for the top step is usually obtainable in rough lengths. Standard wedges are also available. If the mill is furnished with the exact dimensions of the stairwell, the parts can be completely machined and then assembled on the job.

HOW TO LAY OUT AND HOUSE STRINGERS

1. Select stock at least 1 1/16 inches thick and from 10 1/2 to 14 inches wide. Length depends on the length of the stairs. Allow about one foot at each end for the top and bottom cuts of the stringer.

Fig. 20-6 Marking Gage

Note: If regular tread stock is used for the stringers, plane the nosed surface flat so that molding may be fitted to the surface after the stairs are positioned.

2. Plane the bottom edge of the stringer so that it is straight.

3. Set a marking gage on about 1 1/2 inches and gage a line from the bottom edge of the stringer. A *marking gage* is a tool used to scribe a line parallel to the edge of a piece of work, figure 20-6.

4. Lay out the tread and riser marks with a steel square. Use a scratch awl or a fine, hard-lead pencil to mark the stringers.

5. Lay out the right-hand and left-hand stringers. Be sure to check them for accuracy before doing any template or housing work.

   If the layout is accurate, the markings on the stringers will match when they are placed together.

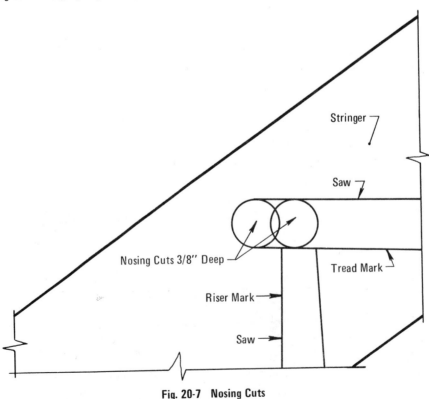

Fig. 20-7 Nosing Cuts

6. Place the straight edge of the tread template over a tread mark on the stringer. Adjust it so that the riser mark on the template is exactly in line with the riser mark on the stringer. Mark a point on the stringer by putting the scratch awl through the hole in the template to locate the center of the nosing. Also mark along both sides of the template on the stringer.

7. Bore a hole 3/8 inch deep, using the point marked through the tread template as the center. Locate the center of a second hole so that it will overlap the first and be within the top and bottom lines of the tread, figure 20-7.

8. Use the back of a 1 1/2-inch butt chisel to chisel along the tread marks between the holes.

9. Make a 3/8-inch cut along the tread marks with a backsaw. Start with the tip of the saw at the holes and continue back the length of the tread mark.

   Note: When using the backsaw to cut the housed joints, tip the saw so that the edges of the joint will be *undercut;* that is, with the edge at an angle but not perpendicular. This will allow a tighter joint between the top of the tread and the stringer cut and will help hold the wedge between the bottom of the tread and the edge of the housing.

10. Chisel out the stock between the cuts. Remove the chiseled stock carefully to a depth of 1/4 inch. The remaining 1/8 inch will be taken out by a router.

11. Set the router to take a cut 3/8 inch deep and use it to form an even joint.

12. Cut the other tread housings in the same manner.

13. Mark the riser cuts by placing the riser template with its straight edge exactly over the riser mark on the stringer. Mark along the opposite edge of the template on the stringer.

14. Cut along these lines with the backsaw. Chisel and rout out the stock as it was done for the treads.

15. Finish cutting and routing for all treads and risers including nosings at the top of both stringers.

16. Make the top and bottom cuts of both stringers with a crosscut saw.

HOW TO ASSEMBLE STAIRS

1. Select clear stock which is free from imperfections and sanded to a finish on all surfaces which will be exposed on the assembled stairs.

2. Square and cut the pieces.

   Note: Assume that the distance between the two walls of the stairwell is 3 feet 6 inches.

3. Check the width of the stairwell at the top and bottom and at several intermediate points to be certain that no distance measures less than 3 feet 6 inches. The assembled stairs will then easily fit between the walls.

4. Deduct from this assumed distance of 3 feet 6 inches twice the thickness of a stringer from the bottom of the housed joint to the outside face of the stringer. Subtract one inch from this figure.

   Note: Assuming that the stringers are 1 1/16 inches thick, the distance from the bottom of the housed joint to the outside face of the stringer is 11/16 inch. Adding 11/16 inch for the other stringer gives 22/16 inch or 1 3/8 inches. Three feet 6 inches minus 1 3/8 inches equals 3 feet 4 5/8 inches. Subtracting 1 inch from this figure gives 3 feet 3 5/8 inches, the length of the treads. The 1 inch is an allowance for fitting the assembled stairs in the wellhole. Also, stairs have a tendency to spread when assembled. The space between the stringer and wall will later be covered with molding.

5. Square and cut the treads and the nosed piece for the stop step.

6. Rip the required number of wedges for risers and treads or obtain them precut.

7. Place the stringers on sawhorses which are toenailed to the subfloor and spaced far enough

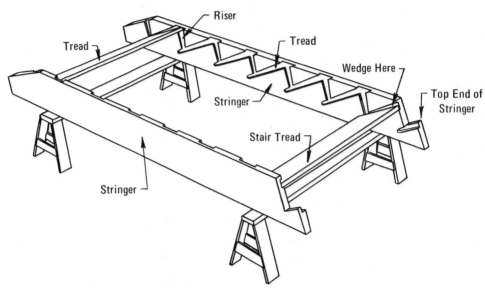

Fig. 20-8 Partially Assembled Stairs

apart to properly support the length of the stringers, figure 20-8.

8. Apply glue to the housed joint in which the tread is to be inserted.

9. Insert a tread in the top housing of one stringer and tap it so that the nosed section fits into the curved part of the housed joint.

10. Apply glue to the wedge and drive it between the bottom side of the tread and the edge of the housing. Drive the tread and the wedge alternately until the tread nosing and the top surface of the tread fit perfectly against the edges of the housed joint that will be exposed in the assembled stairs. The back edge of the tread must also be in line with the riser cut of the riser housing.

11. Pull the stringer tightly against the tread end by driving an 8d common nail through the stringer into the nosing. Drive at least two more nails into the tread. Use more nails if needed to bring the tread tightly against the bottom of the housed joint.

12. Insert the bottom tread in the bottom housing of the same stringer and fasten it to the stringer in the same manner.

13. Insert the opposite ends of the treads in the top and bottom housings of the opposite stringer and fasten them in the same manner.

14. Toenail the top edge of one stringer to the tops of both sawhorses with 8d finishing nails. Be certain that the stringer is straight. Place a steel square between the back edge of the top tread and the surface of the stringer. Bring the stairs into a square position at this point and toenail the loose stringer to the sawhorses. Check the diagonally opposite corners of the stairs for squareness.

15. Insert the remaining treads and fasten them into the housings in a similar fashion.

Note: Be certain that the back edge of each tread is perfectly flush with the front cut of each riser housing. If any are not, chisel off the riser cut until it is even with the back edge of the tread. If the tread projects beyond this point, carefully plane or chisel off the back edge of the tread to form a straight line.

16. Cut the risers the same length as the treads. The top riser should be about 1 3/8 inches longer than the remaining risers since it must be face nailed to the stringers at the top cut.

17. Nail the top riser to the stringers and to the back edge of the top tread. Be sure that the top of this riser is even with the bottom of the housed joint of the nosing.

18. Rip the bottom riser to the proper width and insert it into the bottom riser housings.

19. Install the remaining risers and fasten them in the same manner as the treads were fastened.

20. Nail the back of the risers to the back edges of the treads with 8d common nails spaced about 8 inches apart.

21. Cut angle blocks from a 2 x 4. Glue and nail them in place with shingle nails. Put one block in the middle of the stair width at the intersection of the back surface of each riser and tread.

22. Loosen the stringers from the horses, turn the stairs over, and fit molding underneath the nosing. Nail molding to both the riser and tread surfaces with 1 1/4-inch brads.

23. Nail through the top surfaces of the treads into the risers with 8d finishing nails. Space the nails about 8 inches apart and set.

HOW TO POSITION STAIRS IN A WELLHOLE

1. Place the stairs in the wellhole with the top riser against the header. Adjust the top edge of the housed joint of the nosing so that it is level with the top of the finished floor. It may be necessary to shim the back of the top riser out from the face of the header on one side of the well.

2. Center the stairs between the two sidewalls of the well and nail the riser securely to the header.

    Note: If the finish floor has not been laid, be sure to use blocks of finish floor stock under the bottom ends of the stringers.

3. Locate the studs in the sidewalls. Nail through the stringers into the studs with 10d or 12d finishing nails.

4. Insert the rabbeted nosed piece into the top nosing housed joints and fit it firmly against the top of the subfloor or header over its entire length. Nail it to the header so that it will be forced tightly into the housed joints.

5. Set the nails and cover the stairs with building paper and wood cleats to protect the nosings and other surfaces.

6. Cut and fit molding against the top of the stringers at the sidewalls of the wellhole and under the top nosing of the stairs.

REVIEW

A. Choose the best answer or answers to complete each statement.

1. The treads of a housed stringer staircase extend _____ inch into the stringer.

   a. 1/2   c. 3/8
   b. 5/8   d. 3/4

2. To tighten tread boards in dado joints, _____ are used.

   a. screws   c. nails
   b. wedges   d. staples

3. The top riser is about _____ inch(es) longer than the other risers.

   a. 3/4   c. 2
   b. 1/2   d. 1 1/4

4. A tool used to scribe a line parallel to the edge of a board is called a (an)
   _____ .

   a. marking gage   c. gage
   b. awl   d. square

5. A (an)_____ is used to even out the dado joint of a housed stringer.

   a. awl   c. marking gage
   b. router   d. chisel

B. Place the correct answer in the space provided.

   1. The tread template is laid out on a _____ .

   2. Treads are fastened with _____ , _____ ,
      and _____ .

   3. When laying out a stringer, the tread template is placed _____ .

   4. The tools used in cutting housed joints are _____ .
      _____ , and _____ .

   5. The top riser is about _____ inch(es) longer than the other risers.

C. In the space provided sketch

   1. a tread template.

   2. one section of a housed stringer.

Unit 21 Built-in Furniture

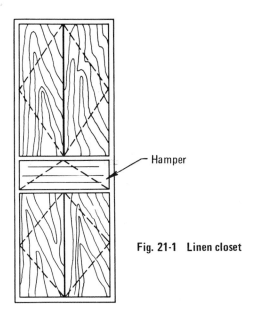

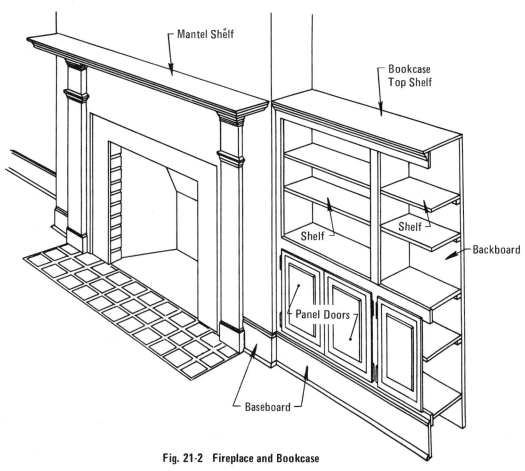

Built-in furniture is furniture which is permanently fastened to the wall of a structure. Linen closets, cabinets, and room dividers are all classified as built-ins.

The built-in features of a house are important in obtaining the maximum amount of convenient storage space. Built-ins may be used in virtually every part of the house to utilize space.

LINEN CLOSETS

Linen closets are used for the storage of blankets, sheets, and towels. The closet may have shelves in the upper part and drawers or a hamper for soiled clothes in the lower section, figure 21-1. If the closet is to be used for storing woolens, it may be lined with cedar.

Fig. 21-1 Linen closet

Fig. 21-2 Fireplace and Bookcase

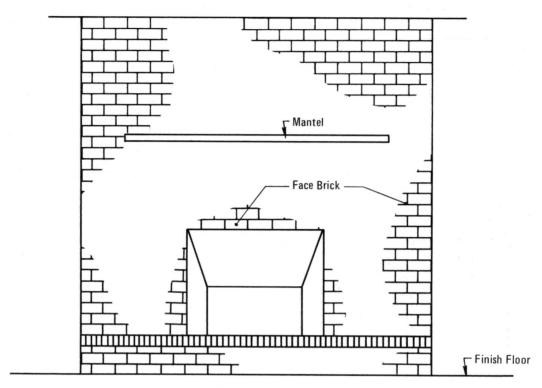

Fig. 21-3 Fireplace Elevation

BUILT-IN BOOKCASES

Built-in bookcases are frequently found in living rooms or dens. They are often built in conjunction with mantel shelves and around fireplaces, figure 21-2. They may be equipped with doors, but more frequently are built without doors and with adjustable shelves. The style and layout of built-in bookcases depend on the availability of space and architectural style, but the general framing and shelf construction is similar to that of kitchen cabinets.

MANTEL SHELVES

Fireplaces are sometimes decorated by placing a mantel shelf above the opening, figure 21-3. The shelf may be almost any height and size, depending on the size and shape of the chimney.

When the brickwork of the fireplace is built flush with the finished wall line, a casing, frieze and cap are built around the brickwork, forming a shelf at the top, figure 21-4.

Mantels and fireplace trim may be built by the carpenter or obtained in standard sizes and styles from mills and assembled on the job.

ROOM DIVIDERS

Room dividers are used to separate a room into two or more parts. Room dividers can be used to separate a dining room from a living room, separate a

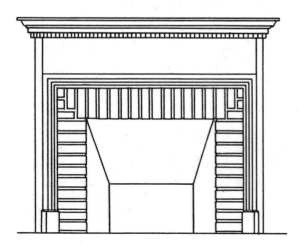

Fig. 21-4 Fireplace With Flush Mantel

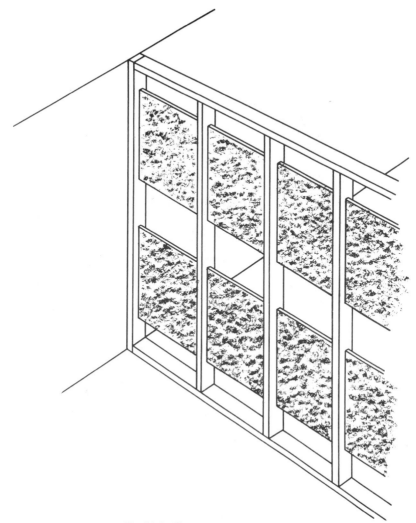

Fig. 21-5   Floor-to-Ceiling Room Divider

room for two children, or provide a wall for an entrance hallway. There are two basic types of room dividers: the divider which extends from floor to ceiling, figure 21-5; and the divider which is a half-solid, half-open construction, figure 21-6. Room dividers can be built on the job, or sculptured grill-work can be obtained assembled on the job site.

HOW TO BUILD A LINEN CLOSET

1. Mark the locations of the shelf cleats on one end wall of the closet. Use a level to mark the opposite end wall the same distance from the ceiling.

2. Nail the shelf cleats flush with the marks on the wall, making sure that the nails penetrate a stud.

3. Cut, fit, and nail the shelves on the cleats. The shelves should be cut 1/4 inch shorter than the width of the closet.

4. Lay out the doors. A lip door, the easiest door to fit, is most often used for linen closets.

5. Cut the door and lip to the proper dimensions.

6. Fit the doors.

HOW TO BUILD A BOOKCASE

1. Build a bottom platform of 2 x 4s, figure 21-7. The width of the platform will vary, but the depth should be a constant 12 inches.

2. Cover the platform with 3/4-inch plywood.

3. Cut two sides for the bookcase.

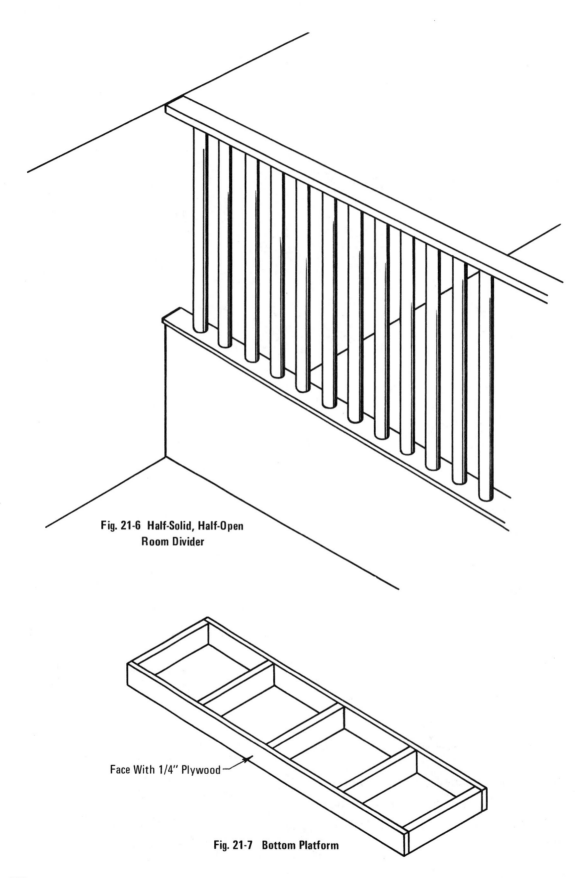

Fig. 21-6   Half-Solid, Half-Open
Room Divider

Face With 1/4" Plywood

Fig. 21-7   Bottom Platform

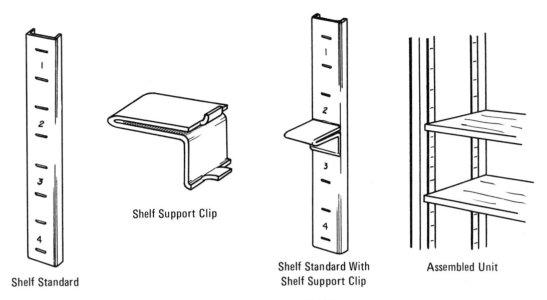

Shelf Support Clip

Shelf Standard

Shelf Standard With
Shelf Support Clip

Assembled Unit

Fig. 21-8 Adjustable Shelf Parts

4. Cut a 1/4″ x 3/8″ rabbet joint in the back of the two sides.

5. Make some provision for adjustable shelves. One of the most widely used methods of supporting adjustable shelves is the metal shelf support strip, figure 21-8.

6. Place and secure a piece of 1/4-inch plywood in the rabbet joints.

7. Place the sides and back in position and secure them to the walls.

8. Cut the shelves to the proper length and place them in position.

9. Cut rails and stiles and place them accordingly.

Note: A furring strip can add a decorative touch to the bookcase, figure 21-9.

HOW TO BUILD A MANTEL SHELF

Note: This is only one of several techniques used for building mantel shelves. Another popular method consists of a 3 x 12 timber attached directly to the exposed brick of the chimney, figure 21-11.

Fig. 21-9 Two Types of Furring for Bookcases

Fig. 21-10 Location of Assembled Mantel Shelf

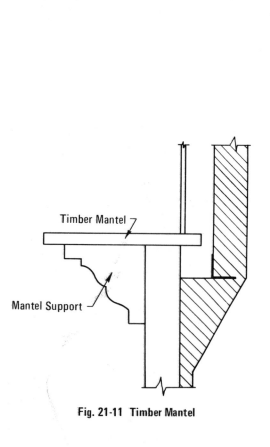

Timber Mantel

Mantel Support

Fig. 21-11 Timber Mantel

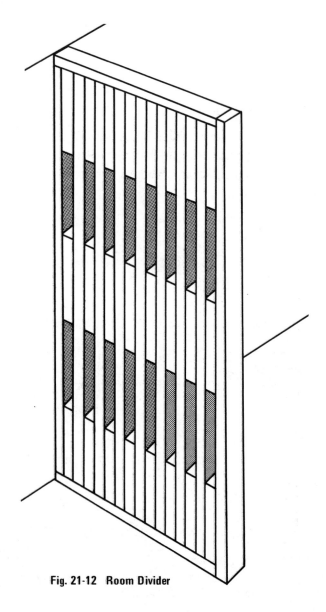

Fig. 21-12 Room Divider

1. Lay out the length and width of the pilasters and frieze according to the size of the chimney. Cut them accordingly. *Pilasters* are the vertical members of the fireplace. The *frieze* is the horizontal member directly below the mantel.

2. Lay out and build the shelf according to the width of the chimney.

3. Assemble the frieze and pilasters by nailing them in a plumb position on the wall. They should overlap the sides of the chimney about 1 inch.

4. Place wooden plugs in the masonry joints so that the mantel shelf may be securely attached to the masonry surface.

5. Place the assembled mantel shelf on top of the pilasters across the face of the chimney, figure 21-10. After making sure it is level, nail it to the wooden plugs in the masonry joints.

   Note: It is sometimes necessary to scribe the shelf to the wall surface. A small piece of molding may be used to cover an unscribed joint.

   The surface of the **pilasters and frieze** may be decorated by *fluting*, a form of channeling for decoration; by forming miniature columns and bases; or by mitering molding in various designs.

6. Set all nails and sand the surfaces.

HOW TO BUILD A ROOM DIVIDER

1. Locate the position of the room divider and snap a chalk line.

2. Nail a 2 x 4 bottom plate in position, using the chalk line as a guide.

3. Place a stud against the existing wall, plumb it, and nail it in place.

4. Using the plumbed stud as a starting point, snap a chalk line on the ceiling parallel to the bottom plate.

5. Nail a top plate to the ceiling, using the chalk line as a guide.

6. Nail an 18-inch block at the bottom, top, and middle of the first stud.

7. Place a full-length board against the three blocks and nail it in place.

8. Repeat the process alternating the three blocks and full-length studs until the desired length is reached, figure 21-12.

REVIEW

A. Place the correct answer in the space provided.

1. Built-in furniture may be defined as _____ .

2. Linen closets are used for _____ .

3. Built-in bookcases should have _____ shelves.

4. A fireplace is sometimes decorated by a _____ .

5. The _____ and _____ are two types of room dividers.

6. Closet shelves are sometimes supported by _____ .

7. The first step in the construction of a room divider is_____
   _____ .

8. To protect woolens, closets can be _____ .

9. Built-ins are used mainly to _____ .

B. In the space provided design a

1. floor-to-ceiling room divider.

2. linen closet front.

3. bookcase.

4. fireplace mantel.

Unit 22 Finish Hardware

The proper selection and installation of hardware aids in the easy and convenient operation of windows and doors. Hardware can be chosen from a variety of patterns and designs to fit the decor of a room.

MATERIALS USED IN HARDWARE

Much of the hardware for both interior and exterior use is made of steel or iron. Since these materials do not present an attractive finish and rust rapidly when exposed to the weather, the hardware is usually given a coating or finish.

Chromium plating over steel hardware provides a rust-resistant, smooth, attractive finish which is easy to clean. Cadmium-plated steel hardware is highly rust-resistant but is not particularly attractive. It is frequently used for interior hardware which is not visible and for exteriors where appearance is not important, such as in garages and cellars. Steel hardware which is brass-plated provides an attractive finish but is not rust-resistant and should not be exposed to weather. Steel hardware is frequently given a first coat of metal primer in the factory, a process known as *prime coating* and is later finished with additional coats of paint on the job site. To obtain an antique or rustic effect, wrought iron is often given a rough black finish.

Any exterior steel hardware, regardless of the coatings used, may eventually rust. Rust prevents proper function of the hardware and causes stains on the surface of the building. To overcome the problem of rust, much hardware is made of a solid rustproof metal, such as brass or bronze. This hardware is considerably more expensive than coated steel, but it is more satisfactory for outside use and may be obtained in various finishes.

All screws for exterior hardware should be rustproof. Brass screws will not rust and present an attractive appearance. They are not strong, however, and tend to shear off if turned with too much force. Cadmium-plated steel screws provide both strength and rustproofing qualities.

HARDWARE FOR DOORS

The hardware needed for a typical door consists of a pair of butt hinges, a mortise or cylinder lock, and a doorstop. Exterior doors are usually hung with three butt hinges and may have an ornamental latch on the outside.

The *butt hinge*, figure 22-1, consists of two leaves and a loose pin. Since the hinges are mortised into the door and jamb, they are slightly offset or swaged so that the leaves are close together, figure 22-2. One leaf of each hinge is attached to the jamb; the other leaf is fastened to the door. When the door is set in its proper position, the loose pin is placed in the opening, holding the two halves of the hinge together. Butt hinges are made in different sizes, weights, and types of bearing surfaces. However, only a few sizes are generally used in light construction. The size of a hinge is determined by the length of the leaf and the distance between the outer edges of the two leaves when the hinge is open. When ordering hinges, the length of the leaf is always stated first.

A *door lock* usually consists of a latch bolt operated by either a knob or thumb latch and a guard bolt operated by a key. Locks are usually placed in the side or edge of a door. A strike is mortised into

Fig. 22-1 Butt Hinge

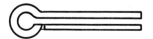

Fig. 22-2 Swaged Hinges

Fig. 22-3 Door Lock

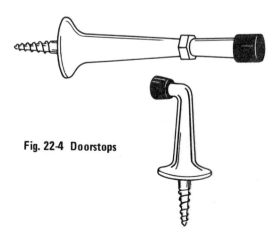

Fig. 22-4 Doorstops

the jamb to receive the bolts when the door is closed, figure 22-3.

Doorstops, figure 22-4, prevent both the door striking the baseboard and the doorknob from striking the wall. They are usually cast iron or brass and have a rubber tip. Doorstops are screwed into the baseboard or floor.

CABINET HARDWARE

Cabinet doors require hinges, a handle for opening the door, and a device for holding the door closed.

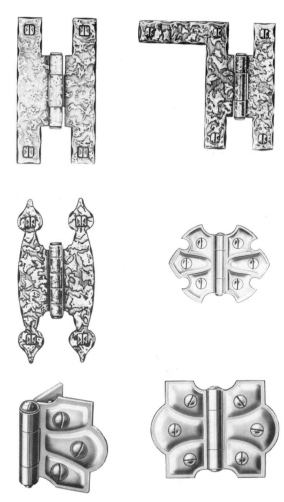

**Fig. 22-5 Ornamental Cabinet Hinges
For Flush Cabinet Doors**

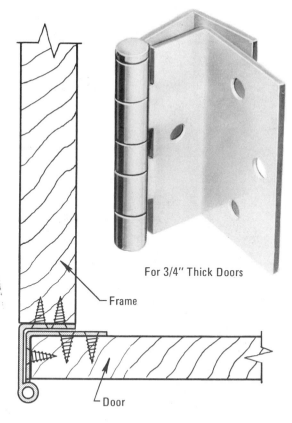

For 3/4" Thick Doors

Fig. 22-6 Wraparound Cabinet Hinge

For flush doors, small loose-pin butt hinges or ornamental surface hinges, figure 22-5, may be used.
If the flush door is constructed of plywood, the wraparound cabinet hinge, figure 22-6, holds more effic-
iently than a regular butt hinge since it is fastened
not only to the edge but also to the back of the door.
If the door has a lip, an offset hinge may be used,
figure 22-7.

　　To hold the cabinet door in position, a roller
catch, figure 22-9, or a magnetic catch, figure 22-8, is
usually used. There are several variations of the roller
catch and the magnetic catch. The magnetic catch
can be used for a pair of cabinet doors or one full-
sized door, figure 22-10.

　　A simple door pull or doorknob, figure 22-11,
is usually placed in the right-hand or left-hand corner

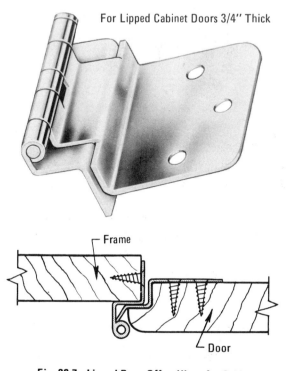

For Lipped Cabinet Doors 3/4" Thick

Fig. 22-7 Lipped-Door Offset Hinge for Cabinet

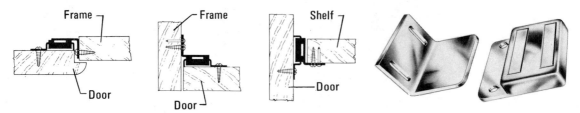

Fig. 22-8 Magnetic Catch for Lipped, Flush, and Overlay Cabinet Doors

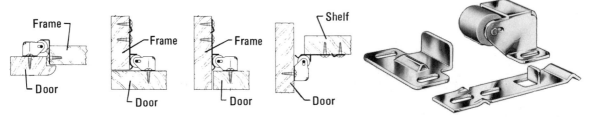

Fig. 22-9 Single Roller Catch for Lipped, Flush, and Overlay Cabinet Doors

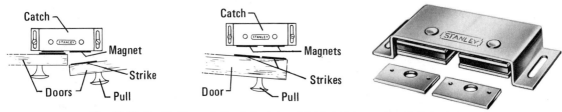

Fig. 22-10 Double Magnetic Catch for Pairs of Cabinet Doors or One Full-sized Door

Fig. 22-11 Door Knob and Door Pull

of each cabinet door to facilitate the opening of the door. A matching drawer pull or knob is placed on the front of each drawer. Two pulls are used for bigger drawers.

Cabinet hardware such as drawer pulls, friction catches, and latch door handles are usually accompanied by instructions for their installation. These instructions should be carefully followed. Templates are also usually included.

HOW TO INSTALL MORTISE LOCKS

1. Mark the location of the lock 36 inches from the floor, figure 22-12.

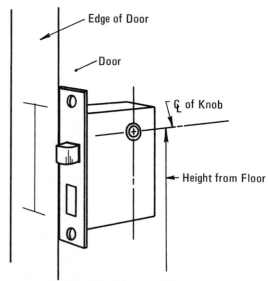

Fig. 22-12 Lock Located On Door

2. Keeping the face of the lock flush with the edge of the door, mark the door through the knob spindle hole. While the lock is in position, mark

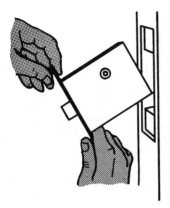

Fig. 22-13 Placing Lock Case Into Mortise

**Fig. 22-14 Installing Self-aligning Knob
and Escutcheon Assembly**

the top and bottom of the case on the edge of the door.

3. Mark a vertical centerline on the edge of the door between the top and bottom mark.

4. Measure the thickness of the lock case. Use an auger bit about 1/4 inch larger than the case to bore holes into the stile of the door. The depth of the holes should be equal to the depth of the

lock. Space the holes so that they overlap and so that the spur of the bit is on the centerline.

5. Use a 1/4-inch and 3/4-inch chisel to clean out the holes in the door stile. This forms the mortise into which the lock case will be inserted.

6. Place the lock in the mortise so that the faceplate fits evenly against the edge of the door. Mark the outline of the faceplate on the edge of

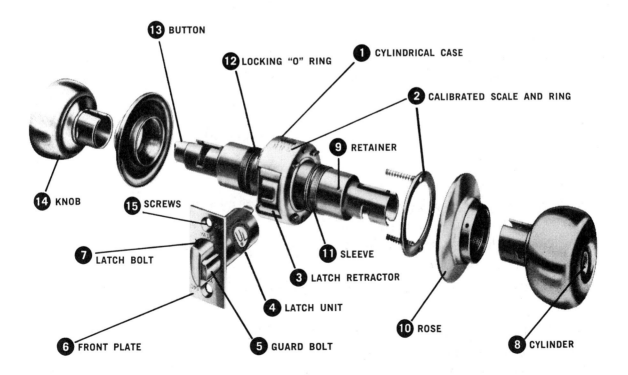

Fig. 22-15 Parts of a Cylinder Lock

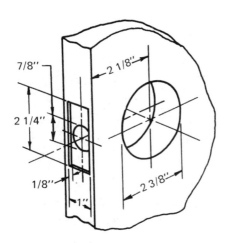

Fig. 22-16 Cutout of Cylinder Lock

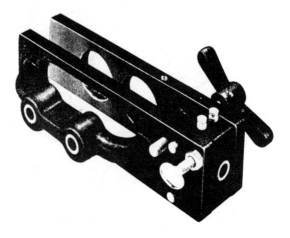

Fig. 22-17 Boring Jig

the door by cutting into the wood about 1/8 inch with a knife.

7. Make a groove in the outline as deep as the thickness of the faceplate.

8. Fit the faceplate flush against the edge of the door and tap it into the opening with a block of wood and a hammer.

9. Remove the lock and carefully bore the spindle hole as marked on the side of the door. Bore from one side of the door until the point of the bit is visible; finish the hole from the opposite side.

10. Replace the lock, figure 22-13. Be sure that the spindle hole is large enough to prevent the spindle from binding.

11. Fasten the faceplate onto the edge of the door.

12. Install the knob, spindle, bolt and side escutcheons, figure 22-14. Adjust the knobs on the spindle bolt to hold the escutcheons tightly against the surface of the door.

13. Be certain the doorknobs, key, and latch work freely.

14. Open the door slightly, turn the guard bolt of the lock out and mark the location of the dead bolt and latch on the jamb edge.

15. Place the strike plate on the faceplate of the lock

and mark the strike vertically along the outside edge of the door.

16. Place the strike plate on the doorjamb and line up the guard bolt and the latch openings of the strike plate with the markings which were placed on the jamb in step 14. Also, keep the vertical mark on the strike plate in line with the edge of the doorjamb.

17. Mark the outline of the strike plate on the face of the jamb with a knife.

18. Make a groove in the outline the depth of the strike plate. Mark the locations of the guard bolt and latch openings on the jamb and cut out the wood so that when the plate is fastened in place, the guard bolt and latch will enter the holes freely.

19. Test all parts for workability.

HOW TO INSTALL CYLINDER LOCKS

Note: Figure 22-15 shows the typical construction features of a cylinder lock.

1. Measure 36 inches from the floor and mark a line on the face of the door parallel to the floor.

2. Measure 2 3/8 inches from the edge of the door and mark a vertical line.

3. Mark a line indicating the height of the lock across the edge of the door and locate the center of the door.

4. Bore a 2 1/8-inch hole through the face of the door and a 7/8-inch hole into the edge of the door, figure 22-16.

   Note: For quick, accurate installation, a boring jig is sometimes used, figure 22-17.

5. Mortise out space for the latch front and install the latch unit.

6. Mark a line indicating height of the strike and cut a mortise in the jamb for the strike and box.

7. Place the strike plate on the doorjamb.

8. Install the lock and knob, adjusting the lock according to the manufacturer's specifications.

REVIEW

A. Place the correct answer in the space provided.

1. Interior and exterior hardware may be constructed of _____ , _____ , or _____ .

2. A disadvantage of iron and steel hardware is _____ _____ .

3. Screws for exterior hardware should be _____ -proof.

4. The size of a hinge is determined by the _____ .

5. The purpose of a doorstop is to _____ .

6. Cabinet doors are held in position with a _____ .

7. A lock is usually placed _____ from the floor.

8. A _____ is used to clean out the mortise.

9. A cylinder lock has a _____ inch hole bored through the face of the door.

B. In the space provided sketch

1. a butt hinge.

2. a wraparound hinge.

3. an offset hinge.

C.   Identify the parts of the cylinder lock in the figure.

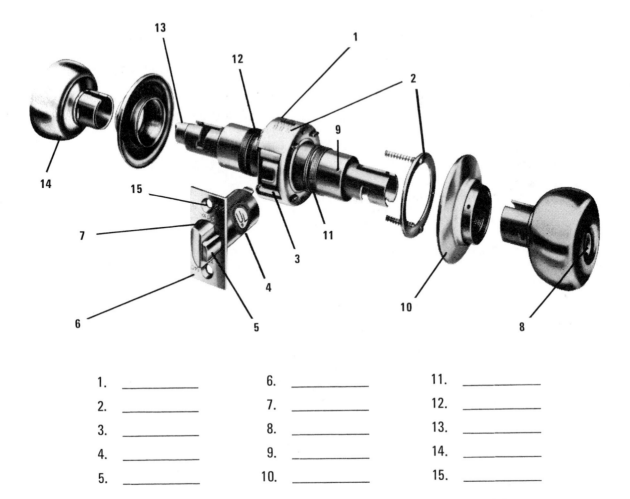

1. _____	6. _____	11. _____
2. _____	7. _____	12. _____
3. _____	8. _____	13. _____
4. _____	9. _____	14. _____
5. _____	10. _____	15. _____

APPENDIX

Table I Common English Measurement Conversion
Linear Measure
12 inches (in.) = 1 foot (ft.)
3 feet = 1 yard (yd.)
Surface Measure
144 sq. in. = 1 sq. ft.
9 sq. ft. = 1 sq. yd.
Cubic Measure
1728 cu. in. = 1 cu. ft.
27 cu. ft. = 1 cu. yd.

Table II   Fractional and Decimal Equivalents to Millimeters

Inches	Decimal Equivalents In Inches	Millimeters	Inches	Decimal Equivalents In Inches	Millimeters
1/64	.015625	0.397	33/64	.515625	13.097
1/32	.03125	0.794	17/32	.53125	13.494
3/64	.046875	1.191	35/64	.546875	13.890
1/16	.0625	1.587	9/16	.5625	14.287
5/64	.078125	1.984	37/64	.578125	14.684
3/32	.09375	2.381	19/32	.59375	15.081
7/64	.109375	2.778	39/64	.609375	15.478
1/8	.125	3.175	5/8	.625	15.875
9/64	.140625	3.572	41/64	.640625	16.272
5/32	.15625	3.969	21/32	.65625	16.669
11/64	.171875	4.366	43/64	.671875	17.065
3/16	.1875	4.762	11/16	.6875	17.462
13/64	.203125	5.159	45/64	.703125	17.859
7/32	.21875	5.556	23/32	.71875	18.256
15/64	.234375	5.953	47/64	.734375	18.653
1/4	.25	6.350	3/4	.75	19.050
17/64	.265625	6.747	49/64	.765625	19.447
9/32	.28125	7.144	25/32	.78125	19.844
19/64	.296875	7.541	51/64	.796875	20.240
5/16	.3125	7.937	13/16	.8125	20.637
21/64	.328125	8.334	53/64	.828125	21.034
11/32	.34375	8.731	27/32	.84375	21.431
23/64	.359375	9.128	55/64	.859375	21.828
3/8	.375	9.525	7/8	.875	22.225
25/64	.390625	9.922	57/64	.890625	22.622
13/32	.40625	10.319	29/32	.90625	23.019
27/64	.421875	10.716	59/64	.921875	23.415
7/16	.4375	11.113	15/16	.9375	23.812
29/64	.453125	11.509	61/64	.953125	24.209
15/32	.46875	11.906	31/32	.96875	24.606
31/64	.484375	12.303	63/64	.984375	25.003
1/2	.5	12.700	1	1	25.400

Table III   Millimeters to Decimal Inches

Mm In.	Mm In.	Mm In.	Mm In.	Mm In.
1 = 0.0394	21 = 0.8268	41 = 1.6142	61 = 2.4016	81 = 3.1890
2 = 0.0787	22 = 0.8662	42 = 1.6536	62 = 2.4410	82 = 3.2284
3 = 0.1181	23 = 0.9055	43 = 1.6929	63 = 2.4804	83 = 3.2678
4 = 0.1575	24 = 0.9449	44 = 1.7323	64 = 2.5197	84 = 3.3071
5 = 0.1969	25 = 0.9843	45 = 1.7717	65 = 2.5591	85 = 3.3465
6 = 0.2362	26 = 1.0236	46 = 1.8111	66 = 2.5985	86 = 3.3859
7 = 0.2756	27 = 1.0630	47 = 1.8504	67 = 2.6378	87 = 3.4253
8 = 0.3150	28 = 1.1024	48 = 1.8898	68 = 2.6772	88 = 3.4646
9 = 0.3543	29 = 1.1418	49 = 1.9292	69 = 2.7166	89 = 3.5040
10 = 0.3937	30 = 1.1811	50 = 1.9685	70 = 2.7560	90 = 3.5434
11 = 0.4331	31 = 1.2205	51 = 2.0079	71 = 2.7953	91 = 3.5827
12 = 0.4724	32 = 1.2599	52 = 2.0473	72 = 2.8247	92 = 3.6221
13 = 0.5118	33 = 1.2992	53 = 2.0867	73 = 2.8741	93 = 3.6615
14 = 0.5512	34 = 1.3386	54 = 2.1260	74 = 2.9134	94 = 3.7009
15 = 0.5906	35 = 1.3780	55 = 2.1654	75 = 2.9528	95 = 3.7402
16 = 0.6299	36 = 1.4173	56 = 2.2048	76 = 2.9922	96 = 3.7796
17 = 0.6693	37 = 1.4567	57 = 2.2441	77 = 3.0316	97 = 3.8190
18 = 0.7087	38 = 1.4961	58 = 2.2835	78 = 2.0709	98 = 3.8583
19 = 0.7480	39 = 1.5355	59 = 2.3229	79 = 3.1103	99 = 3.8977
20 = 0.7874	40 = 1.5748	60 = 2.3622	80 = 3.1497	100 = 3.9371

Table IV   Metric Measure

Linear Measure		
Unit	**Symbol or Abbreviation**	**Value in Meters**
Millimeters	mm.	0.001
Centimeter	cm.	0.01
Decimeter	dm.	0.1
Meter	m.	1.0
Surface Measure		
Unit	**Symbol or Abbreviation**	**Value in Sq. Meters**
Square millimeter	$mm.^2$	0.000001
Square centimeter	$cm.^2$	0.0001
Square decimeter	$d.^2$	0.01
Square meter (centiare)	$m.^2$	1.0

Table 5   Architectural Symbols

IN SECTION

	BRICK
	STONE
	CONCRETE
	EARTH

ELECTRICAL

	CEILING OUTLET
	WALL BRACKET OUTLET
	DUPLEX OUTLET
S_1	SWITCH (Single Pole)
S_3	3-WAY SWITCH

PLUMBING

	COLD WATER
	HOT WATER
	ROLL RIM TUB
	ANGLE TUB
	SHOWER STALL
	WATER CLOSET
	BIDET
	URINAL STALL TYPE
	LAVATORY
	KITCHEN SINK R & L DRAIN BOARD

	COMBINATION SINK AND DISHWASHER
HWT	HOT WATER TANK
M	WATER METER
	HOSE BIBB OR FAUCET
D	DRAIN
R	GAS RANGE
D	DRYER
WM	WASHING MACHINE
	WALL—TYPE DRINKING FOUNTAIN
DW	DRY WELL
WH	WATER HEATER

HEATING AND VENTILATING

RAD	RADIATOR EXPOSED
	UNIT HEATER
	UNIT VENTILATOR
	TRAP THERMOSTATIC
	TRAP – FLOAT AND THERMOSTAT
	TRAP BOILER RETURN
	VALVE AIR LINE

	VALVE DIAPHRAGM
	VALVE STRAINER
T	THERMOSTAT

IN PLAN

	EXTERIOR DOOR (In Wood Part)
	WINDOW (In Wood Part)
	WINDOW (In Brick Veneer)
	WINDOW (In Brick Part)

METAL

	RADIATOR
	SUPPLY DUCT
	RETURN DUCT
	SUPPLY LINE
	RETURN LINE
	RISER
	RETURN

ACKNOWLEDGMENTS

The author wishes to express his appreciation to the following for contributing illustrations which appear in this text.

ALCOA BUILDING PRODUCTS, INC., Figure 5-7

AMERICAN HARDBOARD ASSOCIATION, Figures 9-1, 12, 17, 18; 11-9

AMERICAN PLYWOOD ASSOCIATION, Figures 1-4 - - 6; 5-6; 9-2, 21, 22

ANDERSEN CORPORATION, Figures 7-1 - - 12, 14, 19, 24

ASPHALT ROOFING MANUFACTURING ASSOCIATION, Figures 1-8 - - 16; 3-1 - - 6, 8, 10 - - 12

CALIFORNIA REDWOOD ASSOCIATION, Figures 9-4 - - 6

CELOTEX CORPORATION, Figures 12-1 - - 5, 8 - - 12

COVER PHOTO, Barbara Schultz

EATON CORPORATION, Figures 22-3, 15, 17

GEORGIA—PACIFIC CORPORATION, Figures 6-1, 2, 4 - - 6; 11-5, 7, 8, 12

GYPSUM ASSOCIATION, Figures 10-1, 3 - - 5, 9, 13, 25

H.C. PRODUCTS COMPANY, Figures 6-13, 21 - - 23

JOHNS-MANSVILLE SALES CORPORATION, Figures 9-7 - - 9; 12-6, 7

L.E. JOHNSON, INC., Figures 6-11, 24, 25; 22-16

KNAPE & VOGT MANUFACTURING COMPANY, Figures 17-4, 5

MASONITE CORPORATION, Figures 9-13 - - 16; 11-1, 2, 4

RED CEDAR SHINGLE & HANDSPLIT SHAKE BUREAU, Figures 1-3, 2-1 - - 5, 8; 3-7; 9-3, 25

RIVIERA PRODUCTS, Figures 16-1, 3, 9; 17-2, 6, 8

SARGENT AND COMPANY, Figures 22-13, 14

STANLEY TOOLS, Figures 6-19; 13-6, 7; 15-19, 20; 16-7; 20-7; 21-8; 22-1, 22-5 - - 11, cover

UNITED STATES DEPARTMENT OF AGRICULTURE, FOREST SERVICE, FOREST PRODUCTS LABORATORY, Figures 14-1, 10, 16, cover

UNITED STATES GYPSUM, Figures 10-2, 6 - - 8, 10, 11, 12, 14 - - 24, 26; 11-10, cover

WESTERN WOOD MOULDING AND MILLWORK PRODUCERS, Figures 1-1, 2; 4-5, 6; 5-5; 8-1, 2, 5 8; 11-3, 6; 13-1 - - 5, 10, 11, 13 - - 15, artwork on title pages, and cover

WEYERHAEUSER COMPANY, Figure 6-3

Publications Director
Alan N. Knofla

Source Editor
Mary Grauerholz

Reviewers
John W. Schafer, James Murphy

Technical Advisor
Christopher T. Mahoney

Director of Manufacturing and Production
Frederick Sharer

Production Specialists

Patti Manuli, Jean Le Morta, Sharon Lynch,
Betty Michelfelder, Lee St. Onge

Illustrators
Anthony Canabush, Michael Kokernak, George Dowse, Chris Carline

INDEX

A

Acoustical ceilings, 98-102
Acoustical tile, 99-101
Adhesives and nails, 86
Aluminum siding, 72, 79
Apron, 64
Asbestos cement siding *See* Mineral fiber siding
Asphalt shingles, 17-22
Awl, 126-127
Awning windows, 55

B

Bagasse, 98
Bar clamp, 122
Bargeboard, 34
Baseboard, 110
Base cabinets
  bottom platform for, 130-134
  building of, 134-135
Base flashing, 5
Basement stairs, 157
  building of, 159-160
Base moldings, 105
Base show, 110
Bevel siding, 75-76
Blend joints, 122
Block flooring, 113-114
Bookcase, 171-173
Bottom platform, 130
Boxed cornice *See* Closed cornices
Built-in bookcases, 170
Built-in furniture, 169-175
  See also Built-in bookcases; Linen closets; Mantel shelves; Room dividers
Butt hinge, 177
Butt joints
  defined, 120
  making of, 122-124
Butts, 11
Bypassing doors *See* Sliding doors

C

Cabinet door
  construction of, 146
  sliding, 142
  swinging, 141-142
Cabinet drawers
  construction of, 140-141
  drawer guides, 140-141
Cabinet hardware, 178-180
Calcining, 82
Cant strip *See* starter strip
Cap flashing *See* Deck and counter flashing
Carriage, 148
Casement windows, 52
Ceiling moldings, 105, 107
Cement-asbestos, 98
Center guide, 141
Chair rails, 106, 109-110
Cleats, 157
Closed cornices, 25-31
  See also Snub cornice
Closed valley *See* Woven valley
Common crown molding, 105
Cone molding, 105
Coped corners, 105
Coping saws, 106
Corner guides, 140
Cornice, 25
Cornice members, 25-27
Cornice returns, 29
Cornices *See* Closed cornices
Countersinking, 93
Countertop, 135
Cricket, 5-6
Cripple, 65
Cupping, 122
Cutout stair stringers, 155-157
Cutout stringers, 159
Cylinder locks, 182-183

D

Dado head, 125
Dado joint
  defined, 121
  making of, 125
Deck and counter flashing, 5
Decking, 3
Door frame, installation of, 43-44
Door lock, 177-178
Doors, 41-48
  See also Flush doors; Folding doors; Panel doors; Sliding doors; Swinging doors
Doorstop, 63
Door trim, 63
Double-hung windows, 51-52
Dowel joints, 42
  defined, 122
  making of, 126-127
Drawer guides, 140-141
Drip edge, 25
Drop siding, 76-77

E

Eave, 25

Eaves flashing, 7
Eaves troughs *See* Gutters
End lap joint, 121
Exterior sidewall covering, 69-79

F

Face, 92
Face glazing, 59
Fasteners, 8
Feathering, 89-90
Finish fascia, 25
Finish hardware, 177-183
Fixed windows, 55-59
Flashing, 4-7
Flashing chimneys, 5-6
Flashing eaves, 7
Flashing pipes, 6-7
Flashing valleys, 4-5
Floating corners, 88
Flush doors, 41-42
Flush drawer, 140
Fluting, 175
Folding doors, 43, 48
Frieze, 25-26, 175
Furring strip, 37

G

Gain joint *See* Stop dada joint
Giant shingles
    American method of application, 22
    Dutch lap method of application, 22
Glue block, 148
Groove glazing, 59
Gutter, 31, 36, 38-39
Gypsum, 82
Gypsum wallboard, 82-90
    application of single-ply, 86-87
    concealing of joints, 89-90
    cutting of, 86
    two-ply, application, 87-88
    types of, 82-84

H

Half-turn stairs, 150
Hardboard paneling, 92, 93-94
Hardboard siding, 69, 73
Hardware
    for doors, 177-178
    materials used in, 177
Hardwood strip flooring, 112-113
Header, 66
Headroom, 148
Hex shingles, 21-22
Hips, 14, 20-21
Hopper windows, 55

Horizontal siding, 70
Horizontal sliding windows, 52-55
Housed stringer, 162-163, 164-165

I

Individual asphalt shingles, 17
Inswinging casement windows, 52

J

Jamb, 51
Jointer, 122
Joints, 120-127
    See also Butt joints; Dado joint; Dowel joint;
    Lap joint; Miter joint; Mortise and tenon joint;
    Rabbet joint
    concealment of, 89-90

K

Keel, 86
Kerf, 65
Keyed joints, 122
Kicker, 140-141
Kitchen cabinets, 130-137

L

Lap joint
    defined, 121
    making of, 125
Linen closets, 169, 171
Lip drawer, 140
Lookout ledger, 27
Lookouts, 25

M

Mantel shelves, 170, 173-175
Marking gage, 164
Matched siding *See* Drop siding
Miter box, 65
Mineral fiber fiber siding, 70-72, 77-78
Mineral-fiber ceiling, 98
Miter box, 106
Miter joint, 121-122
Moldings, 105
Mortise, 122
Mortise and tenon joints, 42
    defined, 122
    making of, 126
Mortise hinges, 45-48
Mortise locks, 180-182
Mullion, 51

N

Nails, 84-85
Nosing, 148

O

Open cornices, 34-39
    building the rake for, 38
    construction of, 36-37
    placing beaded ceiling stock on, 37

Open joints, 122
Open stringer stairs, 150-152
Outswinging casement windows, 52

P

Panel doors, 42
Paneling, 92-95
    See also Hardboard paneling; Plywood paneling;
    Solid wood paneling
Pilasters, 175
Pilot hole, 48
Pinned joints, 122
Plancier *See* Soffit
Plank flooring, 113
Plaster of paris, 82
Plinth block, 63
Plywood, 2
Plywood paneling, 92-93, 94-95
Plywood roof sheathing, 1
Plywood siding, 69, 73-74
Predecorated vinyl-covered panels, 88-89
Prefabricated cabinets, 130, 137
Prime coating, 177

Q

Quarter turn stairs, 150

R

Rabbet joints, 42
    defined, 120-121
    making of, 124-125
Rails, 41
Rake, 11
Rake cornice, 25
Return, 29
Return cornice, 25
Ribbon coursing, 20
Ridges, 14, 20-21
Ripping, 135, 157
Risers, 148-149, 162
Riser templates, 163
Room dividers, 170-171
Roofing materials, 1-8
Rough fascia, 25

S

Saddle *See* Cricket
Sash, 51
Saw kerf, 145
Scarf joint, 107
Scribe, 93-94
Semihoused stringer, 155
Set, 92
Setting, 44
Shadowline, 83
Shakes *See* Wood shakes

Sheathing, 1-2
Shingles *See* Asphalt shingles; Hex shingles;
    Individual asphalt shingles; Strip shingles;
    Wood shingles
Side guides, 141
Sidewall shingles, 69
Sill, 51
Simple dado joint, 121
Sleeper, 116
Sliding doors, 42-43, 48, 144
Slipsheet, 135
Sloping soffit, 27-29
Snow slides, 7
Snub cornice, 29, 30-31
Soffit, 25, 27-29
Solid sheathing, 1
Solid wood paneling, 93, 95
Spaced sheathing, 1
Spline, 63
Square, 17
Stair gage, 151
Stairs
    assembly of, 165-167
    basement, 157
    built on house stringers, 162-167
    built on semihoused stringers, 155-160
    defined, 148
    dimension, 150
    parts, of, 148-149
    position in a wellhole, 167
    risers, 148-149
    stock for, 163-164
    treads, 148-149
Stairwell header, 148
Staples, 85-86
Starter strip, 73
Stay, 38
Step flashing, 5
Stiles, 41
Stool, 64
Stop bead, 64
Stop dado joint, 121
Story pole, 151
Straight flight stairs, 150
Stringers, 130, 148
Strip flooring, 112-113, 114-116
Strip floors, 116-117
Strip shingles, 17-19
Strut, 42
Stud, 65
Suspended ceiling system, 101-102
Swinging cabinet doors, 145-146

Swinging doors, 43, 44

T

Tempered hardboard, 69
Tenon, 122
Top plate, 30-31
Total rise, 148
Total run, 148
Treads, 148-149, 162
Tread templates, 162-163

U

Undercut, 165
Underlayment, 3-4

V

Valley, 4, 14-15
Vinyl siding, 72, 79

W

Wallboard fasteners
  adhesives and nails, 86
  nails, 84-85
  staples, 85-86
Wall cabinets, 135-137
Wall moldings, 106, 108-109
Warping, 122

Waste stock, 125
Wind block, 36
Window, 51-60
  See also Awning windows; Casement windows;
  Double-hung windows; Fixed windows; Hopper
  windows; Horizontal sliding windows
Window casings, 64-65
Window trim, 63-64, 66
Wood flooring
  block flooring, 113-114, 117
  finishing of, 114
  grading, 112
  hardwood strip flooring, 112-113
  plank flooring, 113
Wood molding, 106
Wood shakes, 11
  footrest for, 13-14
Wood shingles, 11
  application of, 74-75
  footrest for, 13-14
  laying of, 11-13
Wood stop glazing, 59
Woven valley *See* Closed Valley

488(7C1215F)